the BIG BOOK of independent THINKING

Do things no one does or do things everyone does in a way no one does

Edited by Ian Gilbert

Crown House Publishing Limited
www.crownhouse.co.uk

First published by

Crown House Publishing Ltd
Crown Buildings, Bancyfelin, Carmarthen, Wales, SA33 5ND, UK
www.crownhouse.co.uk

and

Crown House Publishing Company LLC
4 Berkeley Street, 1st Floor, Norwalk, CT 06850, USA
www.CHPUS.com

British Library of Cataloguing-in-Publication Data
A catalogue entry for this book is available from the British Library.

10-digit ISBN 1904424384
13-digit ISBN 978-190442438-3

LCCN 2006923067

Illustrations © Les Evans

Printed and bound in the UK by
Cromwell Press, Trowbridge, Wiltshire

To our wives, partners, husbands, children, colleagues, employers and students who have helped make it possible for us to go out and share with others the ideas and inspirations found in this book – we thank you.

Acknowledgements

Knowledge used to be like gold. The more you had – and hung on to – the more powerful and useful you were. These days think of it like milk. If you hang on to it, it goes off. In this book, we have built on a great deal of great knowledge – adapted it, played around with it, improved it in places and passed it on and encouraged others to pass it on too before it curdles.

We acknowledge the shoulders of the educational giants we are standing on – people over the centuries who have realised that, when it comes to teaching young people, there must be a better way.

Contents

Introduction to Independent Thinking Ltd   vii
Ten Things You Should Know Before You Read This Book   ix

Introducing David Keeling   1
Chapter 1 On Love, Laughter and Learning *by David Keeling*   3

Introducing Nina Jackson   27
Chapter 2 Music and the Mind *by Nina Jackson*   31

Introducing Jim Roberson   55
Chapter 3 The Disciplined Approach *by Jim Roberson*   59

Introducing Matt Gray   73
Chapter 4 'Lo Mejor es Enemigo de lo Bueno' *by Matt Gray*   77

Introducing Guy Shearer   97
Chapter 5 Peek! Copy! Do! The Creative Use of IT in the Classroom *by Guy Shearer*   99

Introducing Andrew Curran   109
Chapter 6 How The 'Brian' Works *by Andrew Curran*   113

Introducing Roy Leighton   137
Chapter 7 Living a Creative Life *by Roy Leighton*   141

Introducing Michael Brearley   157
Chapter 8 Build the Emotionally Intelligent School or The Art of Learned Hope *by Michael Brearley*   159

Introduction to Independent Thinking Ltd

Independent Thinking Ltd is a unique network of educational innovators and practitioners who work throughout the UK and abroad with children and their teachers and school leaders. It was established in 1993 by Ian Gilbert and delivers in-school training, development, coaching and consultancy as well as producing books, articles, teaching resources and DVDs and hosting public courses.

Ian Gilbert is the founder and managing director of Independent Thinking Ltd. Apart from his speaking engagements in the UK and abroad, he is the author of the bestselling *Essential Motivation in the Classroom* and *Little Owl's Book of Thinking*.

David Keeling is a professional actor, drummer, magician, stand-up comedian and committed educationalist who specialises in bringing the best out of some of the hardest-to-reach children in British schools.

Nina Jackson is an opera-trained music teacher with huge experience working in special needs, music therapy, teacher training and mainstream teaching where her research into music for motivation and learning is achieving national recognition.

Jim Roberson is a former professional American football player from the Bronx who is teaching in a challenging south coast school where his role is the 'Discipline Coach'. He also runs a unique 'work appreciation' programme for disadvantaged young people each summer in a number of authorities.

Matt Gray is a professional theatre director and teacher who is currently working at Carnegie Mellon University in the US. Before that he was a leading trainer at the London Academy of Music and Dramatic Arts as well as directing theatre in London and abroad.

Guy Shearer is the Director of the Learning Discovery Centre in Northampton – a centre working to promote smarter learning that sometimes uses new technologies.

Andrew Curran is a practising paediatric neurologist at Alder Hay Children's Hospital in Liverpool. He is on the board of the *Emotional Intelligence Journal* and is leading a number of research projects on the neurological benefits of an education system that teaches – and practises – emotional effectiveness.

Roy Leighton is a lecturer at the European Business School, a coach and trainer to top-level business, author and TV programme maker, his first major series being *Confidence Lab* on BBC television. Apart from his speaking work for Independent Thinking Ltd, he is also a sought-after consultant across the UK, working with senior management on school change.

Michael Brearley is a former teacher and head-teacher who is now a leading trainer and coach in school leadership, effectiveness and emotional intelligence in the classroom. He has been involved in a number of successful long-term school transformation projects across the UK and written several books and programmes.

Ten Things You Should Know Before You Read This Book

1. If you're looking for a quick 'How to …' guide and a series of photocopiable worksheets you can knock out for a last-minute PSHE lesson or because the INSET provider you had booked has let you down at the last minute and you're the only member of the middle-management team who didn't attend the last planning meeting, so you've ended up with the job of stepping in to fill in the gap, then this is *not* the book for you. As befitting a disparate group of people brought together under the banner of Independent Thinking, these chapters are to get you thinking for yourself – thinking about what you do, why you do what you do and whether doing it that way is the best thing at all.

2. Independent Thinking is the company set up by Ian Gilbert in 1993 to 'enrich young people's lives by changing the way they think – and so to change the world'. It has been interesting to see over the years how people have responded to such a mission statement. Some people don't mention it. Maybe the perception that education is about filling young people with knowledge rather than enriching their lives and developing their thinking runs too deep, taking us back to the Industrial Age education system we have all experienced for better or for worse. Others mention the first part but brush over the second in an embarrassed way. It doesn't seem very British to have such lofty ideals somehow. We may have just invented the World Wide Web or the jet engine or the worldwide hospice movement, but let's just have a nice cup of tea and get an early night, shall we?

    Then again, some teachers have loved it in its entirety and can see that *everyone* working in education essentially has such a mission, or else they shouldn't be working in education.

3. Over the last decade and a half, we have worked around the world in all sorts of schools with all sorts of young people, teachers, school leaders, parents, governors and educationalists. We haven't worked with ministers or been asked to advise government (so don't blame us) but believe that individual teachers with the strength of confidence to believe what their intuition is telling them can – and do – change things for the better. Remember, politicians have not chosen a career in education, so you know more than they do; and the education system is just a system and knows nothing of children.

4. Like attracts like and in those past few years we have attracted a growing band of people who now contribute to schools under the Independent Thinking banner. People like Roy Leighton, who featured in one of the very first 'change your life' programmes: *Confidence Lab* on BBC2. He is also a lecturer at the European Business School and a high-level business trainer as well as an educational innovator working with young people and with management teams helping to change radically the nature of schools. There's Jim Roberson, a former professional American football player, born in the Bronx and with the passion and delivery of a Southern preacher, drawing on his work with

seriously disaffected young people in this country to teach us why a focus on behaviour – the 'B-word' – can do more harm than good for the children who need us most. There's Nina Jackson, who is doing some of the leading work in the UK on the use of music for learning and motivation; Matthew Gray and David Keeling and the amazing effect they have when working with young people on motivation and self-belief; Guy Shearer, with his non-techie but radical approach to technology and learning; and, if it's an understanding of emotional intelligence for getting the best out of the people around you you're after, then we have Mike Brearley, one of the UK's leading proponents of the idea that your EQ will take you further than your IQ. There's even a consultant paediatric neurologist from Alder Hay Children's Hospital in Liverpool, who gives the *real* lowdown on the workings of the learning brain and why billions of dollars of research have proved what the old village wise woman could have told us thousands of years ago: you have to love the child. Each of these associates has been given one chapter of this book to describe what they know and what they do in their work with schools in a way that is meaningful and accessible, and each one brings their own unique style, personality and voice to their chapter.

5. Each chapter opens with Ian Gilbert setting the scene, putting the associate's work in a broader context and backing up their ideas and insights with the latest research and understandings. In the way that good teachers intuitively know the right thing to do, the research catching up later, Independent Thinking's associates often have a similar knack for doing the right thing *because it works*, without getting bogged down in academic bickering and theorising. Each introduction steps back and gives some of the background behind the areas that the associates focus on, offering even more ideas and information for the reader.

6. Anybody can read a book or see an expert in action, repackage the information and then stand there and tell everybody what they should be doing. We, however, live by the adage 'show, not tell'. Everything covered in this book – each and every tip and recommendation – is based on the things we do and things we have helped other people to do too. People like you in schools like yours. That way, we know the ideas work, and are workable, in all sorts of settings with all sorts of people, young and old. No one can level at us the accusation that 'it's just theory' or that 'it doesn't work', because it isn't and it does. (The best riposte to the 'old gits' in the staffroom who claim that it's all rubbish is to ask them calmly how they get it *not* to work.) That said, we are not advocating an off-the-shelf answer or a seven-step programme to instant success. Take the ideas, look at the theories behind the strategies and then have a play in your classroom or school setting as you make the ideas your own. Ideally, you will soon forget that you've even read this book, as the ideas become an everyday part of your general repertoire of stratagems and beliefs. We're happy to let you take the credit, honest.

7. This book is meant to be dipped into, with not every chapter being relevant for everybody all of the time. Some chapters are written with the classroom practitioner very much in mind, others with the students in mind, others still with an eye on school leaders. That said, there is something here for everyone, so we encourage you to dip into it with a highlighter pen in one hand and a notebook in the other to capture the main messages and ideas that resonate with you.

8. The motto we use in Independent Thinking is one that is a great spur to our own creativity and determination to experiment, to take risks, to change things for the better and to help move things forward. It is simply, 'Do things no one does or do things everyone

does in a way no one does.' Does the assembly you're about to give, or that lesson on 'forces' you're about to deliver, or that staff meeting you're about to lead, or that new-intake parents' evening you're planning look like everyone else's anywhere else? If so, then what about sitting down with your independent-thinking hat on and identifying how you can make it so that we couldn't drop you into a totally different school on the other side of the country without anyone's noticing the difference? Have the confidence to be memorable – the world of education needs you to be great.

9. If you want any more information about any of the ideas raised in *The Big Book of Independent Thinking* then please make contact with us, via the website (www.independentthinking.co.uk), by email (learn@independentthinking.co.uk) or by phone or fax (0709 239 9617). We'd love to hear from you.

10. And remember: Independent Thinking – we do; do you?

Introducing David Keeling

What's big and ginger and makes you laugh? For those of you who have never seen David Keeling in action, you will have to put aside the image you have now of a carrot in a hat or Chris Evans's latest TV programme being taken off the air, and focus instead on the common sense that David dishes out in his chapter.

For over five years, David has worked with young people who were failing – and being failed by – the system and has consistently achieved the seemingly impossible task of helping many of them re-engage with, and refocus on, their success in school and beyond.

His own story is one that many young people can relate to. He is someone who struggled not only with the narrow academic demands of educational success but also with the relevance of school itself, especially secondary school, where he attended a 'bog-standard comp' somewhere off the M1 to the west of D. H. Lawrence.

A crucial weapon that he advocates and employs himself to great effect is the use of humour. I have seen him win over large groups of disaffected Year 11s within seconds by his self-deprecating wit and his ability to see it – and tell it – how it is.

He points out how important laughter is for the learning process, something that is backed up by recent research revealed in the journal *Scientific American Mind*. Psychologist Kristy A. Nielson of Marquette University was testing her subjects for recall by teaching students thirty new words. However, one group was played a humorous video clip half an hour after the learning process. Both groups were then tested for recall one week later. The group that had followed the learning with the laughing showed a 20 per cent better recall rate than the other group.

You could have a 20 per cent increase in your class's achievements just by using laughter as a learning tool – and now you have the research to back you up when Ofsted come around and accuse you of having 'too much fun' in your lessons. In fact, copy the following sentence on to a piece of paper and stick it in your desk drawer for later use:

> We are not having fun, Mr Inspector: we are simply using positive emotions to obviate negative reptilian brain responses in order to access the limbic system to optimise dopamine release and facilitate autonomic learning.

Having fun and enjoying yourself is not an optional extra for a human being, whatever the age. A *Time* magazine feature in February 2005 took a look at a great deal of the research being carried out worldwide on the benefits of happiness, benefits that include reductions in heart disease, pulmonary problems, diabetes, high blood pressure, colds and infections of the upper respiratory tract. Happy people developed 50 per cent more antibodies after a flu vaccination, and, in a longitudinal study of 1,300 men over ten years, there was 50 per cent less heart disease in the optimistic men. Not to mention the fact that, according to gelotologists (no, you look it up), a hundred laughs is the equivalent of a ten-minute row, and laughter actually produces a significant reduction in levels of cortisol, a stress hormone that can actually impede our ability to lay down memories.

Education is too important to be taken seriously. Teaching children how to be happy – especially by modelling it to them – is no happy-clappy desertion of our duties but an important part of teaching them how to have enjoyable, fulfilled and long lives. Indeed, you may have seen articles in the national press about schools that are already starting to teach happiness to students.

How do we get to be happy in the first place? Although some people are 'born happy', the 'plastic' nature of our brains means that this is no guarantee that they will remain happy. 'Consistent stress can reduce happiness,' the *Time* article points out (although 'moderate doses' of negative experiences help us learn how to cope with life's little knocks and setbacks in a way that helps us bounce back quickly).

Experts suggest that there are three sorts of happiness:

1. Sensory pleasure. A smile stimulates the opioid system but is it transitory? How many have spent their lives chasing after such shadows?
2. A sense of engagement, of being 'in the moment', of 'flow'.
3. Having meaning in our life.

Raise our levels of items 2 and 3 and we raise our happiness levels. Or, in the words of Ruut Veerhoven, professor of happiness at Erasmus University in Rotterdam, 'Happiness is how much you like the life you're living.'

Are you teaching children to like the life they're living and to live a life they'll like? Do you like the life you're living? It's never too late. As Bertolt Brecht said, ' You can make a fresh start with your dying breath.'

Another neurological benefit from experiencing pleasure in your life is the chemical dopamine,

something that David not only taps into in his work but also draws your attention to in his chapter. According to our very own Dr Curran, it's the 'ultimate learning neurochemical' and a key part of the chemistry of memory. A surge of dopamine will help us better remember the fifteen to thirty minutes or so prior to the surge taking place. Perhaps this is what the Marquette University research above was benefiting from. And the adolescent brain is a very dopamine-rich environment. Those young people need dopamine, and lots of it. This explains some of their risk-taking behaviour and their ability to party all night but barely stay awake for your chemistry lesson.

And take heed: if they don't get the dopamine they need with your help they will get it despite you.

Through the 'having a laugh' approach to motivation that David espouses, there are also some very serious and life-changing messages about the need for change – for all of us – why it is necessary and what can so often prevent us from achieving it. If we as adults show resistance to change, what sorts of messages does that portray to young people, people who are setting out into a life where change will be happening for them far faster than it ever happens for us?

And change brings with it the threat of failure. But that's OK. 'We've got to fail faster to learn quicker to succeed better,' as the US head of McDonald's once said. We owe it to our children to embrace change and the effects of it for better or for worse to prepare them halfway adequately for twenty-first-century life.

One final thing. David is an actor by trade and is very much a 'get up and do' sort of teacher. So, there are a great many really simple but effective exercises in here that I have seen him use with young people and teachers alike to get them moving, thinking and changing.

So, push back the chairs, loosen your clothing and welcome to *The Big Book of Independent Thinking*'s very own self-professed Ginger Ninja.

Chapter 1
On Love, Laughter and Learning

David Keeling

Before I leap dramatically into the chapter, I would like to begin by doing this exercise with you, the reader, right now, to keep you on your toes and to make sure that you are not just flicking through to find the pictures.

It is an exercise that I always do at the beginning of my sessions. I do it because my work within education is usually centred on one word: success. So, I like to check with the group to see how successful the one hour, morning or day will be and what responsibility the group are taking to make sure that it is as successful as it can be.

A great pal of mine and fellow Independent Thinker, Roy Leighton (see Chapter 7), trained in Kabuki theatre in Japan and they use this exercise as a technique for getting into what they call a 'state of flow' or a readiness to be absolutely fantastic.

I'd like to put you in this state now by checking three things – your levels of:

- Energy;
- Openness; and
- Focus.

On a scale of 1 to 10, where 1 is low and 10 is high, what is your level of 'Energy' at this moment in time?

I normally get the students to shout their answers out after a count of three, but I suggest you do it in your head so as not to distress those who may be close by.

If you think you are a '1' then please – and I think this is the correct term – 'be arsed' to have a go. If you don't try, how will you ever know? And if you think you're a '10' try not to go through the roof!

Now do the same for 'Openness', by which I mean how open are you to getting involved in your learning, to contributing, to believing that you can change the way you think about yourself, where you are going and what you can achieve?

Finally, do the same for 'Focus'. What's your focus like at this moment in time? Is this the fifth time you've read this sentence? Are you already wondering what's for tea tonight or thinking, 'Does my bum look big in this?'

Many of the kids I come into contact with find it almost impossible to exist in the 'here and now', for they are constantly preoccupied with other things that are not related to the task in hand.

I have been to many sessions where some of the audience (normally those sitting at the back) express that they are here against their will and would much rather be somewhere else. The only problem I have with this is that they can't go anywhere else, but if they continue to focus on what is out of their control then they risk not getting anything valuable done – and what is the point of that?

A Chinese proverb loosely translated puts this argument beautifully: 'If you have one foot in the past and one foot in the future you will piss on today.'

So I ask you again, what is your focus like at this moment in time? Jot your scores down for Energy, Openness and Focus and we'll come back to them later.

Now that we've worked out what sort of state of readiness you are in for a chapter such as this, let's get on with the main thrust of what I have to say. All that you will read in this chapter has come together over a ten-year period to challenge the hearts, minds and spirits of kids from all over the country.

When I say kids, I mean either *big* kids (anyone 16–116), including, parents, teachers, care workers, businessmen and -women), or *little* kids (anyone aged 6–16), this time including high achievers, the gifted and talented, C/D borderline, EBD (those with emotional and behavioural difficulties) or indeed SBQs (smart but quiet kids, the ones who just seem to get on with it and who are often the most neglected).

All of the work I'm involved in is geared towards improving self-esteem, self-expectation, motivation, confidence, goal setting, visioning skills, success, the brain and how it works and how amazing it is, dealing with change and creativity within the individual. These areas are explored and expressed in a unique way incorporating anything from stories, quotes, jokes, games, improvisation, forum theatre, practical strategies, music, magic and boundless energy.

Ultimately, all of the above has been used to help people become more confident learners and enable them to find ways of embracing change, developing the qualities required for success and finding their own sense of happiness.

Oh, yes, I almost forgot: the majority of the work that I do in schools is with disaffected kids. For eight years, involving thirteen schools, and more than eleven thousand young people, Independent Thinking associate Roy Leighton and I have been running programmes alongside the Raising Standards Partnership in and around Northamptonshire that have the sole purpose of enabling these youngsters to feel 'capable' and 'lovable' – two words that for us are the real definition of self-esteem.

We have achieved so much within these schools using a technique called 'forum theatre'. (It's a bit like role play but less damaging.) The main aim of this theatrical device is to set up a scenario based on the ideas given to us by students involved in the programme. During the scene there will always be a point of conflict between the characters, which needs to be addressed by the members of the audience, who have now taken the role of directors. It is their job to stop the action whenever they feel that the characters are doing something wrong, e.g. being disrespectful, arguing, intimidating someone or being ridiculous (this is usually my job).

At this point the directors have the power to give advice to the actors on what they could be doing to improve the scene and generate a more positive and beneficial conclusion. The scene can then be rerun as many times as it takes until the best possible outcome is achieved.

Where this device has really come into its own is when the kids decide that they no longer want to be spectators and instead become 'spect-*actors*'. In this role, the kids get the opportunity to replace the actors and lead from the front in terms of resolving the onstage conflict. This allows the students, within a safe environment, the chance to rehearse their successes. There are no right or wrongs: there is just participation and a desire to transform the action into a more positive direction.

For the kids I have worked with on these programmes, this experience has helped no end in the building of confidence and an openness to look at things differently and to try many ways to create successes. It is through my experiences here and also as an associate of Independent Thinking for over five years working the length and breadth of the country that I feel ably qualified to give advice and suggestions to you in your work with disaffected young people.

My work for Independent Thinking has taken me to some of the most glamorous and exotic places that England has to offer, from Bolton and Stockport to Middlesbrough and Wigan; but, whatever the brief, the outcome and the feedback is always the same. People are genuinely enthused, empowered, excited and enlightened by the information, ideas and theories that they are discovering during these sessions, and there is a huge desire to find out more and at least attempt to do something with this newfound knowledge.

It was my intention, when I started work in education, to 'put a bit back' as they say – and to generate some extra income! It is now a passion to create unique experiences and to enthuse young people regarding the many possibilities that taking control over their life can offer, and to encourage people to think, feel and act in order to create a life they want and dream of, rather than a life that was forced upon them or that was left to chance. It is my aim within this chapter to share with you some of my educational experiences and to provide you with some practical strategies that I hope will support you in your work with young people.

All of this aside, it has also been bloody good fun!

I've made many friends and I have probably learned more myself than anybody I've worked with because, after all, the biggest learner in the classroom should be the teacher – am I right or am I right?

Before I take you through some of the strategies and techniques that I have utilised in my work over the years, let me share with you a couple of thoughts from two heroes of mine (although I know which one I would rather have on my side in a fight):

All great acts of genius began with the same statement, let us not be constrained by our present reality.
– Leonardo da Vinci

Let no way be the way. Let no limitation be limitation.
– Bruce Lee

But less about them and more about me. Let me introduce myself properly. My name is Keeling, David Keeling, or the Ginger Ninja – or, to the thousands of young people I have worked with, the Ginger Man. Not especially creative, or indeed easy to put on the front of my costume, but it suits me and I like it!

Let me give you a bit of my background. I was born in Sheffield in 1973 and was schooled in Nottinghamshire (Dayncourt Comprehensive). I have six GCSEs (failed maths and physics), two and a half A-levels and a diploma in acting from the London Academy of Music and Dramatic Art. It is important to point out that none of the above has ever had any bearing, qualifications-wise, on what I do now as a profession.

On the other hand, my attitude towards myself, the people around me and the environment that I find myself in, most certainly has. I work all over the country and talk to a lot of people about their school experiences, and I never cease to be amazed at how similar their experiences are to mine. At infant and junior school I was having a whale of a time, every day playing with Plasticine and drinking free milk. Occasionally, I had to do PE in my pants and vest, but I've had the therapy and I'm feeling much better for it. I don't know about you, but I found that my polyester two-piece chafed a bit. Especially when I was exiting from a forward roll.

It was a fun-filled creative time that lulled me into a false sense of security with regard to my future educational experiences, because what happened next was secondary school!

When I arrived on my first day, the backside fell out of my universe. Gone was the fun, creative, milk-drinking gymnastics of my primary years, replaced by desks, chalk and talk and textbook after textbook after textbook. For me the creativity, the imagination and the spontaneity had gone and in its place was boredom. Secondary school became, in my experience, a five-year exercise in wasting time. I actually learned more when I left school (not an uncommon event in my experience).

Luckily, three things got me through my comprehensive school experience:

- a good sense of humour;
- the ability to get on with people; and
- a vision.

1. A good sense of humour

Being ginger and chubby at comprehensive school is not a good combination. Fortunately, I've since blossomed into a beautiful swan. A ginger swan, I know. Life can be hard enough, so we should be encouraged to have more fun in everything we do.

Andrew Curran, consultant paediatric neurologist and fellow Independent Thinking associate (see Chapter 6), says quite clearly, if not a little ungrammatically, 'If your heart's not engaged then your head don't work.' So many of the disaffected kids I spend time with are suffering from this dilemma. They feel low or angry within themselves and thus become either reactive or switched off. This disengages the brain and leaves them with a strong sense of feeling incapable and stupid.

If anyone in your life has ever suggested, hinted or quite blatantly said that you are stupid or incapable, then they are wrong and I will willingly pay them a visit to explain why!

Never underestimate anyone – it is the most dangerous form of arrogance.

– Anon

Unfortunately, many of the kids I've seen, for whatever reasons, have spent a good deal of their lives being told that they are thick, stupid and useless and will never amount to anything by the very people they trust and look up to the most: parents, teachers and some friends. This can have a massive impact on a youngster's expectations, self-esteem and perception of what they can achieve with their lives.

The work I do is aiming to create a safe environment for these young people to rediscover their childlike curiosity for learning and to begin the rebuilding of their confidence and expectation of themselves. A good sense of humour and an ability to find fun in learning are, therefore, vital.

We know, scientifically, that if you're having a good time then endorphins, which are chemicals that occur naturally in our bodies, are released to create even greater feelings of happiness and euphoria. Related to that, dopamine is a chemical that is released when you have either been given or are expecting to receive a reward.

According to Dr Curran, dopamine is the number-one, learning-related, memory-boosting neurochemical, and it is therefore essential that we encourage teachers at every opportunity to use fun and creative teaching methods in order to bring about the release of these chemicals within the children and within themselves. The kids can then begin the process of feeling good about themselves and engage fully in the learning arena.

It should, therefore, be the responsibility of every teacher and pupil to ask themselves, frequently, 'Am I having fun?' And, if not, 'Why not?' and 'What am I doing about it?' School should be the best party in town, or, as Socrates once said, education should be a 'festival for the mind'.

2. *The ability to get on with people*

Some would say that I have strong interpersonal intelligence. I strongly believe that education, first and foremost, is about building relationships. If there is a teacher or a pupil whom you do not get on with, what do you think the chances are of any learning taking place when both of you are in a room together? None, because, if your heart's not in it, if you do not care for, or respect, the teacher and hate the lesson, then there will be no emotional investment in time or energy.

If you have a situation like this, then my best advice is to be the adult in the relationship and begin to take steps to sort it out, because, while it's an issue, that issue will always be a block to the learning that could take place. The only person who really loses out in a situation such as this is the pupil. It's their education and their opportunities that will ultimately suffer.

3. *The Ginger Boy had a vision!*

I knew what I wanted to do. Unfortunately, my life as a lap dancer did not work out, but I fell into acting and I am much happier for it.

I had a clear idea of where I wanted to be when I was 21 and I was strong-willed enough and determined, even at the tender age of ten, not to let anything or anyone, especially myself, prevent me from achieving my goal of being an actor. By the way, if you or someone you know is thinking of entering this profession then my advice to you would be this: make sure there is something else you can do, otherwise you will spend most of your waking life sitting by a phone waiting for something to happen; or you can do what I did, which is to get out into the world and make something happen using all the skills that you possess.

From the frequent chats that I have had with students over the years, it has become clear that, for a large number of them, school (in terms of work that is expected of you) can be a very frustrating place to be, especially for those students who didn't really have a clear idea of what they wished to do as a career.

Imagine that every day you are loaded down with work and you don't really know to what end. If students have no idea what they would like to do as a job, then I will ask them if there is a specific area that they would like to work in, such as sport, media or the forces. If they can't answer that, then I ask them how they would like to feel in ten years' time: happy, confident and relaxed, or stressed out, poor and unhappy.

I am pleased to report that everyone would like to attain the former three descriptions (well, everyone except the class comedian). The most frequent comment I hear coming from young people is, 'What's the point?' This is why having a vision early on (even if it changes) is vital in motivating a student to push forward and strive to achieve their goals.

As an exercise in visioning, I ask students where they see themselves in ten years' time. A lot of them have no idea whatsoever (which may come as no surprise), but this can put a huge spanner in the works with regard to their seeing the clear relevance of what they are doing on a daily basis and the impact it will have on where they'll end up.

The work I do is about breaking the habits and beliefs that a lot of these kids have formed about themselves and now feel are set and unchangeable. I encourage them to think that, every moment of every day, they have a choice either to do what they always do or to choose to do something different. It is by choosing to do something new that we grow and change the most, and this is the hardest shift a disaffected child will have to make if they really want to prove themselves – and everybody else – wrong.

As Stephen Covey, author of the international bestselling book *The 7 Habits of Highly Effective People*, says, 'Begin with the end in mind.' If you know what you want, it is so much easier to put all the wheels in motion to get it.

Now, do you remember your scores for Energy, Openness and Focus from the beginning of the chapter? Well, I have used this exercise hundreds of times and very rarely have the scores been high. Normally, they are very similar to this: Energy 5, Openness 6, Focus 5. That adds up to 16 out of a possible 30.

I point out at this juncture that, as a group, we have worked out very quickly that we have a 53.33 per cent chance of getting something positive from whatever we are doing. In other words, just over half a chance. But is that really good enough?

At some point, most of us get caught up in the daily grind of work, school or parenthood and find that we tend to exist on a 5:5:5. This means that we'd love to have more energy but the work is piling up; I had a late night last night and I really can't be bothered. We would love to be more open but to be open requires the facility to deal with change and that in itself requires effort, and, if we have low energy, then openness is not going happen. We would love to be more focused but we are genuinely worried about what we are having for tea tonight and that our bum really does look big in this!

And existing on a 5:5:5 means we're not really having a lot of fun. We are unlikely to remember what it is we are doing and we are very unlikely to want to repeat the experience day after day. For most of the kids I work with, this is school (actually for a lot of the teachers I work with, this is school too).

Often, I ask if anyone in the room has had a 10:10:10 experience, that's 10 Energy, 10 Openness and 10 Focus. I ask them to keep it clean but I'd like to know! I remember one teacher, he was an old boy sitting at the back of an INSET day, who told me his 10:10:10 experience had happened the first time he flew solo in an aeroplane. I asked him many questions, some

apparently more odd than the others. For instance, what was the weather like? Who was he with at the time? And what was he wearing?

He answered them all with aplomb and in so much detail that everyone in the room assumed that this experience was a very recent one. It had actually taken place forty years before, yet he remembered it as if it had been the previous day.

When we have 10:10:10 experiences, we are not only having fun, but remember most of what we are doing in great detail and are very likely to want to repeat the experience, or at least a sense of it, again and again. Energy, openness and focus as an exercise enables the youngsters to take responsibility for their learning and to make everyday things we are doing more memorable – for, as we know, memory is linked to emotion in the brain.

That is why we always remember our first kiss or getting punched and for a lot of young men this happens at the same time! It is not rocket science: if we are coming into an environment without Energy, Openness or Focus then can we really expect to learn anything? If we push to create more 10:10:10 experiences and reach that state called *flow*, then great and memorable things will happen.

Think of an experience, that you have had, where everything seemed to fall into place and you were 'in the zone' or experiencing flow. I bet you the price of a pint you can remember it in great detail, down to even the smells and sounds. I also believe that, if given the chance, you would love to have a repeat of the experience or one like it as often as possible.

This exercise is a great one to use at the beginning of a lesson because it's quick, it encourages audience participation and it involves a lot of shouting! It's always handy to have something for students to do as soon as they enter a classroom, or they will *find* something to do, e.g. destroy furniture or encourage supply staff to leave the room via a window.

Energy, Openness and Focus also constitutes a brilliant way to start your lesson. For instance, if one day your classroom results read Energy 2, Openness 7, Focus 6, then it's quite clear that the first thing you must do is raise the energy by playing a quick game or, failing that, hand out the Red Bull and go for a six-mile run!

Creating a common language and getting the kids to focus on what it is that they are bringing to each session is the first step towards establishing a clear structure and consistent approach to the way a session will run. In my experience with groups of disaffected youngsters, it is exactly this that needs to be laid down, and adhered to, if you ever want learning to take place.

At the outset of a session with young people, I make it quite clear that I work only with geniuses. This remark is normally met with much hilarity and scoffing, as if to suggest I'll be lucky if there's one in the room. But I was once told that expectation is everything, that everyone is born with the potential to be a genius, but that the world spends the first seven years 'de-geniusing' them.

I believe that everyone I work with is a genius in their own right and that there is plenty of evidence to back it up (see all the other chapters in this book!). It is my request to you that, for the rest of this chapter, you think, feel and respond as though your genius had suddenly been unleashed. However, if this proves too much, then just grin and nod knowingly every time I make a good point that you agree with.

I am requested to work with disaffected Year 11s all over the country – mainly to give them one last motivational boot up the backside so that the school can reach its GCSE targets (although I also do INSETs, which work the other way round).

Let me get one thing straight right now: I don't really care about GCSE results. This is mainly because, five years after leaving school, these results will be out of date. So surely there has to

be something else. And I'm a great believer that attitude will determine altitude. If you genuinely care about yourself and where you are going, things such as GCSE results will come as a matter of course.

Look around you: the majority of young people who are failing their exams lack the confidence to do what is right for themselves, or don't see the relevance of what it is that they are doing, or have no idea what they want to do or achieve in life and have a bad attitude towards themselves and the people around them.

My aim is to help these kids raise their expectations, dare to dream, see the relevance of school life, begin to develop self-respect and set themselves targets to attain. Once this has been achieved, the GCSEs will become one step to another phase of our life rather than the be-all and end-all of our existence, which at times they can seem to be.

After all, millions of years of neurological evolution have not geared all of us just to pass an exam. There has to be more to life than just a piece of paper with letters on it. Although the bits of paper have an importance, I feel that we should first concentrate on the individual to build on and strengthen their inherent qualities in order to provide a sturdy platform from which they can leap into their school life and all it has to offer. Everybody I've ever met through my work wants to be happy and successful because that *is* what life's all about, isn't it?

When I use the word *success*, I'm aware that it means different things to different people. To me it is not just about having money or celebrity, but being happy and fulfilled, establishing strong loving relationships, embracing change and feeling as if you've lived life to the maximum. You can then wake up every day, looking forward and smiling at the face that looks back at you from the mirror.

Once we have established high expectations and a sense of willingness to change with a group of young people, I then always ask the following question: 'On a scale of one to ten, with one "low" and ten "high", how successful do you want to be?' I normally brace myself as I'm pinned to the nearest wall by the cacophony of noise created by a room full of young 'uns screaming, 'Ten!'

Everybody wants, and dreams of, success. Some are happier to tell you than others, so why is it that not everyone goes on to achieve it?

Lack of confidence, 'can't be bothered' and social circumstances are some of the replies I've heard. Roy Leighton and I have been looking at the relationship between people and success and, over the years, have come up with and developed six key qualities that everyone needs to have and develop in order to be successful. For this we created the mnemonic 'BECOME':

Bravery
Energy
Creativity
Openness
Motivation
Esteem

My belief is that not everyone achieves the success they desire because these areas are underdeveloped, sometimes severely so.

You may have all the qualifications in the world, but, if you are not brave enough to challenge yourself often, if you lack energy, if you lack the ability to come up with new ideas, if you are closed-minded to new or alternative methods of doing things, if you have no motivation and your confidence is rock bottom, then you may find yourself in the unenviable position of being highly qualified but unemployable.

Think of any job, e.g. a firefighter, sportsperson or actor. To be successful and happy within any of these professions will require you to challenge yourself in each area of BECOME on a regular basis. Where, then, in schools is the space or time put aside so that these qualities can be explored, learned and developed?

Once again, give yourself a score from 1 to 10 for each of the qualities of BECOME. On a daily basis, how brave are you? How energetic? And so on. Which are the areas where you scored highest? Which are the areas where you scored lowest? And what can you do to increase your score in each of these areas? After all, challenging ourselves little and often is one of the best ways to increase our potential and confidently approach change. The way that changes are dealt with can bring about the biggest challenges that face young people, especially boys.

I use BECOME as a creative tool to enlighten and engage young people and help them understand that their attitude to themselves and the things they do has a huge influence over how fun and exciting their educational experience can be.

In working with the students on BECOME, it is vital that, for each of these important qualities, there is a tangible experience that will stimulate their thoughts, feelings and actions. To help with this, we have, over the years, created a large variety of games and exercises to raise the young people's awareness and ability in each of the areas that BECOME promotes. So here, for your delectation, is a taster of the kinds of exercises and games that I use to challenge the kids in each of the areas.

Bravery

Dictionary definition *– 'courage in the face of danger or difficulty'*

Everyone in the session will require one plain sheet of paper (the bigger the better). Down the middle they should draw a line from top to bottom. On the left-hand side at the top, the students must put a plus (+) sign and on the right-hand side at the top they must place a minus (–) sign. For fun they may wish to draw a picture of themselves in the middle of the sheet.

The paper should now look like this:

The students should then be given at least five minutes to write down on the plus side a list of all their strengths, the things that they are good at and what makes them unique. The kinds of answers I've had in the past have included 'funny', 'kind', 'talkative', 'history', 'running', 'eating' and 'good in bed' (I think this was referring to sleep!). They can put down whatever they want as long as it is positive and makes them feel good.

Encourage them to make the list as long as possible. In my experience, the majority will find this first exercise difficult. For instance, a lot of students feel that talking is not a strength. As a nation, we are not encouraged to celebrate the things that we are great at. But, with some gentle coaxing and a few ideas, they'll soon get going.

It is imperative that young people recognise and are recognised for these strengths, so they can then begin to use them as a foundation, which can become a springboard to all kinds of new learning situations.

A good idea, once this list has been compiled, is to get each of the kids to read out their list and then to pick the strength that they feel is their greatest. This all helps to reinforce in the individual that everyone has different abilities and that this is the starting point for their confidence and self-esteem to grow.

Now they can move to the right-hand side of the page and make a list of all the things that they feel are getting in the way of their success, happiness and ability to develop. Some of the classic answers I have seen on lists have been, 'easily distracted', 'can't be arsed', 'never contribute', 'don't like the teachers' and 'don't do the work that's set'. It doesn't mean they are devoid of the abilities listed: it means that these areas will require more time and focus to get things back on track.

To address the aspects on the negative half of the paper it makes sense to draw on the strengths listed on the other half. For example, if you are easily distracted but a good talker, then use this skill to your advantage. Talk it through with your friends and explain that during a particular lesson you would like to focus much more than normal and would appreciate some time on your own. If they are your true friends then of course they'll understand.

The purpose of this exercise is informally to create some time to reflect on what it is we are already good at and on the things we need to improve on in order to become even better. If the groups are working well, you may want to pass the sheets around and have the students' friends add at least one quality to the list.

Everyone needs a starting point and everyone requires the bravery to begin at this point in order to move forward.

This exercise can be as long or as short as you wish it to be, but I recommend it be no shorter than fifteen minutes, since this will create the freedom for time and thought to take place and the lists to be a mile long.

Energy

Dictionary definition – *'intensity or vitality of action or expression'*

Stop/Go is possibly my favourite game for two reasons:

- I don't have to do it because I'm leading it; and
- it's hilarious watching everybody desperately trying to wrestle with years of fixed patterns of thinking.

The other great thing about this game is that you can play it anywhere with any number of people (my record so far is about five hundred!). This is how it goes.

You ask everybody in the room to stand up and explain that you are going to play a game that will require them to do exactly as you say but with no talking. You will be shouting out some very simple instructions that they will need to listen to. When you say 'Go' you would like them just to walk on the spot briskly and with enthusiasm. When you shout 'Stop' you would like them to stop still straight away.

At this point, as a warm up, you can shout 'Stop' or 'Go' as many times as you want and for varying lengths of time and in any order, just to make sure that the group are concentrating.

You can now explain that, since they all found that so easy, you are going to change it around a bit. From now on when you say 'Stop' it means 'Go' and when you say 'Go' it means 'Stop'. The faster you say this, the funnier and more confusing it is.

Check for understanding. If there isn't any, say the sentence again but even more quickly.

You then begin once more and this time you can have lots of fun watching the total confusion, frustration and hysteria taking over the room as the people struggle with this simple reversal of orders.

Now it's time to announce some more instructions. From now on when you say 'Clap' you would like everyone in the room to clap once and together (you may wish to practise this: the older they are the more this action eludes them!) and when you say 'Jump' you would like them to do a little jump, nothing ridiculous, just enough to see the room move. Practise this a few times and, quick as a flash, at least 99 per cent of the room will have forgotten the Stop/Go instruction and the fact that it's still reversed. Drop this back in and you'll catch the whole room out. Continue with Stop/Go and Clap/Jump for a minute or so then get everyone to stop by saying 'Go'!

Confused yet? It gets worse, but it's much easier to play than to explain.

From now on when you say 'Go' you mean 'Stop' and when you say 'Stop' you mean 'Go'; when you say 'Clap' you mean 'Jump' and when you say 'Jump' you mean 'Clap'. This announcement will usually be met with looks of bewilderment and utter confusion mixed in with screams and much laughter.

You can see the pattern forming. As the game leader, you'll really enjoy adding to the mêlée by setting up patterns and then changing them using your voice, intonation and dramatic pauses.

To cause even more confusion create lots more instructions to follow, such as 'Sit Down'/'Stand Up' or 'Left Arm'/'Right Arm'. The more the merrier.

The main purpose of this game is to have fun and raise the level of energy within the group along with improving – or showing problems with – listening skills. It also encourages the use of whole-brain thinking (using the left and right hemispheres at the same time) while, at the same time, demonstrating how fixed our thinking can be and how this limits our ability to be open to new ideas and new ways of thinking.

Creativity

Dictionary definition *– 'originality of thought, showing imagination, sophisticated bending of the rules or conventions'*

Whether you consider yourself to be arty-farty or not, creativity is naturally present in all of us. It is my job to assist the students in uncovering and exercising what is already there. Unfortunately, a lot us, due often to our educational experiences, have allowed this essential tool to get lost at the back of our mind kits.

Get your students to pair up or in the case of odd numbers threes will do. Each pair requires one pen and one large sheet of plain white paper. The pen is to be held over the paper by both (or all three) students using one hand each. (By the way, this exercise works just as well with grown-ups.)

You then explain that they now have one minute to draw a house. When the minute is up ask them to place their pens down. I guarantee that 99 per cent of the pictures drawn will look like this:

If they are feeling particularly artistic you may also encounter a variety of optional extras such as smoke coming out of the chimney, a wibbly-wobbly path, a garage and maybe even some cartoon planting. Basically, you will see a house that you would expect to have been drawn by a six-year-old.

Ask the group why they seem to have drawn the same house? Have they ever seen a house like that? Explain that the brief was to draw a house. The students could have drawn anything they wanted – no restraints, just that it's 'a house'. Tell them that they are going to do the exercise again but this time they can have a couple of minutes to discuss and plan their dream house. It can be any size or shape and anywhere in the world; it can be made of chocolate or, as one boy suggested, a pub floating above Newcastle United's football ground. It can be on the moon, or underwater, one room or a thousand rooms. It simply doesn't matter.

So, as before in their pairs, they have a minute to draw this dream house. You may wish to give them a little longer if you feel it's necessary or need to pop out to make a phone call. When this time is up, you will see a huge difference in the drawings because this time they have used their imagination, they have dared to dream and the results are amazing. Each drawing is unique: mansions, islands, tree houses, fish, biscuits – you name it and the kid wants to live in it.

Take time to go around all the pictures. The kids may even want to talk you through them. Ask them which house they enjoyed drawing the more (it's always the latter one).

This exercise is so effective in not only showing what happens to our brain when we are put under the pressure of time but also how we resort to simple patterns of behaviour without being actively encouraged to break the perceived rules and be creative. Our brain shuts down and we revert to the first thing that comes into our head or will get us through whatever has been set, e.g. a six-year-old's version of a house.

The difference between the two drawings was a couple of minutes. Imagine that we gave the students more time to dream and be creative, thus enabling their imaginations to wander and seek out new ways to do things rather than conforming to what everybody else does.

This is a simple way to engage the students in the art of creative thinking and will hopefully sow a seed in them, which will aid their efforts in other subjects.

Openness

Dictionary definition – *'the quality of being not closed or barred, unrestricted and unlimited'*

One game that I use for openness is called 'Anyone Who?' To play this game students must be seated in a large circle. One person must be standing in the middle of the circle and with no chair to go to.

The object of the game is for the person in the middle to ask a question of the circle (it must also be true of themselves), for instance, 'Has anyone ever been to America?'; 'Is anyone wearing black socks?'; 'Who likes curry sauce on their chips?'

If your answer is 'yes', then you must move across the space and sit in another chair that's been vacated. If you leave your chair, only to find there is no other chair to sit on, it means it's your turn to stand in the middle and ask the next question. The rules (per question) are that you cannot move to the seat next to you and you cannot return to your seat once you have left it. The idea of the game is to find out as much as you can about everyone in the room. The more probing the questions, the more you find out; and, if you are really clever with your questioning, you can get everybody moving at the same time.

This exercise is a great energy raiser and is good at the beginning, middle or end of a session. It requires openness to play and a readiness to ask questions and be truthful in your answers.

The game works well only if those participating are genuinely open to playing it 100 per cent, and over the years this game has proved to be incredibly popular with students and teachers alike.

Motivation

Dictionary definition – *'feeling of interest or enthusiasm that gives an incentive to do something'*

For this exercise, 'Future Interview', the students will once again have to pair up but threes will do. Explain that you would like them all to imagine that they are 25 years old and are exactly where they want to be in terms of career, families and friends and so forth. Give them a few minutes to think about this on their own.

Now you can tell them that, because they have been so successful, Michael Parkinson would like to interview them on his show to discuss their life. The pairs should now decide who is A and who is B. A will pretend to be Parky and will interview B first. If there is an odd number, then the students may take it in turns to be the interviewer/interviewee. At this point you can unveil the five questions that you would like A to ask B.

1. Where are you now (at the age of 25 and not geographically)?
2. How did you become so happy and successful?
3. Who helped you to get there?
4. When did you take responsibility for your life?
5. What advice would you give to the young people who are watching and who dream of becoming successful and happy like yourself?

My advice would be to put these five questions on a flipchart so that everyone can see them even if the pairs are spread out.

When A has interviewed B, then B can interview A. Each time, the person being questioned must give as much detail in their answers as possible. When everyone has finished, it is a good idea to bring everybody back together for a debrief and to find out what some of their answers were.

A lot of young people find it difficult to imagine what is going to happen next week, let alone in ten years. This exercise begins the process of visualising a positive, happy future and, more importantly, gets the students to discuss with each other the various ways in which they can make the future they dream of a reality.

From my experience, the students' answers to Question 5 above is usually what their next step should be in terms of furthering their education. For instance, I asked one young lady what her advice would be to young people. She replied, 'Ask for help, do the work set, go for what you want and don't let anyone get in the way.'

I asked if this is what she does now?

She replied, 'No.'

This is exactly what she needs to be doing if she ever wants to move forward and in the right direction. Her intuitive voice is giving her the best advice ever, yet her lack of confidence and self-esteem is drowning that voice out. Her over-all happiness should be motivation enough, but sometimes we need to break things down into much smaller chunks in order to achieve our successes one step at a time.

Take as long as is needed for this exercise. It's great fun and also adds to the excitement if you count the students down to a live transmission. I must confess to singing the *Parkinson* theme tune, too, but I will understand if you don't feel up to it. I have been trained by LAMDA after all!

Esteem, as in self-esteem

Dictionary definition – *'respect for oneself'*

I normally reserve this space for the kids to reflect on the experiences, thoughts and feelings that they have had during the session and ask them to commit to something tangible that they can do to raise their self-esteem over the next seven days. The students must see their commitment through, because only through experience can we build confidence and through confidence we can then begin to feel better in ourselves and happier to keep this process of self-reflection and improvement an ongoing one.

You will know best how to set this up with a view to assisting the students to go through with their commitments, review what happens and work out what they may wish to do as a next step. Good luck and may the force be with you always!

Meanwhile, let's move away from the fun and games of the exercises and back to the meat of my chapter.

The top ten UK businesses were once asked what six qualities would they like school leavers to possess? *And, yes, it is important to remind the students as frequently as is possible that there is a world going on outside of school that they will very soon be joining and, hopefully, contributing to in a very positive way.*

The results were as follows and in no particular order:

- self-confidence;
- communication skills;
- teamwork;
- evaluating information;
- time/personal management; and
- the ability to cope with – but better yet create – change.

Look at that last one. Two things are constant in life: things change and then we die.

The world has continued to change ever since it was created millions of years ago and it will continue to do so. Yet so many of us 'don't do change' because, to embrace change and even to enjoy it fully requires effort and a good degree of openness and focus – especially as change can sometimes be an uncomfortable and even painful experience.

How good are you with change? Do you like it? If not, why not? What is it that stops you from liking it? How could you change your mind about change?

For those of you who can't last a page without a game to play, here is a great one that explores the process of change and our reaction to it. It's called 'Pass the Clap' (I know!).

I am constantly surprised by the number of people (even young people) who moan, grumble, huff and puff, first in response to being asked to get off their backsides in a session and, second, in response to the idea that they will have to engage in 'play'.

The great man is he who does not lose his child's heart.
– Anon

Most people I work with don't even know at this point what the game will be and yet have already made up their minds about their feelings towards it. This to me smacks of a lack of confidence and an overwhelming preoccupation with how they may be perceived in front of a group of their peers. You see, game playing requires the ability to take risks and to engage in something whereby you are not fully in control. I use games all the time as a tool for the risk assessment of a group. Playing games will very quickly tell you who are going to be the movers and shakers and who is going to be a pain in the backside.

Anyway back to the game.

Very simply, the people in the room must be split into sizable teams and preferably stand in rows. You can decide on team size based on the number of people you have in the room at the time. The clap is then passed down the row from person to person. You receive the clap when the person immediately next to you has clapped once and you pass it on by just turning to the person next to you and clapping your hands together. You are looking to create a ripple of claps if the team is working well together. This is repeated several times and can be improved upon by asking players to unfold their arms take their hands out of their pockets and stand as if they are ready to play. The best position for this is to squat down

with your hands held out in front of you. You may also encourage each team to shout and scream as much encouragement to every other member of their team to energise and motivate their group to win.

However, the last time the clap is passed down the line I suddenly reverse the direction. Such a decision is always met with gasps of shock as if doing it another way would cause their legs to drop off or their clothes to disappear. It's amazing how quickly we develop a pattern that we want to hang onto and how quickly we become challenged when asked to learn a new pattern. Yet this process of acquiring a new skill, reinforcing it and then adding a sudden twist that pushes the learner forward and quickly out of their comfort zone is good learning practice and helps with brain development.

There are three great reasons for playing games in any form of learning:

- They are great fun – except for maybe 'Spin the Bottle' or 'British Bulldog'!

- Your brain weighs 2 per cent of your body-weight but takes up to 20 per cent of the oxygen. By getting up and moving around you are increasing your oxygen supply to the brain by up to 15 per cent. Which means, if you are standing up and moving about you are actually cleverer than you are if you're sitting down!

- Scientists have discovered something called *muscle memory*. We learn so much more by *doing*. It's like riding a bike. We can talk about stuff till we are blue in the face but give a youngster a fun and tangible experience and you can watch them grow in front of you.

'Pass the Clap' creates such an experience and leads beautifully into the ideology of a Japanese educationalist called Tsunesaburo Makiguchi (1871–1944), to whose work and ideas I was introduced to by Roy Leighton.

Makiguchi lived and taught at the turn of the last century and at that time a typical school day for a child was to be up at five o'clock in the morning, then off to school for a two-hour vigorous physical limber (we won't do it now!) and then into lessons all day until five o'clock in the evening with no breaks, not even for lunch.

Makiguchi felt that this was not the best way to learn and so developed the 'Cycle of Change' as a way to approach everything you do in life.

The reason I love this cycle so much is because it's so simple.

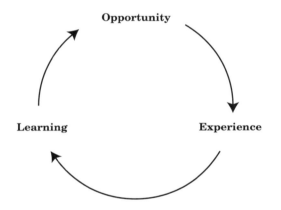

Figure 1. Cycle of Change

Very simply:

- you have an opportunity;
- if you take the opportunity then you'll have an experience; and
- if you have an experience then you'll learn something.

That's it. I told you it was simple.

On the other hand, if you don't take the opportunity, then you don't have the experience, and, if you *experience* nothing, then – you guessed it – you *learn* nothing.

For example, you the reader had an opportunity, which was to read this chapter, and you took it, and I'm over the moon that you did. Your experience was reading the chapter, and the learning may have been that it was the most amazing, thought-provoking and inspirational chapter that you have ever read (I should start to write all my reviews!). It may be, however, that if you ever have the misfortune to read anything like this excuse for a chapter again you will happily take me outside and give me the slap that I so richly deserve.

Whatever your thoughts are, you have learned something and I'd rather you based your knowledge on something you have had an experience of rather than what you imagined it was going to be like.

How often are we guilty of that? Think back to the reactions I described as coming from the people I told were about to play a game. What on earth did they imagine was going to happen to provoke such a response?

Along with the 'Cycle of Change' is something called the 'Emotional Cycle of Change'. Makiguchi says that, in order to take an opportunity, you need *courage*.

Figure 2. Emotional Cycle of Change

Now, hang on a minute. I don't know about you, but I must have had tonsillitis the day this idea was taught at my school. I don't remember any of my teachers sitting me down and saying, 'David, you know what? Before you get good at anything, before you can run a hundred metres, before you can make a quiche, before you can fashion a milk-bottle indicator from Perspex, you've got to be brave enough to have a go.'

Even better, if something doesn't work out the first time, then you've got to be brave enough to have another go, but this time do something different to make a positive change.

The difference between a failure and a *successful* failure is that successful failures will pick themselves up, dust themselves down and work out what they can improve upon for next time. How many people do you know who continually make the same mistakes and never seem to learn from them? As my mother would say of my father, the definition of madness is 'to do the same thing over and over again and always expect a different outcome'. This definition, however, comes from a woman who, for 35 years, has been trying to change my father and now complains, 'He's not the man I married!'

If you live like this you are only ever going to be frustrated and angry at your inability to move forward. I see so many kids trapped in these self-perpetuating cycles of mistakes and wrong choices. I encourage them to look ahead and see what the repercussions of these actions and choices may be.

I was once told, 'Your talent is in the choices you make.' (See Mike Brearley's chapter, 'Build the Emotionally Intelligent School', for more insights into the relationship between choices and achievement.) If we can motivate and inspire the students to stop and reflect more often on what it is they are doing and whether it is getting them closer to where they want to be or further away, we will enable them to move ever closer to the Holy Grail that is being in control of your life.

The more courageous you are the more opportunities you will take. The more opportunities you take, the more experiences you have. The more experiences you have, according to Makiguchi, the more *conviction* you develop and with conviction comes confidence.

Figure 3. Cycle of Change

And, in a world where everyone lacks confidence to some degree (some are just better at hiding it than others), this is vital in order that our young people grow into happy individuals with their self-esteem intact. What's more, the more confident you are and the more you learn, says Makiguchi, then the more *hope* you have for the future.

Figure 4. Cycle of Change

Hope is a great word. 'Hope fires a neuron' (Ian Gilbert, 2002, *Essential Motivation in the Classroom*, RoutledgeFalmer, Abingdon); hope creates a desire to get out of bed in the morning and to do something great in the world. Without effort, however, hope is simply an optimistic daydream.

Within this cycle, Makiguchi has given all of us a foundation from which to launch ourselves into any environment in which we may find ourselves:

- courage
- conviction
- hope

If you are reading this and dream of being, or becoming, more successful, then use these three things as a foundation for everything you do and I guarantee you will be successful at anything you do – or your money back! Even if some of your experiences do not turn out to be as happy-clappy as you'd hoped, you will still have enough courage, confidence and hope to turn them into something positive that will work for you.

Gandhi said something simple, yet profound and amazing: 'Be the change you want to see in the world.' By that he meant that, if you want to have more fun at school, then be more fun at school. Take action.

If you'd like to learn more effectively, then do something about it – don't just sit there and moan or wait for someone else to do it for you. In other words, get off ya butt and do it for yourself!

What is it, then, that stops a disaffected child, and indeed all of us, from being more courageous, trying new things and embracing change? After all, we live in a world that is moving four times faster than our schools are.

According to Ken Robinson in his book *Out of Our Minds*, nanotechnology is *the* major new scientific breakthrough that will revolutionise the world as we know it. Nanotechnology is the manipulation of molecular structures and the miniaturisation of everyday things.

A third form of carbon called C-60 has already been discovered that could revolutionise the worlds of engineering, medicine and travel. C-60 is a hundred times stronger than steel a tenth of the weight, and can conduct electricity like a metal. With qualities like this, it is predicted that we may be able to construct aeroplanes that are up to fifty times the size of your average jumbo jet and build bridges that could span great distances such as the Grand Canyon. If you think that's amazing, you should see the size of the pencil they've created!

Mobile phones are a classic case in point: they are constantly changing and upgrading the technology as well as making them smaller. Most mobiles now take photos and can make small films as standard.

Nokia have already produced a mobile phone complete with a mobile printer, so that when you've taken a great holiday snap you can have a 10-by-8 in your hands in ninety seconds – and not many people can boast that.

In Japan, they have already created a phone that's a wristwatch and when it rings you answer it by putting your finger in your ear. It works using sonic waves up the bones in your fingers to the bones in your ear.

The point that I am making is that, in a world that is being transformed so quickly, what are we doing to make sure that our kids have the qualities and attitude to thrive in such a climate of change?

According to wise old Mr Makiguchi, there is one major block to our successfully circumnavigating the cycle of change – *FEAR*. It is what prevents us from taking new opportunities and learning more.

What is FEAR (the capital letters are deliberate)? Think of it as '*F*alse *E*xpectations *A*ppearing *R*eal' or, as one teacher put it, '*F***k *E*verything *A*nd *R*un', but I think he was having a bad day.

Sometimes what we imagine will happen is so awful that it stops us from ever trying or moving forwards. The fear of what has not happened but could happen stops us from making anything happen. But that fear is imaginary. It is something we have made up in our head.

To prove a point, I will ask a group of students if anyone is scared of spiders. Immediately, several hands go up, already panicking at the prospect that I have with me a large, hairy, man-eating arachnid. I ask them what it is they think the spider will do to them. It is very unlikely that the spider will get them into a headlock, drag them outside and punch their face in!

It may on the other hand crawl in their ear and lay eggs – but that's a different story and a different bug! In other words, the potential *imaginary* threat is far bigger than the *actual* threat when you step back and look at it intelligently. It is our imagination that makes us scared, not the spider.

The point being made is simply that our emotional brain will always override our thinking, creative genius brain if we allow it. And there are similar forces at work, in my opinion, when I look at what is holding back underachieving and disaffected young people. Most of us live off our emotions without even being aware of it. In doing so, we allow them to control our lives and never learn to handle them effectively – again, have a look at Mike Brearley's chapter for more information here. This is why so many of the kids I meet are continually making rash and, ultimately, wrong and damaging decisions.

Living like this means that we are never given the time to think, reflect and take the appropriate action. We thus become reactive instead of proactive.

You gain strength, courage and confidence from every experience which makes you stop, look fear in the face, and do the thing which you think you cannot do.

– Anon

I'm sure the author of this quotation was not suggesting that if you're scared of heights you should throw yourself from the nearest tall building, but that it's the little day-to-day things such as the person you don't quite get on with or the piece of work you always put off, or the thing you'd love to do now but feel that it's too late (yep, we all have one of those).

If we move closer to these problems soon, there will be no problem – but the further we distance ourselves the bigger the problem will seem.

A question was asked of old people: 'If you had your life again, what would you do more of?' The answer was to take more risks – not rusks but risks. They would take more chances, do what's right for them and live the life they wanted. Or as one octogenarian put it in this marvellous poem:

If I had my life to live over

I'd dare to make more mistakes next time. I'd relax. I would limber up. I would be sillier than I have been this trip. I would take fewer things seriously. I would take more chances. I would take more trips. I would climb more mountains and swim more rivers. I would eat more ice cream and less beans. I would perhaps have more actual troubles, but I'd have fewer imaginary ones. You see, I'm one of those people who live sensibly, and sanely hour after hour, day, after day. Oh, I've had my moments and if I had it to do over again, I'd have more of them. In fact, I'd try to have nothing else. Just moments, one after another, instead of living so many years ahead of each day. I've been one of those persons who never goes anywhere without a thermometer, a hot water bottle, a raincoat, and a parachute. If I had to do it again, I would travel lighter than I have.

If I had my life to live over, I would start barefoot earlier in the spring and stay that way, later in the fall. I would go to more dances. I would ride more merry-go-rounds. I would pick more daisies.

– Nadine Stair, 85 years old, Louisville, Kentucky

You have only one life (unless you're a Buddhist), so, wherever you are in terms of age or happiness, make sure you are living your life now and grasping the endless opportunities that come your way every day.

Now comes the tricky part. If we follow the Cycle of Change, if we want our kids to be courageous, confident and full of hope, then we ourselves must be all three and lead from the front. Remember what Gandhi said: 'Be the change you want to see in the world.'

You cannot change anybody but yourself, but in doing so you give permission for the people around you to do the same. This is where the real power of change – and all it brings with it – comes to fruition. We don't just have a responsibility to change for ourselves, we have a responsibility to do it for the people around us. If we can't change, why should they?

I guarantee that, if you embrace the ideology contained within the Cycle of Change and begin to challenge yourself consistently in the areas of BECOME, which we met earlier, you will not only see improvements in your academic achievements but more importantly you will feel significantly more confident in your life as well as your learning.

There are schools that we have worked with who have started by simply using the 'Energy, Openness and Focus' model and have witnessed a significant increase in the students' attitude towards learning and achievement. And as a result, they have also seen the grades of the students rise. This will happen because the kids now understand they have the responsibility – and choice – to turn up for lessons in a positive state, conducive to learning.

After all, the brain is not designed for formal learning. It is designed for survival yet often we assume that young people can learn if we simply teach them. Never assume your children know how to learn. And you know what they say about the word 'assume'.

Assumption is the mother of all f**k-ups.
– Steven Seagal, *Under Siege 2* (1995)

There are other assumptions that follow certain children around school too – negative beliefs and expectations that can hamper a child or a group of students who genuinely want to change and improve their lot. Often, when I enter a school to work with a group of disaffected students, I'm told one of the following:

- 'You'll have your work cut out if you're going to bring about any changes in this lot.'
- 'It's the worst year we've ever had.'
- 'Good luck – you're going to need it.'

More recently, I spent fifteen hours, over three days, in a school in North London with twenty of what the school described as 'the worst kids we've got'. Totally unmotivated, undisciplined, turn up when they feel like it and no respect for authority. Yet, this sounds like most of the teenagers I've ever met – including myself at times.

These kids were, as I had heard Ian Gilbert once say of another group, 'overachieving underachievers'. The group had become adept in the art of doing it wrong. What I discovered while working with and talking to them about their lives and experiences, however, was that they were all highly motivated outside of school, disciplined when they wanted to be and respectful when they felt they too were being respected – and the majority of them turned up on time.

So why does all their good work and effort go to pieces as soon as they enter normal lessons? There are many answers to this one.

To get to a point over three days at which we could entertain a positive working environment and everybody was getting what they needed required my Independent Thinking colleagues, Matt Gray and Jim Roberson, and me to pull on all our reserves of energy, openness, focus, creativity and patience. This, my friends, was no easy task, but from the word go we all led from the front.

You cannot just expect to walk into a room of disaffected youngsters, who think they've got a day off, and believe you will be respected or indeed listened to. So, based on our experiences working with this group as well as some of the more challenging students around the UK, here are David Keeling's Seven Keys to Getting More out of 'Them':

1. You have got to give respect in order to get it. So much of working with young people is about building relationships and allowing these young people to see that you are respectful towards who they are and where they are from.

2. Quickly establish contact by finding out a few names and then from that point forward use them.

3. You ask many questions of them and will happily answer any of theirs.

4. I tend to work in a very energetic and dynamic way that is both physical and punchy. I want the group to feel my enthusiasm and see my passion. I like to create a workshop that will contain something for everyone.

5. There must be something for the thinkers to think about, the feelers to have something to engage in emotionally and something for the doers just to do. I want my sessions to be entertaining and thought-provoking, stimulating and challenging, but most of all I want them to be *fun*! You can never underestimate the mighty power of a good laugh, especially in an environment where the kids don't have much to laugh about. It is the fastest and most successful way to get a group of strangers interested in what you have to say and to get them on your side. It works even better if you are able to laugh at yourself (something I experience frequently).

6. Humour, I believe, is one of the most important and underrecognised qualities that we have. Its power to bring people together, from whatever background, and unite them in the next comedic and funny moment is worth more than a hundred clever quotes and a thousand flip charts (a speaker's third leg). If you want to help educate groups of youngsters who don't want to be in education, start building strong relationships and get a sense of humour. As Victor Borge once said, 'Laughter is the quickest route between two people.'

7. It also helps if you have an interest in young people and show it in every thought and deed. I'm still bowled over by the number of teachers I come into contact with who don't like kids. I'm thinking of writing a book for such people entitled *Get Another Job and Stop Kidding Yourself*.

Whenever I'm with a group of kids, I like to ask them what makes a good teacher. Before you look at what the students I have worked with have come up with, look away and see what you think first. Depending on where you are reading this book, ask a colleague or your partner or the person in the cubicle next to you.

Here are a few of the answers I've been given over the years, and in no particular order:

• well presented (cool not bookish)
• funny
• respectful
• fair
• consistent

- treats us like an equal
- makes lessons interesting
- confident
- always in control
- good-looking (obviously this is subjective according to an individual's own likes or dislikes)
- ginger (OK, I added that one myself)

A great list and not a lot to ask for, surely. It contains everything I would look for in a friend or colleague, so why shouldn't they be found in our teachers, especially when they play such a vital role in the formative years of our children? How many teachers do you know, either now or from your school days, who fit these criteria? No names, just have a think.

I also ask the kids what makes a good lesson and here again in no particular order is a list of ideas I've heard along the way:

- It should be short. (Not sure what can be done about this but in terms of concentration and from a neurological perspective one single topic should not last more than 10–15 mins.)
- It should be imaginative.
- It should not always be in a classroom.
- It should be unpredictable.
- It should be fun/interesting.
- It should involve people from the outside, e.g. other professions.
- It should create curiosity.
- You should be able to play music.
- You shouldn't have to sit behind a desk for fifty minutes.
- You should be able to eat and drink.
- Ginger people should be allowed to skip homework. (OK, OK!)

Next, armed with the answers, I throw the same question back at the kids but ask them what it is that they are doing to make the lesson more interesting and fun. How are they creating curiosity within a lesson? What are they doing with regard to getting someone from the outside in, e.g. parents, brother or sisters?

The answer, more often than not, is nothing.

The kids I work with get into habits of blaming everyone else for their situation – of blocking you when you are genuinely trying to help and of only ever coming up with excuses, e.g. 'I haven't got a pen', 'Someone's nicked my bag' or 'My teacher's crap.'

The difference between the way an adult brain and a child's brain think is this: a child, more often than not, will come up with problems and excuses while an adult – not all of them but most – will come up with solutions. I am constantly encouraging kids to approach teachers with ideas and solutions as a way to build confidence, relationships and successes.

The role of the teacher has changed. A teacher can tell you something in physics, and then you can go on the Internet and find twenty experts in that specific field who've been doing that job for far longer and who can tell you much, much more. A teacher's role, therefore, is not just to pass on information, but to enthuse, create opportunities for new learning and help youngsters find out what's unique about them and how they may wish to use that for their career.

So, when you are working closely with disaffected students, a lot of time will be spent building up their confidence and self-belief before you even get to the teaching and learning part. You have to be aware of the voices they have – we all have – that are usually saying one of two things: either 'You're beautiful, talented, the world is your oyster, go get 'em, kid!' or 'You're crap, you're useless, don't bother, they'll only laugh at you when you get it wrong.'

Which one do you listen to? The positive one, or the negative one? Most of the young people I work with are tuned directly into the latter. And, when that's the voice in your head, no wonder they don't take too well to new challenges in the classroom.

The only way to shift the balance is to provide them with fun learning experiences that put them in control of their achievement, that show them legitimate ways to 'cheat' at memorising or revising (memory games are a great one for showing them how clever they really are), goal setting and problem solving so that they can begin to build up their successes and begin to feel much more capable. Only then can students begin to tune into the positive voice that is always there if only they could shut the other one up for long enough.

A lot of the young people in my sessions are deeply affected by past experiences, both at home and at school, and it's these past experiences that can emotionally weigh them down and, more frighteningly, influence *all* the future choices that they may make. This cycle of poor decision making, coupled with a lack of confidence, can trap kids and prevent them from ever really moving forward.

I run an exercise that was developed as a way of kick-starting this process, one that Eminem once described as 'cleaning out my closet'. It involves the kids in committing to paper the name of someone, or an event, that made them feel one or more of the following emotions: anger, sadness, humiliation, loneliness, frustration, fear.

Once this has been done, they must write down at least two words to describe how they felt at the time. It is important then to remind them that they always have a choice. They can chose to let what has happened to them or has been said to them impact on every decision they make next or just hope in the future that someone, or something, is going to make it better.

Alternatively, they can choose to get rid of these experiences or put them to one side so that they don't have to affect everything they do from this day forth – thus creating a new future in which they are firmly in the driving seat.

At this point, I announce that as I pass each person in the room they must rip up the paper and throw it into the bin provided. As they do so, I ask if they would say one or two positive words to describe how it feels now that they know that this negative event need *never affect what they do next ever again.*

Words and phrases such as 'relieved', 'happier', 'relaxed', 'don't know', 'calm', 'in control', 'good', 'what?', 'You weirdo!' are the kinds of comments I've had back.

This is a very powerful first step in taking control of our emotions rather than allowing them to unconsciously govern our lives. To develop the sort of emotional intelligence that is so necessary for success in school and beyond.

Success is never final. Failure is never fatal. Courage is what counts.
– Sir Winston Churchill

I am always asking my groups what it is that they would like to be, or do, when they are older, since it is vital that they be heading for something – even if they don't like it when they get there. One young man in Bolton told me he wanted to be a helicopter pilot. I answered, as I normally do, with, 'What kind of pilot do you want to be? Do you want to be an OK pilot or do you want to be the best?'

Very quickly and quite sure of himself, he replied, 'I want to be the best helicopter pilot ever!'

'That's great,' I replied. 'So, what is it that you're doing today to become the best helicopter pilot ever?'

At this point the young man looked at me agog. He, like many others before, had not really thought this through. I believe he thought that, if he said it enough, it might just, one day, come true; that someday, maybe when he was eighteen, he'd be given a golden key to the life he'd always dreamed of and at no point would he have to put in one ounce of effort.

I didn't want to be the person to burst his bubble and I don't think I did. I simply made it quite clear that, in order to get to where he wants to be, he needs to be doing something, right here, right now. I further explained that to be a great pilot he would have to have bravery, energy, creativity, openness, motivation and self-esteem by the bucket load.

These are the things he can start improving now, today – moment by moment – by setting himself daily tasks and challenges to achieve. He was already aware that access to a helicopter during term time was nigh on impossible. This in itself would, in consequence, free him up no end to pursue the qualities that would make him a great pilot. I hope he does become a pilot. Somebody has to, so why shouldn't it be he?

A friend once said to me, 'Prove you've got a brain by using it.' This is really what it's all about. We have come to know more about the brain in the last ten or so years than we have ever known. We know, for instance, that we've got three brains (for more information, see Chapter 6). We know that the brain is still far more powerful than the world's most sophisticated piece of computer equipment, and it's between our ears – although in a lot of men it's located somewhere else, but that's an entirely different workshop! We know that if our learning potential – the number of potential neuronal connections a human brain could make – were calculated and then written down as a number, it would be 1 followed by 10.5 million kilometres of noughts. That means there is more learning potential in each of our heads than there are atoms in the known universe. Yes, we know there is a limit to our potential; it's just that we don't know where it is? How high *is* high?

We have the equipment we need to achieve what it is we want to achieve. Which means that it really boils down to those three key questions:

- What do you want?
- How much do you want it?
- What are you prepared to do in order to get it?

Your answer to these three questions (and for more information about them check out Ian Gilbert's book *Essential Motivation in the Classroom*) will determine how successful you will be. And your ability to develop 'BECOME' will determine how long you stay there.

A leader is one who knows the way, goes the way and shows the way.
– John C. Maxwell, American pastor, leadership instructor and counsellor

I hope that you have found this chapter to be both thought-provoking and fun. I know that, from my point of view, it feels comforting to be nestled in among such rich, varied and exciting company.

In the eight years, at the time of writing, that I have been working in lifelong learning and education, I have met many people, young and old, who have all in their own way contributed to assisting me in the work that I do. I would like to thank all of you from the bottom of my heart, even if you may not be aware of your involvement or contribution.

I happened upon a documentary recently, about Ray Mears, the survival expert. He was asked what it was that kept him coming back for more, no matter what lay ahead. In one sentence he summed up what keeps me excited, curious, enthusiastic and passionate about the work I do: 'The more I learn, the more I realise I don't know.'

Before I sign off and revision not being an option – we can't have you forgetting all that you have read within in this chapter – pick a number between 1 and 10. Now, for a bit of fun, create a sentence using that number of words that sums up what you have learned from this chapter. If you cannot think of one, then go back to the beginning of the chapter and start again.

Ah ha! Suddenly I've tapped into your intrinsic motivation and, as if by magic, you've come up with one. Good! You may now proceed to the final few paragraphs in this chapter. Well done!

I'd like to leave you with a story. I was working with a large group of students in a school some-where in the north of England. Among these students was a little chap with red hair (just like me, except that now I am a big chap). I asked an open question of the group. The little chap raised his hand and immediately a group of slightly larger boys began to snigger and make snide comments. I turned to the little chap, winked then looked at the group of boys and said, 'Why you are laughing? Didn't anyone ever tell you, "The future's bright, the future's orange"?'

This comment was met with cheers from the rest of the auditorium and a cheeky grin from my new little buddy. That day a young man left my session feeling unique with a stronger sense of confidence and success and a catchphrase for his life. I'd had those same feelings as a youngster when I realised that I, too, was unique and there was a world out there with a place in it reserved just for me.

Somebody once said to me, 'Find out what's unique about you and sell it back to the world.' The trouble is, if you keep it to yourself, the world may never know you're here. And that would be a tragedy.

Introducing Nina Jackson

Of all the areas we deal with that come under the banner of brain-based strategies for learning and motivation, it is the controversial use of music in the classroom that seems to cause the most waves (pardon the pun).

Having talked to teachers about the use of music in learning for over ten years now, I have seen it all: the teacher who has tried it but been told off for using it; the teacher who would like to try it but fears a possible telling off for using it; the teacher who could in no way countenance any form of music at any point in the classroom (or beyond, sometimes); the teacher who is using it surreptitiously but switches it off if they see the head coming; the teacher who tried it once but the kids kept asking for their own music instead of 'that classical crap', so it wasn't worth the bother; the teacher who would like to give it a go but doesn't know which music to use; the teacher who is scared that the wrong music will have the wrong effect at the wrong time, so they have thought twice about using it at all; the teacher who has heard that it is just Baroque music that you are supposed to use and has already worn out two copies of Classic FM's *Relaxing Baroque Classics* box set and doesn't know whether to buy Classic FM's latest box set, *Baroque Classics to Relax To* or their other latest box set, *Relax – It's Baroque Classics*; the teacher who plays only whale song and Enya's second album ('before she went too commercial') until the entire class lose the will to live; the teacher who uses just Mozart and only for maths, because that's what they heard on Radio 4; the music teacher who feels that having music on in the background degrades the musical experience and stops children from learning to 'really listen' to the music, an argument that would mean the art teacher would have to remove all paintings from walls in corridors (and, talking of which, there will also be the art teacher who has the local commercial radio station on in the background because, 'Hey, the kids love it – call me Dave').

If you recognise any of your colleagues in the above list, or – dare I say? – yourself, then take heart. Nina Jackson's chapter reflects the research she undertook for her MEd – some of the only accredited research published in the UK so far on this subject – and demonstrates that *different sorts of music at different times for different purposes not all the time but some of the time* can and does have a real, *measurable*, positive effect on learning and motivation in an ordinary school just like yours.

But before Nina starts, let me start. Simply looking more deeply at just a handful of the obstacles thrown up by teachers shows that they usually stem from ignorance or prejudice or both. For example, the belief that people need silence to concentrate is both right and wrong. Some people do work better that way. Try a quick show of hands with your colleagues next time you are all in the staffroom. But, for some people, complete silence is not only contrary to their preferred learning style (see the work of Rita Dunn and Kenneth Dunn in the US in the 1980s, in particular *The Complete Guide to the Learning Strategies Inservice System*, 1999, Boston: Allyn & Bacon) but also has negative effects, including inability to concentrate, shortened concentration span, increased stress or awkwardness, greater trouble in starting a piece of work and increased likelihood of messing around during gaps in concentration or once finished. Not to mention the opportunities the teacher is missing to tap into a particular learner's musical intelligence strengths during a lesson, to use music as a resource for improving memory, to use music as a classroom-control mechanism (music in corridors to reduce tension and stress between lessons; setting the right tone as children come through the door; transition music between changes in the lesson as they move, for example, from the back of the class to the front or rearrange the chairs; a three-minute music track for a three-minute activity; clearing-away music; exit music …) and to use all sorts of music from all sorts of cultures to help widen their horizons and 'grow their brains' (Radio 3's *Late Junction* is a good source of this).

When it comes to thinking about which music to play when, there *is* research about the power of Baroque music mainly originating with the hallowed Dr Georgi Lozanov in Bulgaria in the 1960s. His research is the forerunner of accelerated learning today and he used Baroque music to create a 'relaxed concentrative' state in his students' minds, imitating the brain state caused by meditation in the Eastern yogis he was studying, by encouraging alpha brainwaves (the brain state somewhere between crossing the road and starting to nod off). But Baroque music calms and focuses – great for quiet study or memorising and personal review but not always what you want when they are, say, working collaboratively on an exercise or activity.

There is also controversial research on the use of Mozart to improve maths abilities, controversial both because some experts are still not convinced and because some argue that it is Mozart, 'and only Mozart', that can induce the elusive 'Mozart Effect'.

There is yet more research that not only shows how different music produces different effects in the learners but also that different learners will have different responses to the same music. If a track being listened to has lyrics, there is a danger that the left brain – where most people have their language-processing centres – will get sidetracked away from the work being done to listen to the words. So, no music with lyrics argue some teachers. But if the music is well known to the listener they know the lyrics anyway, so no longer use their brain's language centres to listen to the words. So it's OK. But, if you are a musician, then, rather than process the music in the right brain, you will analyse it using the left brain …

And as for allowing them to listen to their own music … The reward of a three-minute track of their choice partway through a lesson will induce dopamine that will help them better remember what they have just been learning (see Andrew Curran's chapter, 'How the Brian Works', for why they need dopamine for learning to take place and be better remembered). On top of that, it will also create a sense of ownership and belonging towards the lesson, the classroom and the teacher. What's more, I have seen classes where normally disruptive students have settled down quickly and worked very well indeed because they were allowed to listen to their own music with their headphones on.

But the teachers involved were then burned at the stake!

In Gabriel Garcia Marquez's autobiography, *Living to Tell the Tale*, the great Colombian writer tells of the relationship between music and writing:

> My limitation was that I could not write to music because I paid more attention to what I was hearing than to what I was writing … But with time … I learned to write with a musical background in harmony with what I am writing. Chopin's *Nocturnes* for quiet episodes, or sextets by Brahms for happy afternoons.

The music he was listening to while writing and the writing itself became so subconsciously intertwined that at one point a couple of young Catalan musicians were able to point out the affinities between Marquez's book *The Autumn of the Patriarch* and Béla Bartók's 3rd Piano Concerto, without knowing that he had been listening to the piece 'without respite' while writing the book.

And if developing the practice of listening to music to improve creative writing is good enough for a Nobel prizewinning author, then it's good enough for us.

So, this chapter is for all of those teachers out there who feel intuitively they want to use music in the classroom, who know that it can improve learning and motivation with all sorts of children, who have witnessed first-hand how music changes everything in a classroom – instantly – and who would like not only to tap into existing accredited research but also pick up a few tips on how they may conduct some action research of their own as they argue their case in school. You can even highlight certain bits and wave it at the nonbelievers next time they come in to tell you to be quiet.

As Ewan McGregor said to Nicole Kidman on top of a large elephant, 'My gift is my song – and this one's for you.'

Chapter 2
Music and the Mind

Nina Jackson

Let me start your journey where one of mine ended:

- 95 per cent of teachers felt that using the *Music for Learning and Focus* catalogues helped pupils achieve better grades;
- 100 per cent of teachers felt that the use of *Music for Learning and Focus* improved study skills;
- 95 per cent of teachers felt that using the *Music for Learning and Focus* helped pupils with improving grades or marks;
- 100 per cent of teachers felt that using *Music for Relaxation and Calm* helped the pupils settle better in their work and studies;
- 100 per cent of teachers said pupils gained better marks and or grades when using *Music for Relaxation and Calm*;
- 95 per cent of teachers felt that when using *Music to Motivate, Stimulate and Energise* (Catalogue 4) pupils were inspired to work;
- 95 per cent of teachers felt that when using *Music to Motivate, Stimulate and Energise* (Catalogue 4) pupils worked at an accelerated pace;
- 95 per cent of teachers felt that pupils enjoyed having *Music to Motivate, Stimulate and Energise* played while working;
- 100 per cent of the teachers felt that the music catalogues had been of use to them in their teaching;
- 95 per cent of teachers said the music catalogues had been of use to them as a teaching tool to enhance learning;
- 100 per cent of teachers said they enjoyed using the music catalogues in their classrooms;

- 97.5 per cent said they always enjoyed using the music;
- 97.5 per cent of teachers said that using the music catalogues did not cause them any extra work;
- 100 per cent of teachers said they would like to have an extended library of music to use in the classroom;
- 90 per cent of teachers said that pupils have improved their study skills;
- 75 per cent of teachers said that pupils retained better concentration during lessons;
- 100 per cent of teachers said pupils had settled better at the beginning of and when working on tasks;
- 100 per cent of teachers felt the music supported them and helped them to relax as well during lessons;
- 100 per cent of teachers responded with positive comments to the use of music in their lessons;
- 65 per cent of teachers felt that the music stopped them from raising their voice towards pupils – especially after playing the relaxation and calm music;
- 95 per cent of teachers felt that the music from film soundtracks was the most appealing to pupils – the pupils were unaware that they were musical excerpts from films;
- 95 per cent of teachers felt that using music in their classrooms made the experience of teaching far more enjoyable.

These were just some of my findings from one of the most detailed studies into the use of music in the classroom ever to be carried out in the UK. This chapter is designed to give you a brief outline of what I did, how I did it and not only why I did it, but also why it worked. And, if it worked for me and the students in my typical comprehensive school in Wales, it can work for you.

As a young child, I dreamed of becoming a teacher and studied hard from an early age to fulfil my ambition. I began teaching in a secondary school in Hampshire in September 1992 and joined the school during this time as a Newly Qualified Teacher (NQT) and teacher in charge of the Music Department.

It was a school that had many challenges, especially for an inexperienced teacher: there was a high percentage of pupils who were on the Special Educational Needs (SEN) Register for Emotional and Behavioural Difficulties; and it was a school whose pupil numbers doubled over seven years. It was in this school that I began to use music to help affect the environment and the physical and emotional responses of pupils. This was done with no thought or long-term objective at this time, but the use of music merely to create a calming effect.

It was in Hampshire that I then used my knowledge of music therapy to create and devise music-therapy programmes for pupils with EBD (emotional and behavioural difficulties). These therapy programmes used creative music making – performing and composing activities using mainly instruments, body kit and vocal development as one aspect of the healing process, while a range of musical extracts from CDs were used to affect a pupil's mood or emotion. My constant need for diversity in my teaching and professional development brought me back to my homeland Wales, where, in September 1999, I took up the post of head of music at Ogmore School in Bridgend.

Then, in 2001, the General Teaching Council of Wales was far-sighted enough to introduce teacher research scholarships, an innovation that gave me the opportunity to bring my ideas and experiences together in a specific research study into the affects of 'Music and the Mind', the title

of my research project and my teaching philosophy.

I wanted to build on my earlier discoveries about the effects of music on young learners and prove what I had always felt about music. Put simply, I wanted to show that:

- listening to music in lessons helps pupils' concentration and study skills;
- listening to music in lessons makes pupils feel happy, relaxed and ready for work; and
- listening to music in lessons helps pupils achieve more.

And where better to set myself such a challenge than in a country where it is music itself that helps us define our national identity?

Musical beginnings

Since music is the only language with the contradictory attributes of being at once intelligible and untranslatable, the musical creator is a being comparable to the gods, and music itself the supreme mystery of the science of man.
– **Claude Levi-Strauss (1970, p.18)**

Those who do not appreciate music think that it has no significance other than providing ephemeral pleasure. They often consider it a gloss upon the surface of life, a harmless indulgence rather than a necessity. This, no doubt, is why our present politicians seldom accord music a prominent place in their plans for education. Today, education is becoming increasingly utilitarian, directed towards obtaining gainful employment rather than enriching personal experience.

The idea that music is so powerful that it can actually affect both individuals and the state for good or ill has disappeared. In a culture dominated by the visual and the verbal, the significance of music is perplexing, and is therefore underestimated. Both musicians and lovers of music who are not professionally trained *know* that great music brings us more than sensuous pleasure, although sensuous pleasure is certainly part of musical experience.

Origins and functions of music

Music is so naturally united with us that we cannot be free from it even if we so desired.
— Boethius (1989, p. 8)

No culture in the world so far discovered lacks music. Making music appears to be one of the fundamental activities of mankind – as characteristically human as drawing and painting. But what *use* is music? Music can certainly be regarded as a form of communication between people, but *what* it communicates is not obvious.

Although science can define the differences between tones in terms of pitch, loudness, timbre and waveform, it cannot portray the relationship between tones, which constitutes music. While there is still considerable dispute concerning the origins, purpose and significance of music, there is general agreement that it is only remotely related to the sounds and rhythms of the natural world.

All of Western music theory is based on an abstract construct by the Greek mathematician Pythagoras that determines which notes go together, in scales, keys and chords, by calculating ratios between their frequencies and overtones. To discuss the rules underlying Western music, from classical to rock, folk and jazz, is to embark upon a dizzying journey of numbers, fractions and series for which you need some neural planning!

In fact, music has often been compared with mathematics; but as G. H. Hardy (1940, p. 26) pointed out, 'Music can be used to stimulate mass emotions, while mathematics cannot.'

If music were merely a series of artificial constructs comparable with decorative visual patterns, it would induce a mild aesthetic pleasure, but nothing more. Yet music can penetrate the core of our physical being. It can make us weep, or give us intense pleasure. Music, like being in love, can temporarily transform our whole existence.

The mnemonic power of music is still evident in modern culture. Many of us remember the words of songs and poems more accurately than we can remember prose. The notion that music facilitates memory has been objectively confirmed by the study of 'mentally retarded' children who can recall more material after it is given to them in a song than after it is read to them as a story (Farnsworth, 1969).

Music, the brain and the body

Music brings about similar physical responses in different people at the same time. This is why it is able to draw groups together and create a sense of unity. It does not matter that a musical dirge or a football or rugby chant may be appreciated in a different way by a musician than by an unsophisticated listener. They will certainly be sharing some aspects of the same physical experience at the same moment, as well as sharing emotions aroused by the game itself. Music has the emotion of intensifying or underlining the emotion that a particular event calls forth, by *simultaneously coordinating the emotions of a group of people*.

It is generally agreed that music causes increased *arousal* in those who are interested in it and who therefore listen to it with some degree of concentration. By *arousal*, I mean a condition of heightened alertness, awareness, interest and excitement – a generally enhanced state of being. We all crave some degree of excitement in our lives, and, if stimuli from the environment is lacking, we seek other forms of pleasure to enhance our existence. This may explain why the desire to chat to friends seems to diminish in a classroom where there is music to satisfy the brain's thirst for stimulation.

Pulse, pace and pattern in music

Everything that lives has a pulse, and so does music. Pulsation means flow, the steady current of energy coursing through and around us. Our circulatory system is an intricate network of surge and release, activity and rest. The pulse of music opens or paces the pulse of the listener.

Although we do not become perfectly synchronised with music merely by listening to it, the pulse of the music does influence the tempo of our thinking and behaviour. At a dance, for instance, the music will stimulate our body movement, and different styles of music will cause us to move in different ways. However, while driving a car and listening to a CD, the body won't harmonise to the same degree. This is because our mind is more focused on the task of driving.

Music creates multiple patterns simultaneously. The structure and design of its tones affect our body and our movement, while its changing harmonies and chords can sway our emotions.

Arousal manifests itself in various unavoidable physiological changes, many of which can be measured. The electroencephalogram shows changes in amplitude and frequency of the brainwaves that it records. During arousal (Storr, 1997), electrical resistance of the skin is diminished; the pupil of the eye dilates; the respiratory rate may become faster or slower, or else become irregular. Blood pressure tends to rise, as does the heart rate. There is an increase in muscular

tone, which may be accompanied by physical restlessness. In general, the changes are those that one would expect in an animal preparing for action, whether it is flight, fight or mating. They are the same changes recorded by the polygraph or 'lie detector', which demonstrates arousal in the form of anxiety, but which, contrary to popular belief, cannot prove guilt or innocence.

Recordings of muscle 'action potentials' on another instrument, the electromyograph (Storr, 1997), showed marked increases in electrical activity in the leg muscles while the subject was listening to music, even when the subject has been told not to move. In a concert hall, the physical restlessness induced by arousal is often insufficiently controlled. Some people feel impelled to beat time with their feet or drum with their fingers, thereby disturbing other listeners. I have since discovered that this is linked with the person's physical response to sound waves in the air, mood and current state of emotion.

Storr (1997) shares with us Herbert Von Karajan's increase in pulse rate while he is conducting Beethoven's overture *Leonora No. 3*. Interestingly, his pulse rate showed the greatest increase during those passages that most moved him emotionally, and not during those in which he was making the greatest physical effort. In direct contrast, it is also worth noting that recordings of his pulse rate while he was piloting and landing a jet aircraft showed much smaller fluctuations than when he was conducting (Harrer and Harrer, 1977). Music is said to soothe the savage beast, but it may also powerfully excite it.

There is evidence that music can reduce headaches and relieve back and posture pains. In a German study, three types of music were used to determine how they affected subjects. They used a rhythmic Strauss waltz, a non-rhythmic piece of modern music by Henze and a highly rhythmic selection by an Indian musician, Ravi Shankar. The one with the highest musical predictability was the Ravi Shankar piece. It was the one that reduced cortisol and noradrenaline levels, where some patients had no more headaches! (Mockel et al., 1994.)

Brownley, McMurray and Hackney (1995) argue that music can also raise stress levels and can increase blood pressure. In one study, following high-intensity exercise, runners listened to one of two types of music – sedative or fast (techno-pop) – or no music (the control group). The group of runners who heard the fast music experienced increased levels of stress hormones, whereas the other two groups showed no rise in cortisol. Evidence suggests there may be a universal response to high-beats-per-minute music – stress levels rise! And, under certain controlled conditions, that may be good if an adrenaline response is needed. This could be used to motivate and stimulate some pupils.

Tomatis (1996) believes that, once the ear (hence, our brain) has been trained to listen to music in an active way, as opposed to passively hearing it, a domino effect can take place where other systems in the human body reorganise themselves. Tomatis says that sound provides an electrical charge that energises the brain. He devised an auditory-stimulation process that identifies various dysfunctional physical or motivational systems related to listening, hearing, communicating and movement, and corrects them via specially filtered classical music, including that of Mozart, as well as selected chants.

Tomatis further discovered that, whereas the higher frequencies powered up the brain, low-frequency tones discharged mental and physical energy (stress). Tomatis's position is that the ear is a major integrator of the nervous system. Many believe that hyperactive children may be in a constant state of motion as a means of 'charging up' their brain. We know that movement stimulates the vestibular system, and this theory would help explain the calming effect music can have on hyperactive children or pupils in our care. On the other hand, lethargic students can benefit from music's recharging influence on the nervous system.

Campbell (1997) explains that Dee Coulter, director of cognitive studies at Narop Institute in Boulder, Colorado, specialises in the relationship between musical patterning and neurological development. She explains that the use of excerpts of Mozart's music was used in some IQ and spatial-intelligence experiments at the University of California at Irvine. These extracts stimulated high-quality beta waves, or ordinary consciousness. But for optimal creativity, and for grappling with issues that do not lend themselves to simple, linear solutions, she recommends jazz. The music of Miles Davies, John Coltrane and the avant-garde composer John Cage can lift the listener into theta consciousness – the highly creative brainwave state associated with artistic and spiritual insight.

In contrast, she finds that rock, rap and other music centred on the beat constitutes an intense statement about *time* – particularly well suited to refining the abilities of children who labour under an oppressive sense of it. Because some children in America live in inner-city environments that are war zones, in order to survive this, the children dare not let their guards down – hence a heightened state of alertness most of the time. This type of rap and rock music can keep them focused. Within a chaotic, unpredictable environment, it sharpens their ability to organise. New Age and ambient music is organised *space*. For people living in a highly mental, structured life, such music helps them to unwind and float freely.

On the other hand, Jensen (2001) believes that music like the hard-core rap and rock in the inner cities can have a negative effect on youngsters. Many students who seem attracted to heavy metal or violent rap music may already be predisposed to inappropriate behaviours. In a study of young male felony offenders, rap music was most commonly cited as their favourite (Gardstrom, 1999). Narrative comments by the subjects suggested that music was more a reflection of their lives than a call to action. Only 4 per cent thought the music was causal in their behaviour, although 72 per cent said that their moods were influenced by music.

A separate study of 121 high-school students (Scheel and Westefeld, 1999) suggested that although heavy-metal fans espoused fewer compelling reasons for living and had more thoughts about suicide, subjects also claimed music elevated their moods. It was suggested previously that listening to heavy metal is not causal in suicides or inappropriate behaviour, though it raises a red flag for potential destructive behaviour (Took and Weiss, 1994).

A variety of physiological scales have been developed to study mood, and they have shown music to be a powerful manipulator of your emotional state. Psychologists were using music to induce moods as early as 1806, when Samuel Mathews first proposed the ISO principle, whereby you could induce mood by matching music to the patient's current state of mind. For instance, downbeat music for a depressed patient, then gradually changing the music's tempo, volume, pitch, melody and rhythm until it approached the desired state for the patient (Mathews, 1806).

I have been able to control this type of change myself in the research project, but by altering the process. Agitated behaviour would warrant a calming track and vice versa. Other studies have confirmed music's usefulness as a mood regulator. While several different kinds of experiment have supported music's mood-inducing effect, it has also been found that people tend to have the same emotional reactions to different kinds of music regardless of age or gender (Adaman and Blaney, 1995).

Music and the 'Mozart Effect'

There has been much controversy over the past decade about the 'Mozart Effect' and its mathematical and spatial intelligence-enhancement theory. Gordon Shaw, Frances Rausher and Katherine Ky began the 'Mozart Effect' experimentation at the University of California at

Irvine, in 1993, following Gordon Shaw's 25-year adventure in the scientific study of the brain.

Shaw (2000) investigated music as a window into higher brain function. Following work on the columnar organisational principle and spatial–temporal firing patterns of neurons, Shaw moved on to work on the Trion model, based on higher brain function. The name 'Trion' was evolved and used because it represented a group of neurons, and had three levels of firing activity.

From the Trion model in 1988, it was noted that memory patterns were enhanced. One of Shaw's students at Irvine, Xiaodan Leng, was interested in mapping computer-generated spatial–temporal reasoning sequences of memory patterns in the Trion model onto music, in order to have another means of understanding these patterns and all their different symmetry relations. Leng's results were totally unexpected: different mappings gave different recognisable styles of music. Leng and Shaw at this time realised that this could be the beginning of their quest to understand how we think, reason and create. This was the birth of using music as a window into higher brain function in Shaw's mind, and this has dominated his research ever since.

Shaw and his colleagues began to perform a series of experiments in which 36 college students were each given three sets of standard IQ spatial reasoning tasks; each task was preceded by ten minutes of:

- listening to Mozart's Sonata for Two Pianos in D Major, K448;
- listening to a relaxation tape; and
- complete silence.

Performance was improved by those tasks immediately following the first condition compared with the second two. The students participated in all three listening conditions. Immediately following each listening condition, the student was tested on one of three spatial tasks from the Stanford-Binet intelligence tests (of which there are four), namely, paper folding and cutting, pattern analysis and matrices.

Ten minutes of Mozart

In the music condition, the subject was exposed to, and listened to, ten minutes of Mozart's Sonata for Two Pianos in D Major, K448. The relaxation condition required the subjects to listen to ten minutes of relaxation instructions (the spoken word) designed to lower blood pressure. The silence condition required the subjects to sit in silence for ten minutes.

One of the three abstract-reasoning tests taken from the Stanford-Binet intelligence scale was given after each listening condition. Converting the various scores into points on the IQ scale, the research showed that the IQs of subjects participating in the music condition were 8–9 points *above* their IQ scores in the other two conditions and that the subjects performed better on abstract/spatial reasoning tests after listening to Mozart than after listening to either the relaxation tape or nothing. The music condition differed significantly from both the relaxation and the silence conditions.

Interestingly, the enhancing effect of the music did not extend beyond a 10–15 minute period during which the subjects were engaged in each spatial task.

Shaw did not expect such a large and overwhelming response from his discoveries, but he was astounded by the worldwide interest in his work. It was the media that soon called their experiment at Irvine, the 'Mozart Effect'. The idea that listening to this sonata could make you smarter, even if only for 10–15 minutes, had captured the world's interest. Mozart as a tool to enhance higher brain function is still used today. Shaw (2000) continues to test pieces of Mozart on larger groups of preschool children as well as postgraduate students to collect further data.

The Mozart Effect was used by Swanson (1992) on groups of students in the USA who had been diagnosed with attention-deficit disorder (ADD) and attention-deficit hyperactivity disorder (ADHD). He noticed that students generally had two types of symptom:

- inattention (including being easily distracted, and difficulty following through with instructions); and
- hyperactivity-impulsivity (including difficulty in awaiting their turn to do something).

While being exposed to Mozart and a spatial–temporal programme developed by Shaw called STAR, there was over ten minutes where there was *no* sign of inattention or hyperactivity in these children.

From Shaw to Gardner

In the early 1980s, Howard Gardner of Harvard wrote *Frames of Mind*, one of the most influential books on education for this generation. In it, he introduces the notion that we have multiple intelligences. In addition to linguistic, logical-mathematical, spatial and bodily-kinaesthetic intelligences, he believes that we have interpersonal, intrapersonal, naturalistic and emotional, with the musical intelligence being the 'master intelligence'.

He cites research showing that infants as young as two months are able to match the pitch, loudness and melodic contour of their mother's songs, and at four months they can match rhythmic structure as well. Science has found that infants are predisposed to these aspects of music, far more than they are to the core properties of speech, and that they engage in sound play that clearly exhibits creative properties.

In examining traditional music education in Africa, Gardner looks at the Anang of Nigeria. In this society, infants scarcely a week old are introduced to music and dancing by their mothers, while fathers fashion small drums for their children. When they reach the age of two, children join groups, where they learn many basic cultural skills, including singing, dancing and instrument playing. By the age of five, the young Anang can sing hundreds of songs, play several percussion instruments and perform dozens of intricate dance movements.

In some cultures, broad individual differences are recognised. Among the Ewew Tribes of Ghana, for example, less talented persons are made to lie on the ground, while a master musician kneels over them and beats rhythms into their body, and it is thought, into their souls. They value the power of music so greatly that it seems it is the master of all skills for life.

In 1997, during the debate on the future of arts education in public (state) schools in the USA, Howard Gardner expanded his earlier views and said that musical intelligence influenced emotional, spiritual and cultural development more than the other intelligences. Gardner believes that, of all natural gifts endowed to people, none emerges earlier than that of musical talent.

He believes that music helps structure people's thinking and working by assisting them in learning maths, language and spatial skills – the other human intellects. Legislators and school boards that ignore music in elementary education, he stated, were arrogant and unaware of how the human mind and brain have evolved.

Since *Frames of Mind* helped bring musical intelligence into the educational mainstream, hundreds of books have elaborated on this theme. Campbell (1983), in his book *Introduction to the Musical Brain*, wholeheartedly endorses the belief that the more stimulation a child receives through music, movement and the arts, the more intelligent he or she will turn out. Of course, stimulating music should be followed by quiet time and reflection, otherwise the benefits may be lost.

As most parents of teenagers know, a steady diet of music alone does not necessarily make children

brighter. It is the way in which it is delivered, fed and digested by the individual that sets the path of musical intelligence. It is this path of correct musical feeding that will be explored further in this study and my own research work.

Music brings a positive and relaxing atmosphere to many classrooms, as well as allowing the sensory integration necessary for long-term memory. It is also used as a background in some classes to mask industrial traffic or sound, and it can be used successfully to instil excitement, release stress before testing and reinforce subject matter.

In a comprehensive review of hundreds of empirically based studies between 1972 and 1992, three educators associated with the Future of Music Project in the USA found that music instruction supported development in reading, language (including a foreign language), mathematics and overall academic achievement. The investigators also found that music enhanced creativity, improved student self-esteem, developed social skills and increased perceptual motor skills and the development of psychomotor development and skills.

When working with the SEN pupils myself to develop their literacy skills, with particular emphasis on reading, I was delighted to see that many of the pupils' confidence had grown in reading aloud – because with the music supporting them rhythmically as they were reading, and taking away the embarrassment of any wrong words (music masked some mistakes), the children wanted to read to themselves aloud much of the time with headphones playing. Their confidence was boosted immensely by this method of support.

Music has also proved useful in acquiring verbal sequencing skills and language development in other countries. In Thailand, the public-school system uses songs to practise tonal aspects of language (List, 1961). In the USA, matching melodies to sentences significantly increased accuracy in verbal inflection for English as a second language (Staum, 1987), while in France, some educators advocate singing pop music to teach vocabulary, syntax and cultural context of foreign language to teenagers (Alberic, 1994).

There has been some debate about music's net impact when it comes to reading comprehension. Some scholars believe that because so much music processing takes place in the right brain, it may compete for attention with language centres in the left brain. But studies also suggest that the types of music I chose to collate and use *can* actually enhance reading comprehension. One experiment found that reading to classical music boosted comprehension, but rock music distracted readers (Etaugh and Ptasnik, 1982). Results from another trial showed that studying to familiar preferred music raised comprehensions scores (Etaugh and Ptasnik, 1982). And, in an experiment with below-average readers, listening to rap music, composing rap songs and discussing the lyrics' message increased reading proficiency for fifth- and sixth-graders in the USA (Tharyll, 1994).

Furthermore, music can facilitate letter recognition, figural fluency, pictorial memory and spatial skills by activating neurons in the right hemisphere. In one study, increasing the music's tempo actually increased reading speed. I observed this with several of my own pupils also.

More recently, researchers such as Shaw (2000) and Campbell (1997) proposed that music helps in the classroom by making connections in the brain and integrating experience into memory. But even more than a classroom tool, music at a young age might develop cognitive skills that have a long-term impact on the mind. Some scientists, including the Irvine team, postulate that musical training at an early age, while the cortex is still 'plastic', may cause permanent changes to the brain.

In one study, musicians who started training before age seven had significantly larger corpora callosa than others (the corpus callosum bridges both sides of the brain and is important to interhemispheric communication). Another found that

string players had larger cortical representations of the fingers of the left hand and the effect was greater, the younger the person has started to play (Elbert et al., 1995). Brainwave coherence, which reflects the number of functional interconnections in the brain, has been found to be greater both within and between hemispheres in people with musical training (Johnson et al., 1996).

A curriculum that uses music to emphasise sequenced skill development from an early age could enhance many aspects of learning in the brain. I propose that music could work as a prelanguage development tool that could be used for higher cognitive brain function.

Much of the earlier research has been carried out in the USA. In the United Kingdom there has been no such research work with any evidence or data to support this theory, just the occasional person using music and saying 'yes, it affected me', but never data or evidence as to 'how' or 'why'. My research study, under the heading of 'Music and the Mind', set out to investigate how music *can* make a difference to learning and life.

'Music and the Mind' – the beginnings

In 2001, I had a most wonderful experience with a GCSE music class at school. I discovered that playing extracts of music with varying styles, timbres and pitches had all the students visualising, reporting and responding *in exactly the same way*. All pupils in my class visualised the same scenes, described the same change in mood and feelings and experienced a spiritual atmosphere in the classroom from a holistic sense.

I was introducing my GCSE music class to a new unit of work – 'Music for Film'. The concept of having pupils compose a piece of music for film was daunting, and I felt that they needed to have good knowledge and understanding of the development of film music in order to appreciate the task that would be set for them. In the first lesson, I played three extracts of music that were all very different: the main theme from *Schindler's List* – John Williams (1993); 'Adiemus'– Karl Jenkins (*Adiemus Live*, 2001); and 'Time Tunnel' (*Sci-Fi Themes*, 1998).

First, I asked them to close their eyes and *listen* (use the directed listening techniques that are adopted in music) to each extract based on the musical intentions of the composer and to focus on the creation of mood and emotional response. The pupils had no idea where the extracts had come from (unless they had been subconsciously exposed to the films previously and had some recollection of aspects of the music, but this was not the case, I discovered a little later).

Pupil responses

Pupils arrived to the lesson after break time. Most, as usual, were very energetic and happy to be in their music lesson. Some pupils were late and there had been some disturbances with friends during break time; but, generally, the majority of the class were quite happy but boisterous. There were sixteen pupils in total. I gave the lesson introduction, including the aims and learning objectives. They were still quite chatty – even though I have a very good working relationship with them. I explained the long-term aim of the unit on film music and we discussed briefly some of their own favourites – some chose films as their favourites because of the storyline, and others because of the excitement with the visual effects as well as a wonderful soundtrack.

I observed the pupils closely as they listened to these extracts. As soon as the first extract of music was played the following were observed:

1. personal focus – listening and thinking skills;
2. physical response;
3. emotional response; and
4. visualisation.

Personal focus – listening and thinking skills

Pupils were noticeably more focused on the task and I noted that they were able to analyse thought processes more successfully. It was as if there were a 'focus tunnel' (as if they had a boards at either side of their ears and could not see – much like tunnel vision, but in this case 'tunnel thoughts') and the pupils responded only to the music. It was observed that pupils were not aware of the environment they were in (classroom) and that there was a visible change in the way they were taking notes and drawing. They did not let anything in the room or the classroom affect their work – they were totally focused.

Physical effect and response

Effects of the music on pupils' physical appearance and body language as they sat in their chairs was clear and evident. As the piece of music became slower, their bodies transformed. Pupils became lethargic, and arms and legs would stretch out in front of them and they physically relaxed more. Some sat back in the chairs, others curled up as if taking prime position in their place of sleep. The physical changes I observed were amazing. The music was actually changing their physical appearance.

Emotional effect and response

When the extracts had finished and there was a question-and-answer session to determine how the music had affected them emotionally, there were some startling results. The emotional effect was astonishing, with pupils expressing the same changes emotionally, both in a physical and spiritual sense. Initially, I could not comprehend how they were all feeling the same way, just by listening to the same pieces of music. Was it due to the age and gender? I was unconvinced, but continued the listening activity over a period of twenty lessons and gathered some initial results through active participation and observational field notes.

All pupils responded with the same strands of thoughts and emotions. Immediately, I began to plot and plan ways of being able to affect the way pupils could respond in lessons. How could I use music to improve standards of learning across the school? Before I could start to answer that question, however, I needed to find some answers to a more profound question – what is it that music does to our brains?

Music and the brain

Music's impact on our minds and bodies begins with the psychological process of hearing. From an evolutionary standpoint, hearing is life itself, and so we have a sophisticated system for processing sound in the brain, body and nervous system. Listening to and processing music in the brain can affect the way in which we socialise, learn, behave and apply ourselves to daily life.

When we listen to music, the sound waves in the air are captured, and the inner ear transforms them into electricity in our bodies. The effect of music on the limbic system impacts on our emotions, motor responses and hormone levels. This is registered in the conscious part of the brain through the *auditory cortex*.

The development of brain-mapping technology has enabled recent breakthroughs in tracing music's pathways through the mind. Most importantly, researchers (Gardner, 1983; Shaw 2000) have identified elaborate neural networks in the cortex, called *feature detectors*, that process music. This means that the music we listen to actually determines the arrangement of neural networks in our brain. Also known as *neural modules* or *auditory-cognitive neural architecture*, these neural networks perform a variety of sophisticated tasks that include encoding and remembering melodies, or recognising patterns.

EEG (electroencephalograph) studies show that listening to music increases coherence, or electrical relationships, between different areas of the brain. Evidence of electromusical networks can also be seen when different brain cell groups are activated with an electrode, which can actually cause people to *hear* different fragments of music. Neuroscientists have shown that listening to music makes connections and forms patterns that enable us to process information more efficiently, and so boost our cognitive powers. The more often we listen to music, the more effective this becomes.

The discovery of music's neural impact is exciting, but music might derive even more cognitive power from its unique ability to access both the left and right hemispheres of the brain. Some people appear to be left-brain dominant, meaning they are more analytical or word-driven, while right-brain dominance favours creativity and visual-spatial ability. In general, the left brain handles symbolic activities, such as language and logic, while the right brain is responsible for direct perception, including spatial tasks and abstract, intuitive leaps. Listening to music actually taps both sides, potentially uniting creative functions in the mind.

Sound waves make brainwaves

In addition to rearranging the neural networks, music plays with your state of mind as the electrical energy generated by firing neurons creates *brainwaves*. The alpha, beta, theta and delta frequencies created by neural activity – brainwaves – determine what operations you are best suited to conduct at that moment.

For instance, alpha states, which correlate with relaxation, make the brain receptive to new information, focus the mind for quiet thought and enable meditation. Beta is best for attentive mental activity. Theta waves indicate stress, pleasure, deprivation or creative effort. Slow the waves to delta speed and you are asleep. The music a person chooses to listen to can influence the waves' frequency and the person's state of mind. Understanding of such events has even permeated into popular culture: for example, in the film *Se7en*, the main character uses a metronome to slow his pulse rate to aid sleeping.

It's not only the mind that is influenced by music: the body also responds, and musical messages travel down the spinal cord, impacting the *autonomic nervous system*, which regulates the heart rate, blood pressure, muscular activity, metabolism and other vital functions. The autonomic nervous system is literally the link between the mental and physical self, and music directly affects its working.

Although the general rule is that loud, fast music increases metabolism, and soft, slow music slows us down, a subject's personal response to music also depends upon autonomic reactivity, determined by things such as age, gender and physical fitness, as well as emotional reactivity and personal attitude towards the music. In other words, the degree of autonomic response to any given piece of music can vary from one person to another.

Shaw (2000) investigated the cognitive and behavioural changes associated with listening to music and found that stimulating music and physiological arousal are associated with increased energy, aggression and anxiety, while soothing music and relaxation can promote calmness, passivity and depression.

It is not actually necessary to be able to hear to be affected by music at the autonomic level. Even people who are mute and deaf show physiological responses to the vibrations of musical sound. Evidence indicates that, even in the absence of the *sense* of hearing to process sound, the human body has an innate *sensibility* to music that reaches to the deepest core.

Research suggests that music can enhance maths, language, reading and memorising facts. However, explanations for *why* music works as a learning aid is lacking. One possible explanation is that music induces a receptive mood that enhances cognitive processes in general. It might serve as a mnemonic memory aid to help the mind encode information.

Whether learning is accompanied by music or the learner sings new words or concepts out loud, research suggests that music seems to help initial learning, recall and transference into working memory. It is exciting to consider that something that sounds good can improve our memories.

In taking the research questions and beginning to map out 'how' to instigate such a large-scale project on a school, I needed to create and produce the relevant tools for teachers to carry out the task. These tools would include the creation of music catalogues that would help guide teachers to use the music correctly.

What music when?

The six music catalogues I produced were:

Catalogue 1: *Music for Learning and Focus – The Mozart Effect*
1. Piano Concerto No. 21 – Andante
2. Divertimento – No. 15 – Adagio
3. Adagio for Violin and Orchestra
4. String Quartet No. 21 – Andante
5. Serenade No. 10 – *Gran Partita* – Adagio
6. *Eine Kleine Nachtmusik* – Romance
7. Flute and Harp Concerto – Andantino
8. Piano Concerto No. 23 – Adagio
9. Flute Quartet No. 1 – Adagio
10. Violin Concerto No. 3 – Adagio
11. Divertimento No. 2 – Adagio
12. Clarinet Concerto – Adagio

Catalogue 2: *Music for Learning and Focus*
1. 'Sweet Harmony' Live the Dream Mix – The Beloved
2. *Eine Kleine Nachtmusik* – Allegro – Mozart
3. *Oxygene 2* – Jean Michel Jarre
4. *Pavane* – Fauré – modern version from *Utopia*
5. Flute Concerto in D – Allegro – Vivaldi
6. 'Love Train' – from *Sounds of Blackness*

7. Concerto in C Major for 2 Trumpets – Vivaldi
8. 'Julia' from *Brideshead Revisited*
9. 'The Hunt' from *Brideshead Revisited*
10. 'Myserium' from *Libera*
11. Divertimento in D Major – Mozart
12. Serenade in D Major – Mvt 1 – Mozart
13. Serenade in D Major – Mvt 3 – Mozart
14. 'Children' – Robert Miles
15. 'Bridge Over Troubled Water' – Hear'Say
16. Rosamunde – Schubert
17. 'Valse' from *Giselle* – Adolphe Adam
18. Symphony No. 35 – Mvt 3 – Mozart
19. 'Sebastian Against the World' from *Brideshead Revisited*

Catalogue 3: *Music for Relaxation and Calm*
1. *Adagio for Strings* – Barber
2. 'On Earth as it is in Heaven' – from *The Mission*
3. 'Falls' – from *The Mission*
4. 'Gabriel's Oboe' – from *The Mission*
5. 'Borther's' – from *The Mission*
6. 'Adiemus' – from *Adiemus Live* – Karl Jenkins
7. 'Cantus Insolitus' – from *Adiemus Live* – Karl Jenkins
8. 'The Wooing of Etain' – from *Adiemus Live* – Karl Jenkins
9. 'Dawn Dancing' – from *Adiemus Live* – Karl Jenkins
10. 'Salva Me' – from *Libera*
11. 'Sanctus' – from *Libera*
12. 'Agnus Dei' – from *Libera*
13. 'Mysterium' – from *Libera*
14. 'Now We Are Free' – from *Gladiator*
15. 'The Heart Asks Pleasure' – from *The Piano*
16. 'Libera Me' – Leon
17. 'Julia's Theme' from *Brideshead Revisited*
18. 'Orphans of the Storm' from *Brideshead Revisited*
19. 'Sebastian's Alone' from *Brideshead Revisited*
20. 'Venice Nocturne' from *Brideshead Revisited*

Catalogue 4: *Music to Motivate, Stimulate and Energise*
1. 'Hooked on a Feeling' – Blue Swede
2. 'In Caelum Fero' – Karl Jenkins
3. 'Missing' – Everything but the Girl
4. 'Gimme Some Lovin'' – Spencer Davis Group
5. 'You Can Make it If You Try' – Sounds of Blackness
6. 'Ceridwen's Curse' – Karl Jenkins
7. 'I'm on My Way' – The Proclaimers
8. 'Kayama' – Karl Jenkins
9. 'Stuck in the Middle With You' – Stealers Wheel
10. 'Never' – Ronan Hardiman
11. 'Dos a Dos' – Karl Jenkins
12. 'American Dream' – Jakatta
13. 'The Blackness Blues' – Sounds of Blackness
14. 'Cu Chullain' – Karl Jenkins
15. 'Best Years of Our Lives' – Baha Men
16. 'I'm a Believer' – Eddie Murphy

Catalogue 5: *Music for 'Learning to Learn'*
For brainstorming (1–6-minute excerpts)
1. 'Captain Scarlet's Theme' (fast)
2. 'Dream Chunnate' (fast)
3. 'Cu Chullain' (fast)
4. '21 Seconds' (fast)

Reflective – individual learning (15-minutes slow mix)
5. 'Time to say Goodbye'
6. 'Aquarium'
7. 'Facades'

Spiritual / meditation (5 minutes)
8. 'An Ending'

Group task (10 minutes)
9. 'Arachnaphobia'
10. 'Hook'
11. Main title theme from *Jurassic Park*
12. Main title theme from *Raiders of the Lost Ark*

Individual task (10 minutes)
13. 'The Breaking of the Fellowship' from *The Lord of the Rings: The Fellowship of the Ring*
14. 'May it Be'

Meditation / supportive
15. 'Capriccio for Chinese Flute'
16. 'Soukka Stars'
17. 'A Tayal Folk Song'

Catalogue 6: *Music for Personal Reflection and Realisation*

Reflection

1. Main title theme from *Schindler's List*
2. 'Like Jesus to a Child'
3. 'Intermezzo'
4. 'Molly'
5. 'Largo'
6. 'Up Where We Belong'
7. 'Feather Fly'
8. Main title theme from *Empire of the Sun*
9. Main title theme from *The Color Purple*
10. 'Where Dreams Are Born'

Realisation – music to enthuse and create personal potential

11. 'Bad Reputation'
12. 'Hallelujah'
13. 'Duelling Banjos'
14. 'Flop Eared Mule'
15. 'Clinch Mountain Backstop'
16. 'City Madness'
17. Main title theme from *Back to the Future*
18. Main title theme from *Mad Max*
19. 'Sudden Impact'
20. 'Eye of the Tiger'

For each catalogue, hours, even days and weeks, were spent analysing the timbres, textures and instrumental constructions and ensembles so that correct extracts would be compiled for the correct catalogues. I had to consider the pitch changes and the core pulsations of each piece to ensure they would change emotions, feelings, directions of learning and the environment as used by the teachers.

In order for the catalogues to be used correctly by the teachers, I needed to intervene and produce a guide pack that would be used by the instigators. After all, the teachers who would be instigating and playing the music to affect learning were not musicians, and many of them did not 'understand' music in a generalised sense. Therefore, I produced the teachers' guide pack and ensured that INSET was given before asking teachers to begin using the music.

Who?

Taking into consideration the work that Shaw (Shaw and Ky, 1993) had carried out with the 'Mozart Effect', I decided that one aspect of the research would focus on the use of Mozart as a tool for learning. In many respects, I wanted to dispute the notion that it was not just Mozart's music alone that could enhance spatial intelligence.

In considering the overall research design, I chose the following as the main areas of focus:

- Mathematics – (Year 9 – two control and two tests groups) testing the theory that the Mozart Effect can raise standards in mathematical deductions, and spatial intelligence tasks.

- Science – (Year 7) – the use of music to enhance scientific recall and higher-level reasoning as well as abstract reasoning. Pupils recalling experiments and data as well as target setting.

- English – (Year 11) – learning specific vocabulary – key to coursework and crucial for the final examination (written exam in June 2002).

- Welsh, Business Education, History, PE, Geography, French and RE would test the use of music to enhance the learning environment through emotional change as well as using certain extracts for 'stimulating' discussion and reflection.

- SEN – I chose to test the use of music in developing SEN pupils' literacy and numeracy skills as well as some behavioural issues. Some music-therapy programmes were also devised for some pupils in line with the playing of extracts of music from the different catalogues.

- Year 7 PSE – the use of music in the 'Learning to Learn' programme, which would support pupils' understanding of:
  1. 'how' they learn;
  2. 'what' they learn;
  3. 'why' they learn;
  4. 'how' and 'why' we all learn differently; and
  5. 'how' I can make myself a better learner.

I also decided I needed to narrow down the focus of my enquiry to the following categories:

- concentration and study skills;
- achievement – academic and personal;
- emotional and behavioural; and
- specific use of music.

The case study was initially one school alone. To begin with, it would be only certain classes, but it soon amounted to more than 650 children and 40 staff being involved in the research in either a research-led capacity or as a secondary source.

Initially, I had intended the research to be small scale, a few classes, but, due to the overwhelming response from staff, I had most of the school involved. This was now a grand-scale operation in comparison with previous work done in this area, and, as a novice, I found it initially rather daunting.

What I found

If you want all the gory details about my research methodologies then please email me at nina.jackson@independentthinking.co.uk. Along with a series of questionnaires and interviews with staff and students alike, we also used a student diary, which you can download from the Independent Thinking website (www.independentthinking.co.uk).

Those impressive results at the beginning of this chapter are from the teacher questionnaires. My findings from the pupil diaries make equally exciting reading:

Concentration and study skills

- 84 per cent of pupils felt that the music helped them concentrate 'all of the time';

- 14 per cent of the pupils felt that the music helped them concentrate 'sometimes'; and

- 92 per cent of pupils felt that the music was 'brilliant' and helped them tremendously with their 'concentration and study skills'.

Academic and personal achievement

- 70 per cent of pupils felt that the music has helped them achieve 'quite a lot';

- 8 per cent of pupils felt that the music had helped them achieve 'loads'; and

- 15 per cent of pupils felt that the music had helped them achieve 'more than usual'.

Emotional and behavioural changes

- 1 per cent of pupils felt that some of the music made them feel sadder;

- 80 per cent of the pupils felt that some of the music made them feel happier;

- 96 per cent of the pupils felt that some of the music made them feel more relaxed;

- 95 per cent of the pupils felt that some of the music made them more excited;

- 100 per cent of the pupils said the music made them feel more like working; and

- 97 per cent of the pupils said the music made them feel better about themselves.

Use of music in lessons

- 80 per cent of pupils reported that the use of music in lessons was interesting;

- 37 per cent of pupils reported that some music was unusual;

- 6 per cent of pupils reported that some music used was odd;

- 75 per cent of pupils reported that the use and choice of music played was good;

- 75 per cent of pupils reported that the use of music in lessons was different from what they had experienced before;

- 95 per cent of pupils reported they would like to hear most of the music again in lessons;

- 90 per cent of pupils reported that they could get used to the use of music in lessons to help them learn; and

- 100 per cent of pupils reported that the idea and use of music to make learning more fun and accessible was brilliant.

Even the parents became excited by the work we were doing. Pupils began to use music themselves at home and were prepared to share with parents its use and consequences on their own learning. Some parents had observed changes in attitude to work and the way that pupils were keen to do homework. Some parents explained that this was due to the information I had passed to pupils about making the brain active, and the way that the sound waves in air made brainwaves. Some parents commented on the detailed manner in which some of the children had explained the firing of the neurons.

Some children's behaviour had also changed. When some of the pupils became frustrated or anxious about home circumstances, the pupils asked their parents to put some relaxing and calm music on. Occasionally, if there was a family row, some children asked the parents to calm down and listen to the music! Parents were astonished at the changes in some of their children and thanked me for the work I had done and for how I had transformed their children into wonderful pupils.

I was flattered and honoured to receive such a response from parents. Now, during some of the parents' evenings, parents just come along to let me know how the use of music in the home is affecting family life – everyone is happy so they tell me!

In some other lessons, teachers have been using music to support pupils' learning. In two other groups, there have been some substantial differences with self-study skills, levels of attainment and motivation towards working. During the pupil interviews, two pupils commented that the use of music had helped them to improve their grades from an average of Ds to Bs and Cs. This could be due to the longer period of time that teachers have used the music with these classes rather then the eight lessons with the test groups – which was not long enough even to make the pupils feel comfortable in the use of music in lessons. However, some teachers could give only eight lessons to test the pupils.

Research findings from lesson observations, audio recordings and field notes

- All teachers who took part in the project and all pupils who were exposed to the variety of music in their lessons responded with a mostly positive attitude to the research work.

- Some Year 11 pupils came to see me following the study to ask me to compile a study CD for them to support them with their revision skills in preparation for their GCSE examinations.

- Since the early research was conducted, more and more schools and educational institutions have conducted further research for me using my 'Music and the Mind' programme. There is now a stronger case to argue that the use of certain types of music, used effectively in a learning environment can impact upon standards.

- Boys and girls respond differently to self-study and the use of music.

- It is clear that boys and girls respond differently in different lessons and situations, depending on the collection of musical instruments, timbre and textures within the extracts played.

- Not all boys and girls respond to the music in the same way.

- Teachers' preference for certain pieces of music influenced their choices and sometimes the overuse of some pieces, which had, and still can have, an adverse effect on pupils.

- The same type of music has different effects on different children.

- There is some evidence to suggest that it has raised standards – with specific reference to Mathematics, Science and English. Numeracy and literacy strategies and interventions have supported SEN pupils. Some pupils' behaviour and attitude to work has also been affected and noted. There have been significant improvements in the ways in which many pupils apply themselves to tasks and their individual studies.

- The use of 'Music and the Mind' has supported both pupils and staff alike.

- The use of 'Music and the Mind' has affected family relationships and family members' attitudes towards each other.

School-based developments

Following the research work using 'Music and the Mind', the school has been the focus of much attention by other educational establishments and institutions. It has enhanced teachers' professional development as they themselves have been developing tools for learning using music.

Teachers themselves are happier in their work and are willing to ask for support and guidance in the application of other extracts of music to develop their own teaching and learning programmes of study. 'Music and the Mind' is part of teacher induction and used in the Initial Teacher Education and Training professional-studies programme.

The impact on colleagues has been tremendous and they are often asked about the use of music in their classrooms. This has motivated some teachers to carry out other small-scale research study themselves.

Impact on pupil experiences

The use of 'Music and the Mind' in the larger framework of teaching and learning at Ogmore School is embedded into the units of study. Pupils are exposed to and happy for music to be used in support of their learning. Some pupils are now so accustomed to the use of music that they rely on it as a support tool for the development of skills, acquisition of knowledge and memory recall. Many pupils request music if they are experiencing behavioural difficulties, especially those who are having anger-management sessions with a counsellor.

Pupils now use music for supporting the completion of homework and are choosing the extracts carefully. Parents have telephoned the school asking for some assistance in purchasing suitable music and its use in the home to support studying for longer-term projects such as examinations and coursework.

Using music for learning in your own classroom – a quick guide

All in all, I worked with six catalogues of different music for different purposes. Here is a taste of what I used and why I used it.

Catalogues 1 and 2 – Music for Learning and Focus

Extracts (all Mozart) included:

Piano Concerto No. 21 – Andante
Divertimento – No. 15 – Adagio
Adagio for Violin and Orchestra
String Quartet No. 21 – Andante
Serenade No. 10 – *Gran Partita* – Adagio
Eine Kleine Nachtmusik – Romance

Oxygene 2 – Jean Michel Jarre
Pavane – Fauré – modern version from *Utopia*
Flute Concerto in D – Allegro – Vivaldi
'Love Train' – from *Sounds of Blackness*
Concerto in C Major for 2 Trumpets – Vivaldi
'Julia' from *Brideshead Revisited*
'The Hunt' from *Brideshead Revisited*
'Myserium' from *Libera*

'Focusing' music can help pupils and yourself with abstract reasoning, learning and recall, problem solving and brainwork (analytical, creative, administrative etc.) and some aspects of motivation. Music can prime your mind for deducing mathematical theorems, drawing conclusions from chemistry experiments, maybe playing chess, or any abstract-thinking challenge. By using the music correctly, you will be able to stimulate aspects of the right brain in order to promote logical and analytical thinking.

Suggested ways of using the *Learning and Focus* music to promote high-level reasoning

Listen to one of the extracts before undertaking a task – the time will vary for you as a teacher – between two and ten minutes. This will be a time for priming and warm-up. Be careful not to use the music as a 'background' effect, or it might actually create a 'dual-task paradigm' and distract the worker. This will then become deconstructive.

When listening to the extracts, get the pupils to focus on the themes and melodies. Get them to remember the sounds, hear them change and pass from one instrument to the other so that they can link sequences of events or numbers.

If your problem-solving process extends over weeks or longer, you might want to use a broader approach to brain tuning through music. For long-term puzzles or problems, use music as a mood-dependent, recall trigger. Pick the extracts that inspired the pupils in previous lessons and listen to them frequently throughout the preparation process. Then, encourage the development of the problem-solving aspect by listening to the same recording on a regular basis – daily or even weekly, depending on the scope of the project. The music the pupils heard as you gathered information about your problem will recall that knowledge at a subconscious level, rearrange it, and allow it to synthesise in new formulations. Stick with this form of 'incubation', listening until 'eureka!' strikes. These extracts must not be played for more than ten minutes at a time, or else they become redundant in their application of developing effective brain tuning.

Suggested ways of using the *Learning and Focus* music for language and logic

Listen for two to ten minutes or so before you begin the cognitive task, then turn off the music. As with right-brain priming, you want the pupils to prepare for, not compete with, their thinking. Teach the aspect of language, then replay the music after the teaching and get them to link words with sounds, pitches or timbres.

With the aid of the music, get them to concentrate on the sequential thought. Listen carefully to the beats and how they are grouped together in time, and how patterns change from one group to the next. This supports the frequency level of words and pitches in our languages and the repetitive aspect of language development.

Refresh the analytical mind once again with musical breaks or snacks. This will rejuvenate the thought process and provide the reflection time or physical break needed to get the brain (and person) ready for the next task.

Catalogue 3 – Music for Relaxation and Calm

Extracts included:

Adagio for Strings – Barber
'On Earth as it is in Heaven' – from *The Mission*
'Gabriel's Oboe' – from *The Mission*
'Adiemus' – from *Adiemus Live* – Karl Jenkins
'Cantus Insolitus' – from *Adiemus Live* – Karl Jenkins
'Agnus Dei' – from *Libera*
'Mysterium' – from *Libera*
'Now We Are Free' – from *Gladiator*
'The Heart Asks Pleasure' – from *The Piano*

We live in an age of high-level anxiety. When stress puts you on edge, music can smooth you out, slow you down and save you from the ravages of tension. Music for relaxation and calm can help you and your pupils with stress and anxiety, patience, people, panic, balance, meditation and sleep.

Relaxing music flows through your nervous system to counteract the effects of stress on your body, while in your mind the right kinds of music can stimulate alpha brainwaves for clear thinking and patience, or delta waves, which signal sleep. When tension gets the upper hand and panic sets in, music can interrupt the negative biofeedback loop between the mind and body and give some room to breathe. And, on the interpersonal front, relaxing music has been shown to promote communication among people, easing

difficult discussions and averting potential confrontations.

Suggested ways of using *Music for Relaxation and Calm*

Play a suitable extract at the beginning and/or end of the lesson to calm the pupils – this will help their heart rate to slow down as well as lower any hyperactivity. You may choose to do this at any point during the learning process. Tell them to close their eyes and place their head in their hands or on the table. Play the music for 2–3 minutes. Then, ask them gently (in a whispering tone) to raise their heads and take a deep breath to relax. This has had fantastic responses from pupils and adults. It sets them up for positive learning.

Use extracts to set the scene – if you're delivering a particularly poignant task. Music can affect the emotions and give us a physical response. Choose your pieces carefully here so that you can link the activity with the mood that the music creates. You can also use excerpts of music other than those in the catalogue to support your teaching, but make them relevant, e.g. for discovering space, maybe an extract from *Apollo 13* or even *Space 1999*.

Give an extract of music to an individual who is displaying unacceptable behaviour in your class. Ask them to wear the headphones and listen to the piece on their own while you continue to teach and this will relieve the pressure from you and that pupil – thus supporting better learning and teaching. It should calm the pupil and prepare him/her to continue the lesson.

Use the extracts to induce relaxation and calm as a medicine tool – Aristotle called music medicine because it worked as a psychocatharsis. Turning to music can help vent anger, frustration and grief. Relaxation and calm music will support you and your pupils with aggression, repressed anger, grief and problem relationships. With each extract, let the fire burn bright and hot for a moment, consuming the anger, until, with the last chord, it burns itself out.

Use music in your classroom at intervals, or long periods of time, to free angry emotions, which are often accompanied by a feeling of being trapped. When your natural reactions are causing claustrophobia, music can provide a quick escape route – remember, relief is only a flick switch away. This can be employed with the pupils, or you might choose this route yourself as a teacher after a challenging lesson.

The extracts of music in this catalogue were chosen for their tempo, timbre and pitch. These were important so that the extracts could be used to slow the heart rate and get pupils to be calmer, or to use the music as an environmental tool while they learned.

Catalogue 4 – Music to Motivate, Stimulate and Energise

Extracts included:

'Hooked on a Feeling' – Blue Swede
'In Caelum Fero' – Karl Jenkins
'Missing' – Everything but the Girl
'Gimme Some Lovin'' – Spencer Davis Group
'You Can Make it If You Try' – Sounds of Blackness
'Ceridwen's Curse' – Karl Jenkins
'I'm on My Way' – The Proclaimers
'Best Years of Our Lives' – Baha Men
'I'm a Believer' – Eddie Murphy

Extracts were chosen carefully to create the sense of urgency, designed to raise the heart rate sufficiently to become stimulated. Consideration was given to the use of voices, lyrics and instrumentation to give force and power behind the music in order to inspire application of thought when each individual was working. This catalogue is designed to help pupils and staff become energised, motivated and stimulated in their work environment.

Energising music can make your brain exercise longer and harder. It increases speed and workload capacity for greater conditioning benefits, while it lowers perceived exertion rate. Choosing suitable music was a task. It needed powerful textures and timbres in order to inspire and energise. The combinations of instruments was very important as well as the structure and length.

Music with a strong steady beat can:

- increase endurance;
- boost effort level;
- regularise pace, movement and breathing;
- enhance muscle control;
- increase motivation; and
- distract from discomfort and agitation.

Suggested ways of using *Music to Motivate, Stimulate and Energise*

Use chosen extracts of music to enthuse the pupils if you feel that they are lethargic or tired. Get them to move their arms and legs or to clap to the beat so that bodily movements become part of the energising and stimulation process.

For accelerated-learning tasks, choose excerpts that mean 'victory' to you or the class – music that has a sense of purpose and pride. Inform the pupils that they have *x* time while the music is playing to complete the task. The choice of music will inspire and give them the sense of urgency. It's the short and sharp tactic to achieving their full potential.

Use focused listening before an activity to get them started or at the end of a task for thoughtful reflection time. This will keep the pupils and yourself fresh and energised.

Tune up with team listening. If you choose to do group work, then use as many personal players as you can to create a sense of team effort within the group. Let them choose music that will inspire them, but they must see this as a triumphant tool, not as a tool for passive listening while they work.

In order to break up activities or tasks in your lessons, then, give them a musical snack: instead of food for energy, music to develop the brain. A short excerpt of a minute will prepare them for the next task/activity and also give you time to reflect and evaluate your work.

These extracts can be used in any way you feel will support your pupils and help them to become more stimulated, motivated and energised in their application of learning and development of thought processes in your lessons.

Catalogue 5 – Music for 'Learning to Learn'

Extracts included:

For brainstorming (1–6-minute excerpts)
'Captain Scarlet's Theme' (fast)

Reflective – individual learning (15-minutes slow mix)
'Time to say Goodbye'
'Aquarium'

Spiritual / meditation (5 minutes)
'An Ending'

Group task (10 minutes)
Main title theme from *Jurassic Park*
Main title theme from *Raiders of the Lost Ark*

Individual task (10 minutes)
'The Breaking of the Fellowship' from *The Lord of the Rings: The Fellowship of the Ring*
'May it Be'

Meditation / supportive
'Capriccio for Chinese Flute'
'A Tayal Folk Song'

This is a collection of music to be used for specific tasks that are linked to the four areas discussed

previously. The extracts in this catalogue are grouped according to which tasks they are suitable for. You will be able to use them in conjunction with:

- brainstorming exercises;
- reflective exercises – supporting individual learning;
- spiritual exercises/meditation – a time for calm and deep thought;
- group tasks (10 minutes);
- individual tasks (10 minutes); and
- thinking time – a time for reflecting on and evaluating work.

Catalogue 6 – Music for Personal Reflection and Realisation

Extracts included:

Reflection
Main title theme from *Schindler's List*
Main title theme from *Empire of the Sun*
Main title theme from *The Color Purple*

Realisation – music to enthuse and create personal potential
'Bad Reputation'
'Hallelujah'
'Duelling Banjos'
Main title theme from *Back to the Future*
Main title theme from *Mad Max*
'Sudden Impact'
'Eye of the Tiger'

As individuals, we continue to live in a world that is fast, furious and often frantic. Too many times we forget about ourselves as individuals and spend hours each and every day working to satisfy our employers. The pupils work hard to satisfy teachers, and families do not have the time to talk or reflect upon the successes and celebrations of life.

Music for Personal Reflection and Realisation was originally prepared for groups of young people who were disaffected with school and life, as well as lacking confidence and inspiration in the skills and individual personalities that they possessed. We are all special in our own way – we have many wonderful qualities as individuals and often we do not celebrate these qualities or give time for us to feel good about what we do in life.

This catalogue specifically sets out to help all ages to feel good about themselves, and for the individual person to take time to reflect on the successes, and sometimes difficulties, that we encounter while living lives that can be turbulent, smooth, disjointed and calm.

Use each extract to help you:

- to reflect upon the successes of the day in work, relationships or family;

- to take time to focus upon what has been learned and revise and recall the successful storing of this information; and

- to boost morale and motivation and the understanding that anything can be done with a little enthusiasm.

Use the music to improve your mood, raise your psychological arousal, preparing the way to be positive and proactive in everything you want to do. Use it to erase negative or unwanted thoughts and let it take you to a place of harmony and inner beauty. Let the music create a positive outlook to clear the negative cognitions from your mind. It will act as a distraction for you and your pupils.

Some pupils or individuals will feel anxious about interacting with others. If so, ask them to jot down three positive points about themselves so it prepares them and motivates them for what they might feel is a difficult time ahead.

Then there is visualisation, the technique of boosting music's mood-lifting power. Think of it as a 'golden light' filling your mind and let each beat that you hear make the light brighter. Use

Music for Personal Reflection and Realisation for any evaluation time, too. You may also utilise the tracks along with the same types of techniques as Catalogues 1–5, if you feel you can use them specifically for 'measured learning' and/or mood enhancers or environmental changes.

Last word

And after all that, if there are still any people out there who remain unconvinced, then consider this. Since completing my work, I have been involved in 37 separate research projects across the UK using music to raise achievement in the classroom and among educators, children and parents involved in these projects.

Perhaps we should leave the last word to Howard Gardner, who has done so much to open our eyes to the many different ways in which we can all excel. In 1997, in an article entitled 'The Musical Mind', Gardner suggested that music might be a 'master intelligence', and should be viewed differently from other intelligences. He said musical intelligence probably carries more emotional, spiritual and cultural weight than the other intelligences. But perhaps most important, Gardner says, is that music helps people organise the way they think and work by helping them develop in other areas, such as mathematics, language and spatial reasoning, and that, as I found out, music can also have a profound effect on behaviour and emotional wellbeing.

Can you afford not to have that CD player in your classroom?

References and bibliography

Adaman, J. E., and Blaney, P. H. (1995), 'The effects of musical mood induction on creativity', *Journal of Creative Behaviour*, 29, 95–108.

Alberic, G. (1994), 'En Chanson: "Pourquoi" et "Comment", Le francais dans le monde', (Paris: Hachette), February/March, 276, 111–116.

Beentjes, J. W. J., Cees, M. K., and van der Voort, T. H. A. (1996), 'Combining background media with doing homework: Incidence of background media use and perceived effects', *Communication Education*, 45, 59–72.

Black, S. (1997), 'The Musical Mind', *The American School Board Journal*, January, 20–22.

Boethius, A. M. S. (1989), *Fundamentals of Music*, Claude V. Plaisca (ed.), Calvin M. Bower (trans.), (New Haven and London: Yale University Press), p. 8.

Brownley, K. A., McMurray, R. G., and Hackney, A. C. (1995), 'Effects of music on physiological and affective responses to graded treadmill exercise in trained and untrained runners', *International Journal of Psychophysiology*, 12, 16–18.

Campbell, Don G. (1983), *Introduction to the Musical Brain*, 2nd edn, (Missouri: MMB).

Campbell, Don G. (1997), *The Mozart Effect*, (London: Hodder & Stoughton).

Davidson, C. W., and Powell, L. A. (1986), 'Effects of easy-listening background music on the on-task-performance of fifth-grade children', *Journal of Educational Research*, 80 (1), 29–33.

Elbert, T., Pantev, C., Wienbruch, B., Rockstroh, B., and Taub, E. (1995), 'Increased cortical representation of the fingers of the left hand in string players', *Science*, 13th October, 270 (5234), 305–307.

Etaugh, C., and Ptasnik, P. (1982), 'Effects of studying to music and post study relaxation on reading comprehension', Nova University, USA.

Farnsworth, P. (1969), *The Social Psychology of Music*, (Iowa: Iowa State University Press).

Gardner, H. (1983), *Frames of Mind*, (New York: Basic Books).

Gardner, H. (1997), 'The Musical Mind', (Irvine: University of California).

Gardstrom, S. C. (1999), 'Music exposure and criminal behaviour: Perceptions of juvenile offender', *Journal of Music Therapy*, 23, 116–125.

Hall, J. (1952), 'The effect of background music on reading comprehension of 278 eighth and ninth graders', *Journal of Educational Research*, 45, 451–458.

Hardy, G. H. (1940), *A Mathematician's Apology*, (Cambridge: Cambridge University Press), p. 26.

Harrer, G., and Harrer, H. 'Music emotion & autonomic function' in *Music and the Brain*, Macdonald Critchley and R. A. Henson (eds), (London: Heinemann Medical Books).

Henry, S. A., and Swartz, R. G. (1995), 'Enhancing healthcare education with accelerated learning techniques', *Journal of Nursing Staff Development*, 11 (1), 21–24.

Hughes, J. R., Fino, J. J., and Melyn, M. A. (1999), 'Is there a chronic change of the 'Mozart Effect' on epileptiform activity? A case study', *Clinical Electroencephalography*, 30, 44–45.

Hurwitz, I., Wolff, P. H., Bortnick, B. D., and Kokas, K. (1975), 'Nonmusical effects of the Kodaly music curriculum in primary grade children', *Journal of Learning Disabilities*, 8, 45–51.

Jensen, E. (2001), *Arts with the Brain in Mind*, (Alexandria, VA: ASCD).

Johnson, J. K., Petsche, H., Richter, P., von Stein, A., and Filz, O. (1996), 'The dependence of coherence estimates of spontaneous EEG on gender and music training', *Music Perception Journal*, 13, 563–582.

Johnson, J. K., Cotman, C. W., Tasaki, C. S., and Shaw, G. L. (1998), 'Enhancement in spatial-temporal reasoning after Mozart listening condition in Alzheimer's disease. A case study', *Neurol Research*, 20 (8), 666–672.

Jourdan, R. (1997), *Music, the Brain and Ecstasy*, (New York: William Morrow).

Kemmis, S., and McTaggart, R. (1992), *The Action Research Planner*, 3rd ed. (Victoria, Australia: Deakin University Press).

Koppelman, D., and Imig, S. (1995), 'The Effect of Music on Children's Writing Content', University of Virginia, Charlottesville, VA. (ERIC Document Reproduction Service No. ED 383 002).

Lenhoff, H. M., Wang, P. P., Greenberg, F., and Bellugi, U. (1997), 'Williams Syndrome and the brain', *Scientific American*, December, 68–73.

Levi-Strauss, C. (1970), *The Raw and the Cooked*, (London: Cape), p. 18.

List, G. (1961), 'Speech melody and song melody in Central Thailand', *Ethnomusicology*, 5, 16–32.

Mathews, S. J. (1806), *On The Effects of Music in Curing and Palliating Diseases*, (Philadelphia: Wagner).

Mockel, M., Rocker, L., Stork, T., Vollert, J., Danne, O., Eichstadt, H., Muller, R., and Hochrein, H. (1994), 'Immediate physiological responses of healthy volunteers to different types of music: Cardiovascular, hormonal and metal changes', *European Journal of Applied Physiology*, 14, 25–36.

Morrison, K. R. B. (1993), *Planning and Accomplishing School-Centred Evaluation*, (Norfolk: Peter Francis Publications).

Nisbet, J., and Watt, J. (1984), 'Case Study', in J. Bell, T. Bush, A. Fox, J. Goodey and S. Goulding (ed.) *Conducting Small-scale Investigations in Educational Management*, (London: Harper & Row), pp. 79–92.

Ostrander, S., and Schroeder, L., 1997, *Super Learning 2000*, (New York: Delacorte Press).

Rauscher, F., Shaw, G., Levine, L., Wright, E., Dennis,W., and Newcomb, R. (1997), 'Music training causes long-term development of pre-school children's spatial-temporal reasoning', *Neurological Research Journal*, 19, 2–8.

Scheel, K. R., and Westefeld, J. S. (1999), 'Heavy metal music and adolescent suicidality: An empirical investigation', *Adolescence*, Summer.

Shaw, G. (2000), *Keeping Mozart in Mind*, (Academic Press USA).

Shaw, G., and Ky, K. (1993), 'Music and spatial task performance', *Neurobiology of Learning*, 6, 455–498.

Staum, L. M., (1987), 'Music as an intonational cue for bilingual language acquisition', *Applications of Research in Music Behaviour*, 6, 45–60.

Stenhouse, L. (1979), 'What is action research?' (mimeo) Classroom Action Research Network, Norwich, 6, 211–215.

Storr, A. (1997), *The Art of Psychotherapy*, (London: Harper Collins).

Swanson, J. M. (1992), *School based assessments and Interventions for ADD students*, (Irvine, California: KB Publications).

Tharyll, W. (1994), 'Using rap lyrics to Encourage At-Risk Elementary Grade Urban Learners to Read for Pleasure', Practicum, Nova University, USA.

Tomatis, A. (1996), *The Ear and Language*, (Norval: Moulin Publishing).

Took, K. J., and Weiss, D. (1994), 'Heavy metal, rap and adolescent behaviour', *Adolescence*, Fall, 29 (115), 613–621.

Wakshlag, J. J., Reitz, R. J., and Zillmann, D. (1982), 'Selective Exposure to and Acquisition of Information From Educational Television Programs as a Function of Appeal and Tempo of Background Music', *Journal of Educational Psychology*, 74 (5), 666–677.

Introducing Jim Roberson

I have just been flicking around the channels on my new television set, getting the hang of how it all works using good old 'experiential' learning. What do you mean, 'Read the instruction book first'? Trying quickly to zap past the various lunchtime news programmes where the news is stretched to fill the time they have (I've always thought that if they made the news reports shorter there would be less news and fewer bad things happening in the world), I caught a caller to one studio berating schools for not sorting out the problem of 'discipline' in the classroom. If teachers would only achieve this, then all children would receive a better education, no matter what sort of school they attended and how many tiers the system may or may not have. The caller went on to describe the situation as being analogous to having a gas leak, where changing service provider won't alter the fact that the gas is still leaking.

If I had a proper job, rather than playing with my new TV, I could well have been spending the time sitting in a staffroom somewhere in the country, discussing similar sorts of problems with my colleagues. However, instead of the word *discipline* I would probably have heard myself using the term *behaviour* instead.

These two words – *discipline* (which entomologically-speaking has experienced a journey that started meaning 'to grasp intellectually' but by the early sixteenth century had come to mean 'orderly conduct as a result of training' and was used by the Puritans in 1585 for their own expediency) and *behaviour* (interestingly from Old English meaning 'to contain') – seem to

be at the root of all the education world's ills. Behaviour is, obviously, what the children are doing wrong and, obviously, what such behaviour needs is discipline, if only the teachers knew how to give it.

Yet perhaps both terms are missing the point and by coming at things in a different way, as Jim Roberson demonstrates in his work and in this chapter, we can fundamentally change the nature of schools for the better. For Jim, *behaviour* is the 'B-word' and he forbids its mention. *Discipline*, on the other hand, is neatly described neither as something others do to you to get you to behave nor even as something you do to yourself.

Rather, discipline is 'what you do for yourself'.

What Jim advocates is a trade-off between children and schools, whereby schools 'open up' to teach children *everything* they will need to prosper at and beyond school, no matter what career and life choices they make. In return, children start to acquire and then implement the strategies and benefits that come with self-discipline on an ongoing basis, following the four steps described in Jim's inimitable fashion as:

1. doing what has to be done;
2. doing it when it has to be done;
3. doing it as well as it can be done; and
4. doing it that way all the time!

Like all the writers in this book, Jim is out there 'walking his talk', working daily with children from some very challenging backgrounds in an area that he says reminds him of home. (Jim was born and grew up in the Bronx.)

For the person in the street (or on the end of the telephone line ringing the news studio to pass the time before 'Countdown' comes on), discipline is something the teachers should be exerting over their class. Interestingly, I often ask students in secondary schools whose responsibility it is to ensure appropriate behaviour in the classroom and they hold a similar view. For many students, the mark of a good teacher is how well he or she can 'control' the students' actions. So, how did we end up in this state of affairs? Why do we have a situation where young people genuinely believe the notion that 'if you don't prevent me from acting in an inappropriate way then my actions are your fault'? To answer that we need to go back a few hundred years and take, as our guide, the excellent book *The Unfinished Revolution* by John Abbott and Terry Ryan.

This book – a book I think should be required reading for all teachers – describes how we've ended up with the education system that we now have in the Western world. That is to say, a factory-method, Industrial Age, outputs-driven model that is very divorced from the nature of real learning in our distant past. And, what's more, it has worryingly little to do with the nature of the future of the world either.

The Industrial Revolution moved the process of manufacture away from an era of skilled artisans and craftsmen to a world of factories and industrial-scale processing, something in turn that led to production-line methodologies where thinking and innovation were sacrificed to the gods of greater productivity and increased profit. In 1911, a man called F. W. Taylor published a book that would change the world, *Principles of Scientific Management*, where he described how the systematisation of a process – from making cars to mining coal – would make that process more productive. But what was vitally important for that systematisation to work with ruthless

efficiency was that the worker was not to think for himself.

Like Charlie Chaplin in *Modern Times*, workers became performers of specific repetitive actions by which their hands, not their brains, were the key to their productivity. (Both our word *manoeuvre* and the French term for workforce, *main d'oeuvre*, come from the Latin *manuoperare*, meaning to 'work with your hands'.)

The success of the method in the factories, mills and mines meant that the powers that be then turned their attention to education. With the outlawing of children working in factories, something had to be done to get the children off the streets and, with the need for a workforce who could do basic maths and English, the 'factory method' was turned in on itself – factory-method schooling to churn out factory-method workers. As Abbott and Ryan point out, 'A primary aim of education became preparing workers for their place in rationally planned manufacturing.' They go on to explain how the government began to use formal education 'to develop loyal, productive and socially contented citizens'.

In other words, to create a society of people who would do what they were told, work hard and know their place: 'For England, probably more than for any other Western country, education of the masses was a form of social control totally separate from the education of the social elite.'

And what better system to produce such model citizens than one based on what had worked so well in the factories? I remember observing a history lesson in a secondary school a few years ago where a TV programme was being shown to help the students learn about life for children in the factories in the early stages of the Industrial Revolution. A list of the factory rules was given along with how infringements were always harshly punished. These rules included things like not being late, not whistling while working, not opening a window without permission.

Remind you of anything?

Education, then, had become a state-run machine for churning out workers, where people were to do what they were told with the minimum of independent thought, where deviance from the system was treated harshly and where discipline carried a large stick.

(And this applied to the teachers as much as the children. Abbott and Ryan quote a spokesperson for the British prime minister as saying, 'We are not convinced that there are enough good teachers so we have emphasised a "teacher-proof" curriculum.' And this was in 1996.)

Abbott and Ryan go on to sum up in one paragraph the starting point for the situation in our classrooms today, where *my* behaviour is *your* fault:

> With the state taking responsibility for schooling, the various pressures that had previously existed on young people to hold themselves responsible for their own development diminished and learning became what the state defined, not necessarily what individuals undertook for their own purposes.

Not only had the teachers become responsible for the students' actions, but the state had decreed what was to be learned, regardless of who or where you were. The whole process of 'learning' – taking on board new information, skills and attitudes embedded in a real-life context and for genuine and pertinent reasons that related to survival in a particular environment – became subsumed by the process of 'schooling'.

The 'game of school' as the Abbott and Ryan call it, had begun.

A hundred and fifty years later, the Industrial Age has come and all but gone and we are dealing with the implications of the Information Age and a world of instant communication and equally rapid upheaval. Yet our classrooms still contain the shadows of another era. I often describe the secret of my success at school as 'waiting to be told what to do and doing it well'. And, if you are a 'good student' like me, that works. But what if you don't want to be told what to do and don't see the point of having to do it in the first place, let alone doing it well?

When discipline no longer works – 'Do this or else' – we then end up focusing on behaviour, or rather *behaviour modification*, to give it its real name: 'Do this and you'll get that; don't do it and you'll get this. Repeat.' But changes in behaviours are not changes in attitude, and controlling another by reward and sanction still leaves the responsibility for the behaviour in the hands of the person wielding the carrot and the stick.

Which is where Jim's Disciplined Approach comes in. Strategies both to help put responsibility back in the hands of the learners and to put a sense of purpose and relevance back into the learning process – and with it the message that it's time to stop playing the old 'game of school'.

As I continued my flicking through the various Freeview channels that I will never need and will never watch again, but that came with my new telly, I caught an advert for a washing powder, asking the question, 'Is gentle something you touch or something that touches you?' Perhaps reading this chapter we can ask something similar about teaching and learning: Is education something you do or something that is done to you?

Chapter 3
The Disciplined Approach

Jim Roberson

Introduction

Ask teachers, parents and the public what they think the big issue in schools is and more than likely they will mention how out of control things seem to be. Teachers are being swamped by the behavioural issues they are dealing with daily, being placed in situations where the priority seems to be controlling behaviour rather than helping the students learn.

Yet I sometimes wonder what behaving has to do with learning. Just because someone is behaving (for 'behaving' read 'quiet'), does this necessarily mean they are learning? And, whose responsibility is their behaviour, anyway? If the children are acting in an inappropriate way, is it the teacher who is at fault? I often come across students complaining about such and such a teacher saying, 'He's rubbish, because he can't control us.'

I realised a while back that these ways of looking at things both lead us down a one-way street. Maybe the way to consider the challenge in the classroom doesn't lie with focusing on behaviour but another word – *discipline*. The word *discipline* conjures up an era of military-style punishment that harks back to the school days of those of us of a certain age, a time of slippers, canes, paddles and a great deal of detaining and shouting.

But there are two fundamental differences in my take on discipline:

1. Let's look to change the focus of what we mean by 'discipline'. It is not what someone in authority does to you. Far from it. It's not even something you have to subject yourself to. For us it means not what you do *to* yourself but what you do *for* yourself.

2. My belief is that school should be the place where you learn all you need to learn – including discipline – to succeed in life, whatever form that success may take. This moves school way beyond just being a place of academic study where if you do well you'll fit in and if you struggle you're in trouble. What are the children who are constantly being punished getting from their education? Maybe by changing the way we look at things, they could get a whole lot more. This is what I mean when I talk about 'opening up' school.

So, let's open up school so that it becomes – for all students – the place where you learn what you need to be successful, where you learn how to get it right. The Disciplined Approach has been put together over 21 years' experience as a teacher, a coach of American football (as well as a player) and – the most important job – as a parent and husband.

Rather than being something you do to children, the Disciplined Approach is the slow bit-by-bit process of getting someone to see the sense in good *self*-control and *self*-discipline. With the Disciplined Approach, it's all about the individual.

In this chapter, I want to take you through some of the basics of such an approach so you can understand the way it works, the reasoning behind it and the benefits to the children of using it – both in school and beyond. And, because at the centre of the Disciplined Approach it is not the system or the teacher but the child, we have to start with what that child is bringing to the table as he or she enters your classroom. What is the attitude the child has to learning? What is the luggage – or baggage – the child brings to school that will affect the way that child learns, reacts and behaves?

(And, when I talk about 'baggage', bear in mind that I work in a school on the south coast with some seriously disaffected and challenging children, not to mention the work I have done in central London with schools experiencing major 'behaviour' problems in their classrooms. Examples of the sort of 'baggage' I am dealing with in children is things such as 'school is shit' and 'teachers are racist'.)

No matter what baggage they have, remember that the ethos in the Disciplined Approach is that 'school is for learning'. Period. No argument! This can be a challenge for some of the children I am working with. But the real challenge is the one I throw down for schools: 'School is for learning – *whatever is needed for success.*'

In other words, it can no longer be a question of some children passing and some failing using specific academic criteria. It has to become a situation where all children will benefit from their time spent at this school in a way that will equip them with *whatever it is* they may need to be successful beyond school, regardless of their academic achievements or aspirations.

What this means is that we can work with the child to help them discover what they want and then work with them to help them achieve it, something that immediately moves the goalposts away from the situation where we are trying to coerce the child into sitting still while we try to teach them material that they perceive to be irrelevant, impersonal and uninspiring.

The first thing we need to do here is to get us all on the same page. Let's define terms here. When I am taking teachers through the Disciplined Approach in my INSET sessions, I ask them to identify a list of 'behaviour issues' that we can work with to help move them into 'discipline issues'. This list usually includes things such as swearing, being late, being rude, disrupting lessons, uniform problems. The task is to shift the way we look at the issues so we can approach them from the point of view of the Disciplined Approach. By doing this we are able to offer immediate tips and advice to help the students help themselves. This idea of helping individuals to help themselves – to become their own doctor – is at the core of this approach.

I also ask for a definition of discipline. What often comes back is a sense of its being something that one person does to another or, if they consider *self*-discipline, then it is something that you make yourself do.

*For us, though, remember: discipline is not what you do **to** yourself but what you do **for** yourself.*

In the era of children's rights and newfound freedoms, with opportunities for all, young people will not achieve what they are capable of without discipline.

Without discipline, freedom is self-defeating, one cannot attain one's goals and therefore neither can one fashion a good life. Freedom without discipline becomes freedom to not reach your goals.
  – John F. Covaleskie, 'Dewey, Discipline and Democracy' (Northern Michigan University Philosophy of Education, 1994)

So, what does such an approach give to young people? It gives empowerment; it is the key to success; it gives self-respect. Let's look at each in turn.

1. Empowerment

It gives the individual the power to accomplish their goals and it is these accomplishments that give you confidence. In other words, you grow by doing. Elsewhere in this book, self-esteem is defined as being 'capable' and 'lovable'. You will never know how capable you are if you do nothing, but it is when you actually accomplish something – in many cases even something quite small – that you begin to feel more positive about yourself. The American professional basketball player Michael Jordan once said when he scored fifty points that he couldn't wait to do it again.

Teachers often say, 'It'll be all right' and let children off the hook of trying, even if trying means you fail and try again. But I've got news for you: it won't be all right!

What builds confidence is accomplishments. And it is this confidence that helps you build self-esteem! You see, you start to feel better about *you* – because you are accomplishing something. It could be as small as learning a new word, how to spell it and use it, or a maths problem or learning three new French words – they can all have the same effect on the individual. And it is because of this that the teacher shouldn't 'ride the bike for them', in other words care too much so that they end up doing it all for the child without letting the child to it for him- or herself, even if this means the child fails first time around. If you never get the chance to try, fail, try again and succeed, how can you ever develop self-esteem? So, we start to open up school as the place you learn to get it right.

2. The key to success

If you have discipline you know what to do, or you'll find out how to do it if you don't. You will see the difference between the way that someone without discipline approaches a problem compared with someone with discipline. People with discipline don't sit around feeling sorry for themselves. If you lose your job, you get another. You do what it takes to pay the bills. If the big exam is coming up, you don't wait until the night before because you know you have to prepare! You move from a problem-based to a solution-based focus.

The key to success is, with discipline you'll always find a way!

3. Self-respect

With self-respect you make the right choices for *you*. Because of this, the Disciplined Approach sees self-respect as a vital ingredient.

Consider the scenario of a student coming late to class. The teacher gives the verbals: 'Why are you late?'; 'What time do you call this?'; 'Thank you so much for gracing us with your presence.' The student returns the verbals: 'You're always picking on me'; 'Jordan was late the other day and you didn't say anything to her'; 'I won't bother turning up at all next time.'

The Disciplined Approach looks at breaking down the scenario with the first question being: Who was late?

Self-respect means that you feel good enough about yourself to do the right thing. You know the rule. You know you were in the wrong. You say sorry. Full stop. End of story. You are responsible for your actions. It's part and parcel of respecting yourself. Feel good enough about yourself to do the right thing. Have the self-respect to do what you need to do. If you didn't like the reaction of the teacher, then maybe you could see him at the end of the lesson and say something like, 'I think you had a go at me, sir' and clear the air that way. But being late and being rude is not what someone with high self-respect does. The Disciplined Approach works towards helping students understand that *actions cause reactions*; therefore, the right action causes the right reaction. So, be on time!

In some schools, I have heard headteachers say that the children misbehaved in a particular lesson because of the poor quality of the teacher's lesson plan. While I'm all for making lessons positive and enjoyable experiences for all learners, I think such a view misses the point. It reinforces from the top down the idea that a student's behaviour is the sole responsibility of the teacher. How will children ever learn discipline in such a climate?

As with so much in this book, it all boils down to what's going on in their brains. So, let me quote from the fascinating article in *Time* magazine mentioned elsewhere in this book, 'Secrets of the Teen Brain'. There's a part of the brain just behind your forehead called the *prefrontal cortex*. It's the part of the brain that says, 'I wouldn't do that if I were you,' and is sometimes referred to as the 'area of sober second thought'.

The human brain matures through a series of sprouting connections between brain cells and then either strengthening the connections that are used or often pruning away those that aren't needed. This process starts at the back of the brain in the baby and over time works its way to the prefrontal cortex. How long does it take a brain to develop in this manner? How long before we can say, 'This is a mature adult brain'? Current estimates are that it takes 20–30 years.

The *Time* article quotes UCLA neuroscientist Elizabeth Sowell as follows:

> Scientists and the general public had attributed the bad decisions teens make to hormonal changes. But once we started mapping where and when the brain changes were happening, we could say: aha, the part of the brain that makes teenagers more responsible is not finished maturing yet.

Now, the brain is like a muscle and needs to be 'worked out' to develop in a healthy way. It has to be used to grow. In other words, young people have to use their developing prefrontal cortex in order for it to develop effectively. There is a huge growth spurt in this area that starts in girls at around age eleven and in boys around twelve and a half, with thousands of new connections being developed. This is followed by a massive pruning process whereby those neural pathways that aren't being used are lost.

School is the most important vehicle for training this part of the brain and developing the young mind, a task that in the grand scheme of things is more important than teaching a child facts from particular subject matter.

Practices in schools that involve control, punishment and behaviour manipulation miss the point because they do not allow the developing brain to learn how to control *itself*. We don't train them how to be adult but we do expect it of them, and, when they don't come up with the goods, we punish them. A focus on behaviour ends up with our punishing children for being *childlike*. When you open up school, you train the prefrontal cortex and young people learn to make better decisions. School is the place where you learn to get it right. Or it should be. So, is your school actively and professionally teaching self-discipline?

The Disciplined Approach is all about taking children carefully through this critical time in their development in such a way that they wire up the prefrontal cortex to be able to make critical judgements for itself about what it should or shouldn't do.

Another aspect of the Disciplined Approach is that of the *myth of motivation*. Schools spend a great deal of time trying to get children motivated, but we feel that motivation on its own is not enough. There are many things we are motivated to do but don't have the discipline to actually do them. We may be highly motivated to lose weight but have no discipline when the cake trolley comes round. We may be highly motivated to get fit but not have the discipline to get up 45 minutes early each day to go for a walk. Look around you. How many things can you list that you have been motivated to do but haven't?

What the Disciplined Approach preaches can be summed up in the following equation:

$$\frac{D}{M} = S$$

In other words, Success comes from the Discipline in your Motivation. You can be motivated to play football, but do you have the discipline to work at it to be the best you can be? You can be a motivated teacher, but do you have the discipline to lesson-plan, to know the individual personalities of your classes, to prepare every lesson?

Think of discipline as 'motivation in action'; they go hand in hand. If motivation is the Ferrari, discipline is the open road. You can own the wonderful car, drive it round the town and receive some envious glances. But you won't know what it's really capable of until you take it on the open road. Then there will be no stopping you! Motivation alone is not enough.

In sport, we talk a great deal about getting 'in the zone'. When you are in the zone, time flies by, work seems effortless and you achieve great things without seeming even to think about it. Discipline and motivation have major parts to play in getting you into such a state. You are motivated to do something because you like doing it and you have the discipline to work at being good, to practise and to become the best.

In the model in Figure 5, the starting point is at the bottom left: we do something because we are motivated because we like it. Because we like it we have the discipline to harness that motivation and work at it and, because of this effort, we start to take pride in ourselves and build up our self-esteem. We are starting to enjoy some of the rewards of discipline. And, because of this, we end up wanting to do it more.

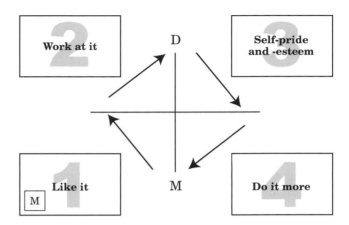

Figure 5.

Yet in schools so often we head straight for the second box – the 'Work at it' box. Now perhaps twenty years ago we could do that, tell children that they had to learn their Latin or their algebra or whatever it was so they may as well just knuckle down and get on with it – or else!

But times have changed. There is a greater independence of spirit in young people these days and they are much more likely to ask that question that proves so challenging to many teachers: 'Why do we have to learn this?' Rather than dismiss them with the old staple, 'Because it's in the syllabus', we need to be working on our selling skills, showing students the relevance of learning and working with them to answer their question. This is the WIIFM? approach to motivation: What's In It For Me? If we want to get children into the 'zone', we do have to invest time in getting them actually to like what they are doing. But, once you are off the starting blocks, you are developing pride in yourself and what you're accomplishing, adding to your self-esteem, and then you want to do it more.

You can't get much done in life if you only work on days you feel good!
– Jerry West, basketball player

I'm sure David Beckham doesn't want to get out of bed every morning, but he knows that, if he wants to stay at the top level, he must have the discipline to work. So it's up to meet Johnny Wilkinson at the park, whose also been practising kicking six days a week.

I am passionate about the ideas behind the Disciplined Approach because I see the sorts of benefits to young people that it offers. In an 'opened up' school, it teaches things such as:

- *being accountable*: learning to make up for messing up, taking responsibility for your actions;

- *dealing with pressure*: exams, revision, performing, high-power jobs, and sports;

- *how to be a competitor*: to find the 'zone' and be the best, whether that's a bricklayer or a football player;

- *how to make sacrifices*: revision, homework and uniform;

- *the development of self-expectations*: learn to want the most from and for yourself, whatever that may be: just be the best you can be;

- *respect for others*: treat people as you want to be treated; know right from wrong.

This is what I have seen in my experience working with children from some really challenging backgrounds. I'm not a psychologist or sociologist. I'm a teacher and a coach. I feel confident dealing with issues in school from a discipline standpoint. I have found less aggression when dealing with problems because the Disciplined Approach has no grey areas. The bottom line is that we all remember we are in school, a school with rules and policies in place that the Disciplined Approach expects us all to follow. No messing. In return, that school will train us to work in a way that will be of immense benefit to us in our lives, whoever we are. You have the discipline to learn and the school will teach you what you need.

In a nutshell, here are three of the main legs on which the Disciplined Approach stands:

1. Discipline is not what you do *to* yourself but what you do *for* yourself.
2. School is where you go to educate yourself.
3. School is where you can learn whatever you need to learn to be successful in whichever area you want to be successful in.

This is what I mean by 'opening up' school. So, let's open it up and take the roof off. Let's make a school a place where the student comes in Year 7 with low reading skills and learns enough to become the lorry driver or computer technician he wants to be without making him strive for – and fail to reach – some spurious academic goal that is irrelevant to his life both now and in the future. This is a very different scenario from the 'failed' students who ends up in a low-paid menial job. What we are talking about is using school as a place where students learn about themselves and learn what it takes for them to be what they *choose* to be – whatever that may be.

It's about creating more able learners, helping children to learn how to learn. It's about finding the gifts and talents that all students have and creating successful school leavers in so many ways. And in doing so, let's aim for a school that doesn't exclude children or use detention as a bullying technique. The Disciplined Approach is not concerned with detention. Yes, we take on board the fact that there will be some things that justify detention, but what we don't want is that school ends up for some students as a place of punishment. They miss five minutes of your lesson, they owe five minutes to their learning, they put the five minutes in after school. Then they go. You are neither punishing them nor detaining them. Instead, you are simply making sure they have the discipline to do their part of the bargain, helping them learn to be accountable and training them to make better decisions.

Remember what I said: school is the place where they come to learn whatever is needed for success.

Even the word 'detain' has huge implications across a range of different cultures in this day and age. For many of the people in our overcrowded prisons today the very first 'jail' they knew was one called 'school detention'. What's the missing word in this phrase: Guantánamo Bay _____ Centre?

And there is another message from our prisons: punishments alone do little to change the behaviour of the individual. According to *The Times* (22 December 2005), '58.5 per cent of adult offenders released from jail in the first quarter of 2002 … were convicted of a further crime within two years.' And for young men between 18 and 22 this figure is even higher. Very little is learned except perhaps a lasting resentment for the authorities that put you there in the first place. Even the act of kicking a misbehaving child out of a lesson is counterproductive. Yes, take them out when necessary to calm them down, to get their brains balanced again; work with them on exploring different possibilities, on actions and reactions, on doing the right thing. But just turfing them out is so counterproductive to the purpose of school as a place of learning for success in life.

Once outside the classroom, they will then miss an important link in their learning. Next lesson, apart from the resentment they feel towards the teacher, the subject and the school, they also have the fact that they missed some of the learning from last lesson, so they are even more behind and frustrated and cross. And an adolescent brain in such a state does not yet have the neural hardware to deal with that in a way that doesn't involve the amygdala kicking in – the part of the brain that deals with primal feelings such as fear and rage and that is relied on for making decisions in adolescent brains more so than with adults, who have a mature prefrontal cortex to help them do the 'right thing'.

And that's just the harm that punishments can do. What about rewards?

The ultimate reward for self-discipline in schools is the life you will lead beyond school. You learn to look beyond the horizon. This is where your selling skills will come in handy again. Selling them the idea that, with self-discipline, you can achieve whatever it is, deep down, that you really want to achieve. That's got to be so much more rewarding than a McDonald's voucher, don't you think? In the Disciplined Approach we don't give such rewards – no vouchers, no pens, no crutches. Why should we be going out of our way to reward children for bringing a pen to school? It's school. It's the place where you come to learn. You need a pen. Bring the damn pen!

The traditional ways of doing things lead to disaffection and demotivation. We talk a great deal about how to motivate young people but often we need to consider what we are doing to *de*motivate children. They don't necessarily start out switched off. Something down the line 'disaffects' them. They don't do it to themselves. We do it to them! The Disciplined Approach is about 're-affection' – switching them on and not punishing them for being switched off.

Teaching discipline cuts through all that behaviour-modification, reward and punishment garbage and actually teaches young people how to work in a way that is appropriate, transferable and even highly moral. (There's no need to give children a lecture when all you want to say is summed up in one of my favourite sentences: Do the right thing!) It is preventative and pre-emptive. It doesn't wait for what is perceived as 'poor behaviour' and then leaps out and punishes it. It works with young people the minute they walk through the door to help them develop the habits that will assist them in achieving their goals.

Remember, school is a place for learning. Period. That's it. Our concern is the gaps in learning that misconduct could bring about. Our concern is to fill that gap. Our concern is that the school work be done. It's teaching young people to be accountable for making up the work if they need to. It's doing not only whatever it takes to achieve what you need (i.e. about what you do *for* you, not *to* you) but also doing the right thing.

The Disciplined Approach works to prevent disaffection, not promote it.

D versus B

I've mentioned a few times already the B-word: *behaviour*. So let's have a look at how this approach doesn't work. We define behaviour as 'a way of behaving, manners, to act or react in a specific way'.

When I first looked at this definition I realised that, as a teacher, I could not see what this had to do with learning or with school. Why the hell do we use the term so much in education?

As I said earlier, I'm not a psychologist or sociologist: I'm a teacher. And I love teaching and working with young people. When in school, I do not comment on behaviour and I try never to use the B-word in school. With the Disciplined Approach we prefer to use some of the following terminology:

- conduct;
- misconduct;
- discipline;
- self-control;
- self-discipline.

Now, try taking a look at 'discipline' as defined in the dictionary: 'Discipline – Training or a way of life aimed at self-control.' Doesn't that make more sense? As a teacher, I adhered to a way of life aimed at self-control, training for a way of leading a life. Shouldn't this sum up the process of being a teacher and working in education, of training young people to have the self-control to do whatever it takes to have the life they deserve?

The Disciplined Approach, then, uses discipline as the vital ingredient to the learning process. A disciplined individual is one who is able to stick with the pursuit of a goal over time. Once I fully grasped the power of 'discipline' over the B-word, things really started to flow. I suddenly realised how I could make a genuine and lasting difference to the lives of young people who were being badly served by the education system under the traditional regime of behaviour modification, punishment and reward.

One of my biggest tools in working with young people, especially with boys, is the idea of what I call 'crossover': taking skills from one area of life and applying them to another. The Disciplined Approach is perfect for this transfer of attitudes and skills. Many young people know exactly what it takes to be successful in, say, football or playing an instrument. Yet it is the very skills they have in attaining high levels of achievement in these areas that seem to desert them when it comes to their learning. By talking in terms of crossover – 'you don't revise for your exams: you *train* for them' – you can show how they really do know what they need to do without being told by a teacher all the time. Crossover helps get students into the 'zone', that wonderful state of flow mentioned in other chapters in this book.

And, when you know what it takes to be successful, you can learn another hugely important life skill that comes out of the Disciplined Approach: you learn how to 'be your own doctor'. Being your own doctor is about knowing what to do for yourself if you need help. You know the skills involved to get things sorted and to get you moving again quickly.

What I wanted to do with the Disciplined Approach was to create tools that the people could use to check themselves, to help them get back on track – tools that would equip students for success in life, tools to help assist them to become their own doctor.

With that in mind I identified four elements of self-discipline (I have them as a poster on my classroom wall and I make sure all my students know the mantra by heart):

1. Do what has to be done
2. Do it when it has to be done
3. Do it as well as it can be done
4. Do it that way all the time

We feel that, if they follow this advice now and practise it throughout their lives, they will succeed. We ask the students, 'If you do these four steps, do you think you will be successful?' Most say yes.

Using the four steps will not only help create more able learners but also make for more effective use of classroom time.

Apart from the four steps above there are also four formulas that I use in my work with young people that really seem to help them focus in on what they are doing, what they should be doing and how to bridge the gap between the two. By using them yourself, they will help make sure that 'discipline' is integrated into your decision-making process, as well as model to the learners you are working with how they work and how important they are. They are:

1. A+C
2. C+R
3. CAF
4. TCB

1. A+C: appreciate and criticise

This helps the teacher acknowledge the effects, for example, of peer pressure on student conduct without either criticising the student for being subject to it or letting it take over. For example, in the classroom you may say – without the use of that favourite tool of the old regime: teacher sarcasm – 'I appreciate that you and your friend want to talk about *Coronation Street* but, [with a smile] ladies, I have a lesson to teach.'

Such an approach is not aggressive or confrontational, is not a threat to the reptilian brain and the ever-ready adolescent amygdala. It should not do too much to trigger the testosterone in the teenage boys. (High levels of testosterone in adolescent boys are natural and necessary. It does not mean that the boy will go actively seeking trouble and confrontation, but if it is triggered it means he is more likely to react in an aggressive way. Your job as the professional who has chosen to work with young people like that is to do whatever it takes to avoid the situation where the trigger gets pulled! Don't make 'em mad, make 'em think. Which is where the Disciplined Approach can help.)

You may also say, 'I appreciate that you have a friend, but I have to criticise the time you choose to talk; discipline, please'; and 'I appreciate that your friend wants to take you in a stolen car, but I criticise your decision to get in.'

Discipline, is about making the right choices for you.

2. C+R: consequences and repercussions

Help students to see the bigger picture. Just think through the consequences of poor attendance or not revising for an important test – again, not in a threatening way but in a matter-of-fact, businesslike way.

'If you carry on missing school, what will that mean? What will happen? And if you have no GCSEs what might that lead to? Prison? No job? A poor-quality job?

'And what, then, are the repercussions of such a job? What sort of house will you live in? What sort of car will you drive? What sort of partner will you have? Where will you have your holidays?'

It's important to highlight short-term as well as long-term benefits from self-discipline. A part of the brain called the *nucleus accumbens* in that slow-to-mature prefrontal cortex is the part that directs our motivation to seek out rewards. Research shows less activity in that region in adolescents than in adults. So, a focus on short-term benefits as well can help here, as can doing things for the fun of it, building relationships with children, getting them to like what they are doing, celebrating success (not rewarding it), helping them become excited about their future – all these things are part of this process.

Another C+R example could be with the child who is not revising for that all-important exam. As the stress of the exam gets close, the low self-esteem is going to take another knock because you know you're not doing what you need to.

Consequences of not revising: not doing well in exams, looking stupid, stress. *Repercussions* of not passing the exam: not getting the course you wanted in college, which in turn will affect your standard of life.

It is also important to get the emotional brain involved in this process too, so it is not just an academic head-based exercise. Ask them what each of the consequences and repercussions will feel like. Indeed, it is only when our emotional brain is switched on that any lasting change can be made. Remember that when you are giving one of your 'pull your socks up' lectures!

3. CAF: consider all factors

This is such a useful tool for decision making and understanding what is at stake and one that Edward de Bono advocates. It means that you get the facts – all of them – to help you make decisions to achieve success. You can do this as a big brainstorm on the board and aim to fill it with ideas.

Try doing a CAF exercise with students on having no education. I teach them CAF so they can learn to identify and process information before making a decision that will affect their lives.

4. TCB: take care of business

Doing what you *have* to do will give you time to do what you *want* to do. TCB is putting life in your hands following the four steps, using the four formulas. TCB is taking care of *your* business. And your business is your being successful in life. You can do it, no matter what your background. Be your own doctor. Get yourself right.

- Will you TCB?
- Will you S=D/M?
- Will you use the four steps?
- Will you remember the four formulas?
- Will you be accountable for your actions?

- Will you remember that discipline is the key?
- Will you help students see the sense in having a little discipline in their lives?

And remember: a disciplined individual is one who is able to stick with the pursuit of a goal over time. *If you want to be successful you must have discipline and with discipline you will be successful.*

We all get the same 24 hours. It's the only fair thing in life. It's equal to all. From the highest achievers to the 'failures', we all get exactly the same allowance of time. The key is what we do with it, and what we do with it is up to us.

So, we don't say, 'Use the spellchecker'. We sit down and help them learn to spell. There are no crutches in the Disciplined Approach. There are no excuses for misconduct, no crutches to lean on that let the individual off the hook. There's no culture of, 'Don't blame me, it's not my fault – blame my parents, the community, the police, the teacher's lesson plans, the supply teacher.' As a great American football coach once told me, 'Excuses are for losers.'

The Disciplined Approach is about the level of self-discipline you show, learning how to do it. The Disciplined Approach is about the choices you make, learning to make the right decisions. The Disciplined Approach is about your learning to do the right thing.

The Disciplined Approach also doesn't believe in gifts and rewards for good conduct. We think the rewards come in the type of life that you will lead and attitude to the success you have in life. And messages such as these come from the top down in a school. I recently read in a survey of American schools that the biggest issue was the lack of discipline from teacher to students all the way down to the caretakers. The entire school site in these schools looked a mess. The better schools all had clear policies, with staff consistently applying the rules and where whole-school discipline was the expectation.

So how can you immediately start to apply the Disciplined Approach in your teaching? As a start, here are some common issues that crop up in nearly every school and the way in which I have used the Disciplined Approach in my work to deal with them. You will see, I hope, that it's not rocket science.

Attendance

Both in class and in school. The Disciplined Approach links what goes on in school to life beyond school, to the bigger picture that someday the student will have a job. You must go to work to keep the job. This isn't moralising or preaching, and teachers should avoid falling into those traps, because they are self-defeating. No one likes being moralised to and children get enough of that elsewhere. Just give it as a statement of fact. Attendance prevents gaps in learning, and so helps prevent disaffection.

Note: If he attends 100 per cent and is still disaffected, what is he disaffected by?

Being on time for class

The fact that you are here is great, but now you must have the self-discipline to be here on time. Again, this is linked into the bigger picture of what's needed to be successful beyond school; that it's not just petty school rules that are being discussed; that it's nothing personal, but just the way of things.

Uniform

TCB (taking care of business). Make sure you have it ready. It's your uniform and it's your responsibility. Don't go blaming your mother. Get it ready the night before if you need to.

Equipment for school

Again – TCB. What will I need for the day to learn. Do I need PE kit? Have I got a pen and pencil? It's my responsibility. I'm at school to learn, so do I have what I need to achieve that? Why should we 'reward' children for turning up at school with a pen?

The Disciplined Approach in the classroom leads to positive reinforcement in school, better support between students, teachers achieving more in lessons and all children getting more out of lessons and learning more. What I have noticed is that, when you use the 'Discipline, please!' approach on little Johnny in the corner, the five people around him are sorted out straightaway at the same time.

And remember at all times to keep to the 'moral high ground', relating all that you are doing to what school is for – learning.

Note that the Disciplined Approach uses classroom techniques designed to *prevent* misconduct through keeping students on task and engaged in classroom learning. Rather than use behaviour management to deal with 'misbehaviour', we do our best to prevent problem situations arising. And when they do, as will happen from time to time, the Disciplined Approach means we can work on rehabilitation rather than punishment. Punished children do not necessarily learn not to act in that way again. They may learn how not to get caught, how to play the system, not to care about being punished or that everyone is against them, but they are not being supported in an effective way to learn how to alter their behaviour for the sake of their learning and their success beyond school.

I know from my experience as one of the country's top American Football coaches that what is important is *development*. You don't punish the bad stuff. You work to develop it so it can be better. In sport we are developing skills and the body. At school we are developing, among other things, the prefrontal cortex.

With that in mind, here are some classroom-management tips that I use and teach to others that allow me to use the Disciplined Approach quickly and effectively in my classroom:

On point

This is a phrase from the Vietnam War and relates to the soldier who is at the front of his unit going into the jungle. In other words, the 'on point' teacher knows what's going on in his or her class; that teacher treats the classroom as his or her domain and has the finger on the pulse at all times. And that means with the quiet girl as well as the disruptive student. I know different teachers have different ideas but I certainly very rarely sit down when I am in my classroom – if ever. I am too busy 'owning' every bit of space in my room.

When you are 'on point' you pick up on the 'little things' such as the child on the mobile phone, the student not on task, the two students chatting. You can then address them instantly, quickly, consistently: 'You know the rules. Discipline, please!' You don't let things go that can cause disaffection with children when some are *told* off and others doing the same things seem to be *let* off. You are not dragging out the process of reprimanding, it is not personal ('You're always picking on me!') and you can get straight back to the real matter of the learning. Ian Gilbert talks about 'surfing' the classroom and it is a similar thing here. You are not fazed by what they are doing; you are not taking large parts of the lesson to moralise or lecture; you are not missing anything; you are on top of whatever comes your way; you take their energy and channel it back at them quickly and with good humour.

'Jordan, I appreciate you have a new mobile and the head says they have to be turned off in class and put away during school hours. Discipline, please! Thank you.' This is the 'preventer'. The next stage is the 'caution', but she is aware that she has chosen that and that you are following up on her lack of discipline, nothing else. After that, I would move her to a different part of the room followed, as a last resort, by removal. However, in all my eight years as a teacher of children as hard-nosed and disaffected as they come, I have never once had to write a referral or have anyone removed from my room.

'John, if you keep passing notes to Dale, I'll have to take the note and send it to your mum! Discipline, please!' Humour is another good way of diffusing a situation. A giggle alters the neurochemistry in the brain and is one of the best ways of building rapport with a class. As Victor Borge once said, 'Humour is the shortest route between two people.'

Dealing with what's going on right away gives the impression that nothing gets past you. And often, when you are dealing with 'challenging children', impression is everything. Research from several years ago found that, in the way that those who looked most as if they thought they were going to be mugged *were* mugged, teachers who looked most as if they were expecting trouble ended up with trouble.

Casino dealer

Casino dealing is attending to different things going on in class without totally focusing on one thing at any time. The key to achieving this is preparation. Different students will move at different speeds through different lessons at different times. The challenge is helping to keep all of them on task at all times in order to learn. This will happen when the teacher tends to a variety different situations in the classroom at once, showing a high level of commitment to *all* students as well as high levels of enthusiasm and energy, giving each student as much – or as little – focus and support as he or she needs.

Remember, surf that class!

Working the room

This is similar to casino dealing but with the big difference being that you are focused on the whole class. You may be at the front of the class but in reality the front of the class is wherever you happen to be standing when you speak. You may be the police officer on the beat, walking and talking at the same time. You may be teaching from right next to the child who you know needs the extra attention to stay focused. You also know whom you can't turn your back on!

Imagine you are doing a cover lesson and what you've been left has all the making of a pretty boring French lesson. If the lesson needs a bit more juice, you need to supply it – before they do!

Positive language

The Disciplined Approach uses positive language. Research has found that children hear far more negative words than positive words in the average classroom, almost to the ratio of ten to one. The language of the Disciplined Approach always deals with the big picture – the reasons for self-discipline and its uses in life – and the role that school can play in the future of the child. It doesn't use threats that undermine the relationship between the teacher and the class, especially when that is all they are and everyone knows they will never be followed through.

Positive language also means that you focus on what the specific problem is and solutions to that problem, that the problems are problems of conduct, not personality. And positive language is also used when dealing with colleagues about a child and with parents at all times: 'I know your son doesn't like PE but it is mandatory. If there are other problems then let's look at them.' You focus on the reasons for doing something as opposed to accepting that the student does not like it.

It's important when dealing with a parent, too, that you show that you care about the future of their child, that you are helping them develop skills for use for ever, not just in school: 'We all have to learn, don't we, that sometimes it's not about what we want to do but what has to be done?'

What you are reiterating through word and deed is that someday they might not only get a job but also *keep* a job because of their experience at school, where they learned to be on time – not because that made them a 'good student' but because it was expected and necessary.

This is another example of the crossover I mentioned earlier: showing the child how skills used in one area of life are equally useful and valuable in others; that what you learn on the football pitch can be applied in your lessons; that what you learn at school can be used throughout your life.

And remember: when you use threatening language you are activating their reptilian brain's primitive fight-or-flight response. And neither fighting nor fleeing will help the child learn.

So, don't make 'em mad: make 'em think.

The Disciplined Approach is as useful for a whole school as it is for an individual and should be part of a school's discipline policy. It's not a magic wand – anyone who claims to have a magic wand for dealing with behaviour in school is usually touting the snake oil of behaviour manipulation and control, often backed up with exclusion. Nothing to do with teaching young people to see the sense of self-discipline. And, if they don't learn such vital skills and attitudes from you, where will they learn them?

To draw my chapter to a close, let me sum up the Disciplined Approach in a few key lines.

Ethos: Discipline is not what you do *to* yourself but what you do *for* yourself.

School: A place where you come to learn something about the world and yourself and open things up, not close them down. The expectation is that school is about learning. Period. This drives all interactions and expectations between teachers and students and helps us, as professionals, create more able learners and not just have learners who are more able.

Learning: What you are learning is not just for school but for ever. You are working to secure a good future. Because what you are learning is – or should be – more than just facts and figures, formulae and dates. The brain is designed for learning and with the right neurochemistry the brain can do nothing *but* learn. But what is that brain learning when it is in the head of a child who is disaffected, excluded and angry? Whether it's learning that you can't always have what you want, how to feel good about working to achieve something or that there are *always* C+R – consequences and repercussions – to your actions, for better or for worse, it's our professional, moral and ethical responsibility to make sure the learning is always at the heart of our actions and theirs.

Discipline v the B-word

This is the real challenge for schools, especially given the data that has recently come out from Ofsted about how student discipline is still *the* big issue that schools need to address despite years of 'behaviour management'.

By selling discipline and all its many crossovers in life outside and beyond school, you are teaching the young person vital tools that will help throughout life. As well as working to improve conduct in lessons and across the school.

$$\frac{D}{M} = S$$

Success comes from the discipline in your motivation. Neither on its own is enough.

Language

All positive with a real sense of caring about the future of the child and a focus on the Big Picture.

Above all, high moral standards

Despite the things that I have experienced as a black man growing up in New York, despite the experiences of my parents under segregation, when they weren't allowed to drink from the same water fountains as the white folk, despite what I know about where I come from and how 'my people' have been treated, I can tell you quite categorically *there is no such thing as racism*.

There are, however, things called 'high moral standards'. My treatment of another human being is down to my morals, no matter what the colour of their skin, their social standing, the team they support or their IQ.

When you follow the Disciplined Approach you are consistently and explicitly taking the moral high ground. You demonstrate how to treat a fellow human being and you demonstrate how you want to be treated as a human being, without excuse.

I've been working on the Disciplined Approach over the past 21 years, as a teacher, coach and parent. And I'd like to think I'm winning at all three. I still teach in a classroom as well as doing the work I am increasingly being asked to do teaching teachers. I love teaching and can't give it up! Because of this I like to look at myself as a practitioner using the Disciplined Approach every day in all types of situation. Like all the writers in this book, I show, not tell. We're not here telling you stuff that we don't use daily, consistently and successfully.

And, like everything else in this book, it's not rocket science. But, if you love children and love teaching, you will be amazed how the Disciplined Approach can really help you bring the best out of all the children in your care.

So, go on, do the right thing.

Introducing Matt Gray

The UK government has the ambition that 50 per cent of young people will be going into further education by the year 2020. There seems to have been little discussion as to whether this goal is actually in the interests of those young people, whether there is a genuine link between how qualified (as opposed to 'skilled') a country is and its productivity, or even what, specifically, they will be learning while there. Not to mention the fact that the 'academic'-versus-'vocational' debate is still raging strong.

In the 2005 Interim Leitch Report, a review of skills in the UK commissioned by the Chancellor, the need for increasing the skills base of this country is put across strongly:

> The proportion of adults in the UK without a basic school leaving qualification is double that of Canada and Germany; over 5m people of working age have no qualification at all; 1 in 6 adults have [sic (ironically!)] low literacy levels and half have low levels of numeracy.

Interestingly, only 2 per cent of that last group felt that their lack of ability in maths had resulted in any negative effects on their working lives. Coupled with that, you also get messages such as this one from business 'guru' Tom Peters: 'Never hire people with exceptionally high grades at university and secondary school.' This is something he put to an assembled audience of 500 top business leaders in London in 2004, adding in his own imitable style, 'If they're not screwed up by the age of 23 they're not going to do anything interesting by the time they're 83!'

Whom would you rather employ – a very qualified dullard or a less well-qualified individual with a spark of life, initiative and ambition? Can you have both? Not easily, when success in the education system is reliant on your doing what you are told, playing by the rules and conformity, as Sir Ken Robinson points out in the article I cite in my introduction to Roy Leighton's chapter, 'Living a Creative Life'.

He also argues that, with so many people going into HE and FE, 'the value of academic qualifications and skills is tumbling … it's not that there aren't enough graduates to go round, it's that too many of them can't communicate, work in teams or think creatively'.

And before you point out that there are many jobs out there that need people *not* to think creatively, just to go through the process they are paid to do, let me say one word to you: 'Fungible'.

If you read only one book this year, read *The World is Flat* by Thomas Friedman. Read it and tremble. By looking at the history of 'the globalised world in the 21st century', he paints a stark picture of the challenges facing Western economies as a result of a number of events 'converging', such as the explosion in technology, the ability to link all this technology through the World Wide Web and the 3 billion new people entering the job market from India, China and Russia, to name but three. (He actually names twelve.) And with regard to this last one, new entrants to the job market, these people won't *physically* enter our job market but, thanks to the other convergences, *will* take jobs from us from the comfort of their own call centres, business parks or even homes. This means the very nature of our privileged place at the top of the world's economy is under threat. As Friedman points out in an interview in *Wired* magazine, 'The entitlement we need to get rid of is our sense of entitlement.'

He uses the word 'fungible', originally used in relation to movable perishable goods such as grain and wine, to describe work that can be 'easily digitized and transferred to lower-wage locations', going on to add, 'Michael Jordan's jump is nonfungible. A bypass surgeon's technique is nonfungible. A television assembly-line worker's job is now fungible. Basic accounting and tax preparation are now fungible.'

If you don't like change, you're going to like irrelevance even less.
– General Eric Shinseki, Retired Chief of Staff, US Army

It is into this maelstrom of challenge and change that we are thrusting our young people, hoping that the length of their qualifications certificates will be enough to help them survive and cranking up the pressure on them to stay in school as long as possible. So, for better or for worse, schools and colleges will find themselves dealing with a great many more young people between sixteen and nineteen years of age who may in turn find themselves in education with a bit of a motivation problem. And, if the students have got a motivation problem, so have the teachers.

Matt Gray's chapter draws on his experience not only working with young people on motivation and aspirations in school and beyond but also his success as a theatre director, where the cry, 'What's my motivation?' is one that has to be addressed before the curtain rises or the leading

dame flounces back to his dressing room. (In fact, Matt has been so successful as a theatre director that, since writing this chapter, he has been 'poached' by Pittsburgh's Carnegie Mellon University, where he is currently an assistant professor of acting.)

For Matt, motivation is more than just carrots and sticks or whipping them into a frenzy of 'go get 'em' self-belief. The motivation of young people asks questions about the attitudes of the older people working with them. It calls into question our approaches towards change. It asks searching questions of the young people themselves that touch on their sense of identity, their courage to be all they are capable of and their willingness – or lack of it – to set goals and have meaningful expectations and aspirations.

This chapter is designed not only for those working with post-sixteen students but, in many ways, speaks directly to them too. Questions such as, 'What picture do students have in their heads when told to buckle down and get on with the work?'; 'What happens when I fail?'; 'How does your community value success?'; and 'What did Alan Titchmarsh ever do for us?' are designed to make you think as well as help you ask questions of the young people you are working with to help them evaluate – re-evaluate – what it is they want, why they want it, how much they want it and what they are going to do in order to achieve it.

One of the questions I often ask groups of sixth-formers when I am working with them on motivation is, *how*, exactly, they mange to underachieve at such a high level. If underachievement is measured by the gap between their achievements and their potential, and they seem quite happy to have a significant gap there, how, I ask, do you do it? Teach me the secret of your underachievement success. I was no good at underachieving when I was at school due to my overachievement. In fact, you could call me an underachieving underachiever. Once they manage to get their heads around what I am asking, they are always able to give me an extensive list of strategies they use in order not to be as good as they could be. These range from being disorganised, forgetting to bring work to school/take it home and not asking for help when they don't understand something, to having a part-time job and working too hard and too often, partying too hard and too often and being in the common room/bed/other world when they should be in lessons. They are always amused by approaching underachievement in this way, but my approach is to highlight the most serious of messages: they *choose* to underachieve by employing one or more (usually more) of these strategies. So, by the same measure, they could also choose to achieve by employing different strategies to produce different results.

But choosing and following through takes motivation. Fortunately, motivation is also in their hands. As Matt points out, personal responsibility is a big part of success.

Occasionally, with students, I have to ask them the meaning of the following: 'Don't water the rocks.' It doesn't take long for them to work out what I mean here and what the implications of such a sentence are on their relationship with, for example, the head of sixth form or a particular teacher. If, despite all the best efforts of everyone around them, a particular student still languishes in a morass of thwarted expectations and self-imposed indolence, then walk away and let them fail. 'Tough love', as Andrew Curran refers to it in his work with seriously damaged children. Sometimes the kindest thing we can do to a developing mind it is to make it stand on – and maybe fall from – its own two feet. After all, if the only way they are going to be motivated is when you motivate them, what will happen when you are no longer in the room? They have not learned *self*-motivation and, as research points out, external motivation can actually inhibit the development of intrinsic motivation.

As I say to the students I work with, 'I want you to be successful – but I can't want your success for you more than you do.'

It is with this focus on intrinsic motivation that I urge you to read Matt's chapter and use the ideas and strategies he propounds with both yourself and your students straightaway. After all, Matt, like David Keeling and Roy Leighton elsewhere in this book, expends a great deal of energy on the all-important but often hardest-to-achieve element of motivation: taking action. Beginning today. 'Being arsed'. Actually doing.

So go on, start starting now.

Chapter 4
'Lo Mejor es Enemigo de lo Bueno'

Matt Gray

The title above translates as 'The best is the enemy of the good', and it is a Spanish proverb.

A few days before I wrote this, my friend Bruno and I were having a coffee and a chat. He's an extremely talented actor, who had just finished shooting a TV film with Glenn Close. He is originally from Antequera in Spain, and has had to fight his way into English-speaking roles by hook *and* by crook. But, instead of talking of his amazing achievement, and his bright future, we were talking about his recent lack of will. Although he has fought hard in the past, being on the cusp of a real 'break' (to use the 'biz' terminology), he is meeting each day with lethargy, lack of desire, and nothing is really getting done in his life.

This interested me, because the situation seems to echo that of many sixth-formers I've met. You know the ones I mean: glazed eyes and collapsed bodies and minds. But, after visiting almost three hundred schools in the UK, I have yet to find any sixth-former totally *devoid* of motivation or achievement. The fact is, they're obviously motivated to a point, because there they are in the sixth form! 'Ah!' I hear you say. 'But they're not motivated *in the right way*.' That's what the proverb above is about.

The enemy of the sixth-former is not necessarily a bad choice. It's a series of OK choices that just aren't the best ones. And it is this internal battle between the mortal enemies of Best and Good that leaves your students looking and sounding as if they'd had a lobotomy. 'What do *you* think?' I have often heard a teacher ask a sixth-former. 'I dunno' is usually the response. That battle of the Best and the Good (not a movie starring Clint Eastwood) has created a state of 'stasis'.

Once, while leading a cluster INSET session, I asked all the teachers to tell me the obstacles to learning in their respective schools. A teacher hushed the other answers to declare, 'The biggest problem is that our young people have absolutely no values.' He then added, 'And they're so *ignorant!*' The irony was lost on him. The young people *I* have had the privilege to work with all have very strong values. I would even go as far to say that their values are often stronger than most adults'. Fairness, equality and justice are all fiercely defended and upheld among most sixth-formers I've met. But so are the values of 'chilling out', 'being with my friends' and 'textual relations' (yup – the mobile-phone issue).

The problem isn't a lack of values: it is *what* they are valuing. And where can they value it, or be valued for it? School?

All too often, I am asked by the school to come in and 'motivate' them. I have even been introduced as 'Mr Motivator'. Which is puzzling because I'm a short, bald Canadian guy who doesn't own *any* spandex. What I confront these sixth-formers with is therefore not motivation, but what they are valuing, because human beings are remarkably adept at placing value on almost anything (how else do you explain Pedragolli's 'swimming umbrella' or Peter Andre?). This must mean our value system is built on something deeper, something more revealing about ourselves. The eminent business coach Stephen Covey calls this bedrock from which values grow 'principles'

(Covey, Merill and Merrill, 1996). For reasons that will become apparent later in this chapter, I'm going to link them more specifically to 'the vision, motive or mission'. But more of that later.

Instead, let me get back to my story. I suggested to Bruno, as I suggest to all of you reading this, that his problem was starting. When '*mejor*' and '*bueno*' have a war, as we have already seen, the state generated is stasis – crippling to any act of beginning. It is also a state distressingly adept at creating a *false* start. Once he had started correctly, I argued, Bruno then would need to continue consistently.

Starting, then continuing consistently

I use the abbreviation 'SCC' for this, because even though I have a Bachelor of Fine Arts in Acting and a Diploma of Directing from the London Academy of Music and Dramatic Arts (LAMDA), my first job in the UK was with a now defunct coffee chain known as Seattle Coffee Company – or 'SCC'. Every day, I'd get up at 5 a.m. ('starting'). The work was hard, and involved long hours with a lot of extremely 'tricky' customers ('continuing' endlessly – I mean 'consistently'). How could I stay focused on my goals of theatre and film? How could I maintain my value system in a world completely unlike the one I was trained in? How do you make a triple skinny Viennese mocha-latte? I started by redefining the abbreviation of the company I was working for, into an abbreviation for the life I wanted to work for me.

In this chapter, I'm going to look at 'S', because the 'CC' is what Jim Roberson talks about in his chapter, 'The Disciplined Approach' (see Chapter 3). I believe the effectiveness of this discipline is defined by the choices you make at the 'starting' stage, however. So I will draw the connections between the 'S' and the 'CC's, but will not go over what Jim can say far more eloquently and effectively than I can. And, anyway, you are now

several paragraphs into a chapter about starting, and I'm only just starting myself! Imagine all the other stuff we could put in the way before we got going! Imagine how long it took for me to figure out how to start a chapter on starting! As Alanis Morissette so poignantly sang 'Isn't it ironic, don't you think…?' So let's go.

Ninety per cent of directors get in the way of starting.
– John Barton, Shakespearean director and classical dramaturge

Starting

Any machine needs a greater expense of energy to begin than it does to keep going. The New Zealand rugby player Jonah Lomu can sprint 100 metres in 10.7 seconds, which rivals an Olympic sprinter's ultimate speed. But consider the size of him, compared with the average sprinter. He's 6 foot 5 inches tall and 120 kg. The energy to get him going must be incredible. That is the energy needed to begin.

And, to begin, you must do something. Go and get a pen and two pieces of paper. No, I mean now. Yes, you. Yes, now! Why are you still here? The paper's only over there. I tell you what, I'll make it easier for you: it doesn't have to be a pen. You can get a pencil instead. OK? So *why* are you still here? We're about to do something that could change your whole approach to beginning. So why can't you move?

My guess is that there are two varieties of crippling thought stopping you. The first is: 'I'm perfectly happy here not moving, so let's just see how far Matt will go in this paragraph before I have to participate.' The second is more militant: 'Why should I? What is the relevance of this?'

As one headteacher I worked with once announced: 'I came here to learn a few new ideas, not to change!'

Try this. Fold your arms and cross your legs, the way you normally do. Be careful not to drop the book. It's big and could damage your foot. OK. Now fold your arms the other way (not all the way around: *the other way*). Now cross your legs the other way. Feel strange? Threatened? Threaten*ing*? Do you suddenly feel incompetent at simply sitting with folded arms? That's the energy needed to change how you sit, so imagine what you'd need to change your patterns of learning and thinking. Let alone putting down this book, getting up and getting the paper, hunting for a pen and returning to the book. All without being lured by the TV or the biscuit tin!

And what's most interesting to me is that I bet now all of you have folded your arms and legs back the way you always do. 'Yup,' your brain and body are saying, 'I've learned that bit.' But have you really learned? If your behaviour has not changed, what have you learned? Starting is always so tricky because it feels so uncomfortable to your brain, body and emotional state. But that's your central nervous system making itself vulnerable for a change. If it isn't continued consistently, your central nervous system will fall back on previously established patterns. That means the starting process is one where the central nervous system remains vulnerable.

We learning guys refer to this period of discomfort as *consciously incompetent*. And it makes us feel like intellectual donkeys.

As a director of student actors, I find this is something fundamental to teach. An actor's strength comes from their vulnerability – their responsiveness to the text. A great actor is one who is responding truthfully to the text, the other actors and (in the case of theatre) the audience and the space around them. This constant 'rediscovering' is what makes an audience feel what that actor is saying is 'truthful'. The cries early in rehearsal from actors of 'What does that mean?' or 'What's my motivation?' are often the discomfort of being vulnerable enough to explore for the answer inside themselves.

As the director, I *can* answer their questions. But that usually destroys their own discovery process, and closes down their vulnerability. If they know I answer all the time, they will turn off their own ability to answer. That sends profound messages to their central nervous system that no change is necessary.

So picture the scene. An actress (Kirsty) is cast in a role that is difficult (let's say, Lady Macbeth, because I don't believe the superstition). With myself as director, the whole cast reads the play. Kirsty inevitably reaches a line in the text she doesn't understand. Afraid of seeming to be ignorant, she reads the line quickly and loudly, without really considering it (something Mike Brearley's chapter, 'Build the Emotionally Intelligent School', might well have described as an 'unconscious incompetent' use of her acting technique). Nobody else in the cast questions her choice, but instead laud her (insert long-winded actor-like praises here), and reward her for working so well with such a challenging role on the first reading. Her unconscious incompetence, in other words, is rewarded.

Later, in rehearsal, I point out to her that, on that *one* line, she is getting fast and loud. I don't understand her. I sense her embarrassment, so I suggest an alternative reading. She realises that she's been covering up her lack of understanding (conscious incompetence). I overexplain my reasoning for the choice, Kirsty accepts willingly because she is embarrassed, and I feel better because I think that, by accepting my choice, Kirsty understands it. And even more worrying is that this change in choice probably reinforced strong feelings of inadequacy and mild stupidity in Kirsty. So, when under duress (opening night), Kirsty will confront the fact that lack of change means the actor will revert to old 'tricks'. We learning guys call *this* period of *renewed* comfort *unconscious incompetence*. When the audience applauds, her choices are all reinforced, and so she won't change.

But it doesn't *always* have to go this way.

Even though I'm a director, who says my ideas are always the 'best' ones? Maybe they're just 'good' ones? And am I a director or dictator? Instead, I could have simply alerted Kirsty to her unconsciously incompetent choice of getting faster and louder. After all, it is an *unconscious* choice. Awareness will no doubt lead her to *conscious* incompetence all on her own. This means that Kirsty can now have a stab at her own, better, *consciously competent* choice. I will reinforce this new choice of hers with increased praise, and so strengthen her brain's desire to use it. And so, when Kirsty gets to opening night and the line is clearly understood, and the audience claps, the applause is for *her* choice and so will ultimately become an unconsciously competent choice.

So, try to remain vulnerable as we move to the next 'task'. And this time really go and get those two bits of paper and a pen or pencil, because now you at least know why you feel so resistant! And perhaps, most controversially of all, turn off your mobile phone *now*. Keep it off until you have reached the section of the chapter when you can turn it on again. Gasp! Yes, as crazy as it sounds, many of us still couldn't even consider turning *off* our mobile phones. No matter what our age is. So take the plunge and boldly go where few have gone before. Beyond the silent mode on your phone.

Vision/motive/mission

Try this exercise with your students. It works particularly well at the beginning of a week, term or a fiercely tricky section of their course. It's even fun to pretend it's you who could benefit from this exercise, not just your students. It may stop those nightmares of being naked in an A-level exam that you didn't study for.

Anyway, imagine this world: you aced all your A-levels. Well done! Nice work! Can you imagine this, or are you already saying to yourself, 'Yeah, right – like that would *ever* happen!'? Push past the cynic. Cynicism is there to protect you from change, but change is what this exercise is about.

If, at the end of the exercise, you want to pick that cynic up again, please feel free to. But, for now, leave it behind. So, you've aced all your A-levels. There's an article about you in the local paper. The world is your oyster. Now imagine it is five years in the future from the day you aced your A-levels and write down your answers on one of the sheets of paper.

1. Which three places in the world could you be studying/working in?
2. Which three jobs could you be trying?
3. Which three undesirable personal qualities about yourself could you have eliminated?
4. Which three new, desirable qualities would you be able to cultivate in yourself?
5. Which three things can you do now that you couldn't do five years ago?
6. Which three things could you do five years ago that you can't do now?
7. Which three things did you do before sitting your A-levels that changed your life?

OK. Turn that piece of paper upside down. Get the other piece of paper. Stay vulnerable. Now imagine, you *don't* get any of your A-levels. No article in the paper. It is five years from the day you messed up.

1. What are three things you can't do any more?
2. What are three places you can't visit?
3. What are three jobs you'll never be able to do?
4. What are three positive character traits you have lost?
5. What are three negative character traits that have got worse?
6. What are three things you do now that you *never ever* wanted to do?
7. What were the three things you refused to change that led to your downfall?

Which life do you like better? Erase the one you don't like – burn the sheet of paper the answers are on. Now. Make sure a fire extinguisher (or fully trained fire crew) is nearby. Watch the life you don't like burn up. Keep the one you like. Look at your answers again. Copy them. Put one copy in a frame and hang it up. Fold the other copy up, and put it in your wallet or handbag. Look at the answers before you go to bed tonight. Look at the answers before you start *any* revision. We'll get back to this later.

Smoke gets in your eyes

'Yeah, but …' is probably the phrase I hear the most, no matter whom I am working with. I'll often quote the first line of Dr Benjamin Spock's *The Common Sense Book of Baby and Child Care*: 'You already have all the answers.'

What I say is stuff that some part of you already knows. But that isn't enough. How many smokers do you know are unaware of the dangers of smoking? When were 'new initiatives and strategies' by the senior management team ever enough to convince you that their ideas were good ones? The solutions aren't always enough – it's those darn problems that need knocking down one by one. 'Yeah, but …' usually precedes a problem. And the problem is often phrased in such a way that the solution I have suggested isn't something that would happen 'in the real world'. I promise all of you now: the things I write about here are all things that have worked in the real world. I use them myself.

So what are the problems? I have asked sixth-formers all over the country what they think is stopping them. I have then been fortunate to put that same question to the teachers of those students, and occasionally the parents. Three things come up all the time: attitude, stress and time.

Attitude

There seem to be two diverging 'stems' to this one:

The teacher/parental perspective

Here the adults are at the end of their rope, exhausted by 'pushing their child' or 'driving' the learning of their sixth-formers. 'They won't do anything for *themselves*!' (Though this is still better than, 'They won't do *anything*!') 'They always want me to spoon-feed them.' This will usually unearth the 'mother of all phrases': 'They won't take responsibility!' Lack of responsibility is often an issue with many young people, and I won't dispute that now. However, I will go on later to describe what I see as a misuse of the word *responsibility* by some teachers and parents. This 'mother of all phrases' is sometimes used as a 'mask' for another statement: 'They make *me* feel responsible.' But we'll look at this later.

My favourite complaint made by adults of adolescents, however, is, 'They won't do what I ask them to!' It's as if, when an adolescent says 'No' (and hence gives 'attitude'), they have shut their brains off and have *no* intention of returning to the subject. This often leads adults to assume the young person is being 'difficult' for the sake of it. However, there are lots of other issues going on here. First, there is a lot of talk of 'learning styles' out there, so I won't go into that here. But Ian Gilbert mentioned something in passing to me once that I have held onto: 'Matt, there are only two learning styles: "Yes" and "No".'

'No' can often mean 'Not now', but even more likely is, 'I'll do it myself when you aren't looking.'

When I was thirteen, my father bought me a Walkman. They were just starting to become fashionable. To have one was to be envied by your peers, and lauded by the Sony Corporation. However, when I got mine, I grabbed my screwdriver and opened it up. My father screamed at me, 'What the hell do you think you're doing, you ungrateful boy?' (Or words to that effect.) I simply replied, 'I want to see how it works!' What was to *me* a way of learning something was to *him* an act of disrespect. Ian is right: there are two kinds of learner in the world. There are those who, when asked to do something, simply get on and do it. Inside their head, the word 'Yes' responds to the call to action by an adult. But there are some of us who, when asked to do something, start by saying 'No' or 'Why?', 'What for?' or 'You have got to be joking!' We call these people 'cheeky' – or use other terms from the French canon.

Teenagers are often learning by making the adults around them believe that they are not learning at all. This is a technique I call *parental control*, which I'll get to later on.

The student perspective

'I can't be *arsed*!'

As David Keeling says in his chapter (Chapter 1), 'attitude will determine altitude'. So, if your attitude is that you can't be 'arsed', your altitude is probably around waist height, which for a lot of boys makes perfect sense! The lethargy they are talking of is not just physical (though that is a huge issue: consider their hormone levels, diet, exercise etc.). Not being 'arsed' to do something usually comes from a bad 'start'. There's no point (in their minds). It's too hard. All they can see is how much more energy it would take them to start. In other words, they've already figured out how not to do it. As adolescents, we all discover that, if we can picture ourselves getting out of something, then we get out of it. In a recent study in the US, 60 per cent of teenagers polled know that cheating and plagiarism are wrong, but they do them anyway (Clairol, 2004). It's less energy expended, which is really frightening only if you need the kind of energy boost that a good start to something requires.

Stress

'Results', 'league tables', 'minimum requirements', 'school reputation', 'family tradition', 'high expectations' (not to be confused with 'limited' expectations: these are summed up by, 'You will be a doctor/lawyer, won't you?') – these are all sound bites that trickle through the 16–18-year-old brain and lodge deep in the centre. Their brains have a few highly effective barriers to all

adult communication. I will call it *parental control* (told you I'd mention this again), since it limits the amount of parental communication getting into the conscious mind. One of these parental controls is the ability to convince an adult that absolutely *nothing* that has just been said has gone in. It begins with breaking eye contact, repeating what *you* just said in a lifeless tone, and then finding something else to do (start a text message, chew a pen, proceed to plot the downfall of mankind …).

But *any* phrase that is laced with a standard of attainment that may imply an adult's pride at their achievement goes directly to the centre of a young person's consciousness. All this talk of 'results' and 'expectations' mixes with their own perception of what their ability is, and what thoughts they've had about their future. What remains is a huge chasm that separates what *they* think they can do, and the ominous echo of somebody else's expectations.

And as I said earlier, young people often have very strong value systems. This means they can be ruthlessly hard on themselves. If they aren't as good as *they* think they should be, a very dark mood can erupt. These value systems, while laudable in their intensity, are often unachievable. They tend not to tolerate mistakes, for example. I believe that a fundamental human need is the need to be understood.

This is why our receptors for others' emotions are usually quite strong. But in a teenager the nerve activity in the brain is increased to such a degree that it has been suggested that all teenagers go through a mild form of autism (defined as 'the inability to recognise or reproduce emotions in others'). A 'stressed' teenager is often unaware that others have figured out that they are stressed. And others around them will quickly assume that therefore the teenager is stressed because of something someone else has done. But the teenager is usually attacking her- or himself from the inside.

Time

How sour sweet music is
When time is broke, and no proportion kept!
So is it in the music of men's lives.
And here have I the daintiness of ear
To check time broke in a disordered string;
But for the concord of my state and time
Had not an ear to hear my true time broke.
I wasted time, and now doth time waste me.

*– William Shakespeare, Richard II (well, I **am** a director)*

Fairly self-explanatory. Robert Kelley of Carnegie-Mellon University (my new spiritual home) carried out a study that aimed to estimate the amount of information about their job a working professional could hold in their head. In the mid-1980s, his research estimated the figure to be 75 per cent (Kelley, 1985). In contrast, in 2001, that figure had shrunk to a staggering 15 per cent (cited by Goleman, 2002). Today, there is a veritable plethora of information out there, and so the implication is that there is less time to learn it all. The national curriculum has structured content in a highly challenging way, as a means to try to meet these new demands of the workplace. Gone are days when there would be 'free' periods, contemplation or reflection 'time', and even reading 'week' has been shrunk (in some schools) to a long weekend. Where do we find the time to educate ourselves?

Also, I watch a lot of teenagers (and adults) exist in two states of time: panic and procrastination. Each of these gives rise to the other. Consider Table 1.

Panic	Prevention
Procrastination	Purposelessness

Table 1.

When allocating their time, our students will usually spend it on what is most urgent: the test that is in twelve hours' time, the essay due in three hours, the phone that rings and rings and rings. However, these things increase their heart rate, raise their skin temperature, quicken their fidgeting. These tasks also demand more brain energy, so that means more glucose. And usually it means a lot of running around, which means more carbohydrates.

When it's all done, they're knackered! So what do they do? Procrastinate. The justification is to call it 'a well-earned break' or 'a present to myself'. But is seven hours of television a nice present to give to anybody?

That covers panic and procrastination. The purposelessness area is also damaging. I notice that a lot of the sixth-formers I meet never, *ever* turn off their mobile phones. A lot of adults fail to do so, also. When I ask the sixth-formers why they can't turn their phones off they respond with, 'What if it's an emergency?' (In other words, a call from the first area: panic.) Surely, if it *is* an emergency, whoever is calling you would be better off calling the police, ambulance or fire service. Without getting too glib, these phones are little more than excuses to become more involved in somebody else's life rather than our own. A mobile phone ringing *pretends* to be important – it has an annoying ring, and an invasive effect on us, and it is expensive! But how do we really know that call is as important as the ringtone suggests it is? Purposelessness means spending our time on other people's unimportant activities – the last area we'll get to last.

First, let's reword Table 1 to explain what I mean. Imagine time as fire prevention. Panic, would be an actual fire. Time to act. Immediately. We all have things that become immediately important to deal with. Otherwise we'd be seriously in trouble. And, instead of procrastination, let's put a fire-extinguisher duel. By that I mean, there is little (if any) purpose in it. Society gains little from it. It also ties up their hands when a real fire happens. If the fire extinguishers have been exhausted in a duel, they won't be full to fight the fire. Which means that, when a fire occurs, your only option is to run. Escape.

On the other side of the table, instead of prevention, imagine a fire drill. These are done in times of calm. Everyone usually has a giggle as you go through the actions of what should be done. They provide safer and better alternatives for when a fire is nearby. And, under the fire drill, is the false alarm. This is someone running down the hall shouting, 'Oh, my God! Oh, my God! Oh, my *God*!' It makes us respond immediately, though it detracts us from what we were doing. The table would look like Table 2.

Fire	Fire drill
Fire-extinguisher duel	False alarm

Table 2.

Which of these areas is both the most effective at saving lives *and* enjoyable? I used to love fire drills at school. It was multisensory learning: The bell rang deafeningly (audible), we laughed at the teacher's angered face (visual) and then we all got up and walked calmly outside (kinaesthetic). The mood was always fun and entertaining and introduced me to people in my class I never even knew were there. We were all rehearsing how to respond effectively in what could become a panic-filled event.

Time is endless when it is purposeful.

– Socrates

Be honest with me: how much time do *you* spend in fire, false alarm or fire-extinguisher duels? If you spent more time in the fire-drill stage, both

your and your students' options would open up. They would stay focused on the things that help them. You would work in a calmer, more purposeful way. We all have enough time. And we all have the strength to choose how to spend it. Often, I am challenged at this point, as rest and breaks are not really clear from the table. I would put rest and breaks in the fire-drill box, because rest is purposeful and essential. It gives both them and us the energy and creativity needed to plan escape (from the fire, not the work!).

(If this model of time management intrigues you and you want to know more, see Covey (1999) and McDermott (2002).)

Break time!

Now, let me put my money where my mouth is. I say breaks are purposeful and essential, so let's have one. You've been working hard. Put the book down and go and make yourself a cup of tea. I'll see you in five minutes.

Welcome back.

Just before we leap back into this chapter let's make sure your brain is in the best possible state for learning. And one of the quickest ways to the brain is through the body. Try this. Draw a figure eight in the air with your nose. Keep it going. Now draw the number six in the air with your right hand. Keep the nose going. And, if you're really brave, try drawing the number nine with your left hand while you keep the nose and the right hand going (easy!). When your mind melts, pick up the book and let's go onwards and ever upwards.

Acting is simple. But that means it is very, very difficult.
– Lee Strasberg, 'Method' acting guru, on why Marilyn Monroe had so much trouble

Before the break, I was banging on about the problems or obstacles. I have heard the pleas of the students themselves, their teachers, their parents, the universities and colleges. I've even talked to (and worked with) the businesses looking to hire these sixth-formers when they leave education. And I hear three very different kinds of problem. They say the problems are 'attitude', 'time' and 'stress'. But I say the problems are quite different. I think they are unclear vision, fear and responsibility.

I want to explain each one, and even some solutions to each – though I warn you: my solutions are often simple. That does not mean they are either (a) easy or (b) simplistic.

> I wouldn't give a fig for the simplicity on this side of complexity; I would give my right arm for the simplicity on the far side of complexity.
> **– American physician and poet, Oliver Wendell Holmes, Snr, talking himself into the most complicated defence of simplicity**

Problem 1: Unclear or bleak vision

> The boxer learns to aim his blows, not at the point of contact, but somewhere beyond it.
> **– Muhammad Ali**

Any time I start a session, no matter who it is with, I begin with thumb wrestling. No 'joke to warm them up'; no 'intro'. I start by doing. It can often galvanise the pervading sentiment of a room in less than a minute. I often hear huffs and puffs, groans, mumbled outrage and dissent. But they'll often all have a go. Why do I do this? I was struck about five years ago when I became aware of a study in the US. It looked at the link between finger strength and visualisation. For four weeks, half the study group worked out one finger on their left hand. The other half simply visualised themselves doing the finger workout. After a month, the group who actually did the workout had increased their finger strength by 30 per cent. The group who visualised their workout had increased their finger strength by 22 per cent (Robertson, 2000).

There are also numerous other fascinating studies linking visualisation and performance. Sven-Göran Eriksson uses 'Mental Training Plans' and documents their impact in his book, *On Football*. Flipping through my library at home, I discovered that five of the six books I have on memory skills dedicate entire chapters to it. And even the former Austrian philosopher (now turned Californian governor) Arnold Schwarzenegger says, 'If your brain can *envisage* you doing something, then you can do it.'

Visualisation has been used widely in competitive sports, and there are numerous accounts of its use throughout history. Victor Frankl (1963) cites the capacity of consistently visualising a better future as the only factor that decided whether or not an inmate of a Nazi concentration camp would survive. He should know: he was in one, and was experimented on in one, for years.

When a sixth-former is asked to buckle down and work, what is their first picture in their head? What vision do they have? What are the perks? I have heard teachers and parents start their appeal to their child to study by setting this vision with, 'Now, *look* [notice the visual syntax?], I *know* this isn't fun …' or 'I *know* this is boring …'

If you type in 'study skills' into Google on the information superhighway, chances are you'll get one hell of a response. And, though I can't claim to have checked all 8,310,000 sites my search threw up, the ones I *did* look at address two things: 'what' is on the test (the knowledge) and 'how' to do it (endless bullet points of skills to try). I assume the rationale is that, if you know what to study and how to study, you *will* study. But you all know that exercise is important. And you all know how to run. But how many of you run regularly? There is a bigger and much more effective question: 'Why?' Why should you go for a run when you have my sparkling prose to read?

Answering 'Why?' or 'To what end?' first, we unleash a greater source of energy. And it is more potent than either 'What?' or 'How?'. If every A-level student were offered £2 million and a first-class round-the-world airline ticket upon completing their A-levels, what would the league tables look like? Now, before you shout me down with, 'Yeah, but that ain't going to happen', think about what I just said. If your students could see themselves getting As and Bs in your A-levels because the incentive is that much cash, then their brains have the capacity to get those grades. End of story.

It is the power of the almighty 'WIIFM' – not a bad smell made by boys in the locker room: it stands for 'What's in it for me?' WIIFM is a great substitute for 'Why?' with adolescents. As a question on it's own, 'Why?' can be quite daunting. It throws open a lot of doors, invariably with many more questions behind each of those doors. So 'I dunno' will usually be their response. Asking what is in it for them will often reap much richer responses. Certainly more decisive ones!

However, sometimes just asking *them* what their 'Why' is can actually be enough. Most sixth-formers I've met are used to crying, 'Why do we have to do this?' – and being answered by the teacher. I firmly believe we *can't* answer that question for them. If they can't think of one, get them to go back to the fourteen questions I asked earlier. What would their world *look* like (notice again the visual syntax?) with those grades they want? Aren't they worth that life?

There are too many pitfalls to just asking 'What?' or 'How?' when *starting*. The beginning of

something needs that extra bit of mental oomph. The 'what' is clearly going to be a part of the beginning process, but the goal isn't enough. The 'how' becomes essential as soon as the 'what' is defined. But they are not enough. The 'why' combines and activates them.

When faced with beginning something, you state your goal. Is that enough? Stating the goal usually succeeds in terrifying most adolescents. 'An A in maths', 'more study time' or 'Oxford or Cambridge – take your pick' can actually demotivate somebody getting ready to begin.

In a similar way, if you have got as far as stating your goal, and it is scary and sizable, the brain will begin to visualise and rehearse obstacles. If you start by saying, 'That's great, Matt, but *how* could I do that?', your brain will actually start running through a complicated diagnostic risk assessment for achieving that particular goal. It will show you how exhausting, boring and intellectually demanding the goal could be to achieve. It will cross-reference with your (distorted) picture of yourself, highlighting every time you've been lazy, asked a stupid question or been disappointed with yourself. In other words, by asking 'How?', your brain shows you 'how hard' the goal will be to achieve.

You need more. 'Why?' can turn the 'how' into a creative process. 'Why?' can eradicate false starts, because it can challenge a weak 'What?'. And, most importantly, 'Why?' can open up 'hows' you hadn't previously deemed possible. 'Why?' is what is in Jonah Lomu's head as he makes a break for the touchline – winning *feels* amazing, and he wants that feeling very, very badly.

And our brain doesn't want us to find things without purpose that are that difficult. So, instead, it comes up with reasons why you couldn't *ever* achieve, and so protects you from that (distorted) vision of 'achievement' in your head. But who says that is the way it's going to be? If the prize at the end of all that hard work and sacrifice is something that changes the direction of your life for the better, doesn't that in turn change the way your brain 'sees' hard work and sacrifice? After all, it could be a lot worse.

A-levels as death wish

There is an apocryphal story doing the rounds of actors I know about Mike Leigh. He is an eminent, brilliant director of British films, including *Abigail's Party*, *Secrets and Lies* and *Topsy-Turvy*. The story goes that he hired an actor straight out of drama school. He didn't have much to do, but did have some text to do on camera. When the actor's big moment came to film his dialogue, he panicked. He forgot his lines, or delivered them badly. After numerous takes, Leigh cleared the set of the crew and went up to the actor. Leigh told him, 'Two things, mate. One: it's only a film. Two: a hundred thousand people lost their homes today in Bangladesh.' The crew was called back and the camera set up. The actor then did a perfect take.

I don't know if the story is true, but I love it. Perspective is essential when dealing with vision. By all means, have a life-affirming reason to go after your goals. But remember: to use the fear of a fate worse than death if you *don't* get the grades you want is tantamount to a death wish.

There is so much to be grateful for, and the human brain has to learn how to notice that. A common frustration that parents confide in me is how their daughter or son is 'ungrateful'. What I have to remind the parents is that we have to *learn* how to be grateful. It doesn't just happen one day. Everybody has to see and feel what grateful means to them. The perspective of one person's gratitude rarely equals another. How many unhappy millionaires would the *Sun* have us believe there are? A close friend of mine who is Swedish has a mother with the greatest perspective shift I've witnessed. Whenever someone in her family is getting heated over something, she puts her arm on their shoulder and looks at them with her piercing Scandinavian eyes. '*Ingen har dött*,' she says, in the quietest, kindest and most reassuring way ('Nobody has died').

What is brilliant is that she never becomes condescending.

Solution: raise expectations

I claim to be no more than an average man with below average capabilities. I have not the shadow of a doubt that any man or woman can achieve what I have if he or she would put forth the same effort and cultivate the same hope and faith.

– Mahatma Gandhi (freed 300 million people, which sounds anything *but* average to me)

Try this with your students. Get them to write down every subject they are being examined in. Next to each subject, they need to write down what grade their teacher would predict for them. Then, they must write down what grade *they* think they'll get. Then they increase the highest grade by one. If they have any As, make them A*. Then, ask them to grab the darkest, thickest pen they can find and scribble out the first two grades. Then look at what is left – one grade higher than before. Ask them how it feels looking at these higher grades, and what kind of life is waiting for them with those results.

Then I tell them to write these new grades on a new piece of paper, twice as big as the first piece. I then ask them to write down the following passage:

It is August [insert date of published exam results]. I am walking to school. It is sunny and very hot. I am wearing [insert favourite clothes]. The sun is warm on my face, I hear an ice-cream

van in the distance, and I can smell the grass –
and suntan lotion. I am smiling from ear to ear.
As I get to the school gates, my phone goes off – I
have a text message from [favourite person]. The
text says [I ask them to write the best possible
text message they can think of getting before
reading their results]. I walk into the hall, walk
up to the piece of paper with my results and
see [they fill in their higher grades *three* times
larger than the last time].

Then everybody stands up. I often put on music –
Aaron Copland's *Fanfare for the Common Man* or
'Mars' from Gustav Holst's *The Planets* will do
the trick. When I give the command, everybody
shouts their completed passage at the same time,
continuing to the end of their last grade. We then
can do it again – twice as loud. Before the repeat,
I add the following to the questions I asked earlier: What would their friends, parents, teachers
think/say when they ran home with these
results? In short, what could they *not* go on and
do in their life?

Is this enthusiastic, shouting display of confidence enough to get those results? Absolutely
not. But it almost is. There's hard work and discipline as well. But, like time, the capacity for hard
work and discipline is limitless when the goal is
purposeful. Raising your expectations pushes you
and your students out of comfort zones and
touches the parts of your brains mediocre goals
can't. Higher expectations don't mean higher levels of stress. They just mean being smarter with
your expectations, rather than just scarier. After
all, our brains work best in high-challenge, low-
stress environment. With lower expectations,
there's less challenge and so our effort is wasted
on stress and last-minute work bursts. That
means a low-challenge, high-stress environment.
Which one would you prefer? And which one gets
them closer to the grades (and experience) they
shouted out in the exercise mentioned above.

There's another benefit to high expectations.
Extensive research in professional sport shows
that fatigue can set in 80 per cent of the way into
achieving a goal (football fans: Arsenal's
Champions' League and FA Cup failings at the
end of the 2004 season?). If the goal is 'realistic',
it's believed the brain already starts to think it
has achieved it, and the amount of energy
expended is greatly reduced. By having a clearly
visualised, higher-challenge goal to go after, that
natural energy dip is smaller. This keeps your
energy level high when you really need it – with
only one-fifth of the work left to do. Think what
happened to you the week before your exams last
time.

This is why I now don't believe in 'realistic goals',
and never knowingly use the phrase. All goals
can be realistic. Only time frames are unrealistic.
Anyone can learn an instrument, or another language, or do their own taxes (without cheating).
Not necessarily in the same amounts of time. We
all learn in our own ways at our own speeds. However, I've noticed that, as the challenge becomes
greater, people achieve it faster. The lower the
challenge, the more procrastination there is along
the way, maybe because, as the challenge
increases, so does the amount of energy needed to
achieve it. And energy begets energy. But, as the
challenge decreases, it just reaffirms our overactive imagination's belief that we aren't really
that smart and couldn't achieve something great.

Problem 2: Fear

*Bara de döda fiskarna simmar
med strömmen.*
– Swedish for 'Only the dead fish
swim with the current'

Fear takes two forms: fear of failure and fear of
success. The first one has become a problem only
because a failure is seen, heard and spoken about
as an 'end'. Predicted grades, poor GCSE or A-
level results, dropping out of university, losing a
job – these are all widely perceived as 'end-of-the-
world' events, except for those individuals who
were cheeky enough to swim *against* the current
of public opinion and use it to help them. You
know the kind of no-good punk kids I'm talking

about: Jamie Oliver, Richard Branson, Bill Gates, Alan Titchmarsh … What have they ever done for us, eh?

But how did they do it? They started something others had decided had finished for all of them. And, when people *continually* told them they couldn't go any further, they took their 'advice' with a pinch of salt and kept going anyway. To keep the cooking and seasoning metaphor going, Jamie Oliver was ridiculed for his learning difficulties (he's dyslexic). At fifteen, he was cooking a hundred meals a night. He *started* in a professional kitchen when he was eight because he wanted to earn extra money. That decision to start something fuelled him through all the many knocks and mistakes along the way.

I am not discouraged, because every wrong attempt discarded is another step forward.
– Thomas Edison, kicked out of primary school for asking 'too many questions'

What happens when I fail?

I have learned one major thing in my time as an Independent Thinking associate: mistakes are the way we learn; failure is when learning stops; success is when the lessons of mistakes are first noticed, and, second, acted upon productively.

I have yet to encounter the following scenario. Somebody crawls up to me on their hands and knees. I ask, 'Why aren't you standing up?' They reply, 'Well, when I was a baby, I tried this walking "thing". But I kept falling over. Again and again. So I thought, "I'm rubbish at this" and I dedicated my life to scuttling around on my butt.'

Learning is persistently confronting and handling failure. Mistakes are a failure only when you stop after the mistake is made. Mistakes are teachers. Or they are warnings that something bigger could be wrong. Asking why the mistake was made, or even what you could have done to make a bigger mistake, can help to reframe the mistake into something you learned. And you strengthen your character for the all things you'll learn going through your A-levels.

Try. Fail. Try again. Fail again. Fail better.
– Samuel Beckett, cracking an Existential-Modernist joke (oh, stop it, Sam, you're killing me)

But what about the second type of fear – fear of success? It sounds crazy. But think about how much a 16–18-year-old will stand out from their peers if they become a fully focused study machine? And how much would they stand out from society if they were to set high standards for themselves, and refuse to compromise until they achieved them?

Ambition is frowned upon at many levels of our society. Is it the remnants of the class system returning to haunt us? I think it is even deeper than that: we are afraid of success, because it implies a massive change. Our brain's purpose is to protect us from such a change. After all, change could threaten our survival.

Before we look at our third and final adolescent obstacle to achievement, let's pull over and take a quick pit stop for all those who blanch at words like 'self-esteem'.

Self-esteem versus therapy culture

We consult troops of specialists on the question of how to live, when memory alone, heard with common sense and empathy, will tell us what we need to know.
– Robert Grudin, remarking on the touchy-feely going topsy-turvy

Our self-esteem grows at a steady but fragile rate in our adolescence. Contrary to what we are told, adolescence years are not always the 'the Wonder Years'. Hormones rage. Our bodies turn on us. In the UK, two teenagers commit suicide every day. Suicide has become the number-one killer of men under 21. Britain has the highest teenage pregnancy rate in Europe. Eating disorders affect over 1 million people in the UK under nineteen – that's one in fifty young women and one in five hundred young men. The self-esteem of today's youth is taking a beating, before it has had a chance to ripen.

Let me define what I mean when I say 'self-esteem'. It is not the happy-clappy definition of many self-help books. It is not the constant poring over your successes. It has been suggested by some that looking in the mirror and telling yourself you are wonderful is the answer. To me, that is conceit, not self-esteem. It leads to an illusionary world in which we arm ourselves against life by telling our brains that we can't handle it. One term for it is 'mollycoddled'.

And self-esteem is also not arrogance. On the contrary, the syntax of the arrogant betrays itself: 'I can do that better than you'; 'I'm bigger/faster/stronger/hairier than you.' Do you hear it? They are trying to steal somebody else's self-esteem to make up for lack of their own. Self-esteem is a lot harder than either of those two.

1. Awareness

First, it is awareness of yourself. Awareness of what you can and cannot do. That means separating the voice of instinct from that of the overactive imagination. The overactive imagination says things such as, 'You are rubbish at maths' or 'You aren't really a leader' or 'People don't really like you.' Instinct, however, says things such as, 'What could I do to be better at maths?' or 'What do I need to do to be a leader today?' or 'What is it about me these people keep attacking, and why is it threatening them so much?'

Instinct asks questions that provide character-building answers. Overactive imagination destroys fragile, illusionary conceits. This is a huge issue for actors I work with as well. Controlling the internal dialogue of the overactive imagination is key to any actor's success. I often say to them, 'There is nothing less interesting than watching an actor beat themselves up.'

2. Vision/motive/mission

Second, self-esteem is a vision, mission or motive we set for ourselves. We talked of this earlier in the chapter. A vision/motive/mission is actually intrinsic to our self-esteem. Our vision is like a movie of our life. Would you pay to go back to see the same depressing, repetitive and upsetting movie? Then why do you tolerate it as the movie in which you star every day inside your own head? Our vision is the course we steer ourselves through, with our instinct and principles as steersman and captain respectively.

3. Physical and emotional safety

A vision, mission or motive leads us to protect both our emotional and physical safety, which is the third key element to self-esteem. Contrary to what Year 8 boys may say, being hit repeatedly is not something any of us actually enjoy. In fact, it sends profound messages to the overactive imagination that we aren't worth anything more than being hit. And that, in turn, will alter our course – back to the vision, mission or motive.

4. Capability

Fourth, we need to train our focus to notice what we are capable of. It has been estimated that, every second, as many as 2 million different pieces of sensory information strike our brains. For example, through this entire chapter, your heart has been beating – hopefully. We tune it out with the aid of our reticular activating system (RAS). But we can tune our RAS manually as well. The constant dialogue in our heads shapes our self-esteem by either noticing what we are doing or by ignoring it. As I mentioned earlier, mistakes are how we learn. If the dialogue in your head after a mistake is simply, 'Well, I'm rubbish at that,' the brain has been given a clear message about how to look at what's just been done. If I get five out of ten in a spelling test, and the first thing my brain focuses on is how I didn't get ten out of ten, I could be heading for failure. The definition inside my own head of my spelling ability is becoming fixed. But I can also interrupt that dialogue with questions. What did I get wrong? Why? How did I prepare for the test? How did others in my class do on the test? When is the next test and what can I do differently? Does the teacher hate me? (Just kidding.) The questions we ask become the dialogue that reshapes our own belief in ourselves. And this can radically change how much we think we can do, what we are capable of.

My persistence is the measure of belief I have in myself.
– Walt Disney (who has the same birthday as I do, so I'm biased)

Our focus is like precious cash. If we treat it like that, we start to get what we pay for. But, unsurprisingly, if we focus only on things we find painful,

horrible, useless and offensive, that too is what we have spent our energy on, and so it is what we get.

When I was learning to drive in Canada, I was taught to handle black ice. With Canada's climate, it's quite common. The instinct that tends to kick in when you hit black ice is to focus on what you're about to hit with your car. If you do that, however, you skid and hit something. You have to train your focus to be on where you want the car to go, and turn *into* the skid. Your head will try to pull you to look at what you might hit, but you have to stay focused on the road. As I mentioned earlier, the dialogue of the overactive imagination would kill you. Instead, you have to train your instinct.

When we are approaching 'black ice' in our lives (silly metaphor, I know, but I am Canadian), our focus can wander. Approaching A-levels, all students start thinking of all the things they haven't done yet or things they've done badly. They may entertain thoughts of how unhappy they, their parents and their teachers will be if they don't do well. But that's the wall we will all hit if we keep focusing on it. We have to encourage these students to go back to their vision – the life they chose for themselves by answering the 14 questions outlined earlier in the 'Vision/motive/mission' section of this chapter (see page 80). And steer themselves into that vision. Under their own steam. It's difficult, but it saves their life.

5. Community

But Marge, I'm not popular enough to be different!
– Homer Simpson

The fifth and final element of self-esteem is community. A human being is a communal animal. We also have the longest period of childhood in the animal world. And, particularly in childhood, we look to the community we are in to see how and where we fit in. If a place is not there for us, we simply leave to find a community that *does* have a place for us. Behind the bike sheds, at the skate ramp, at a mate's garage where she keeps the drum kit, an Internet chatroom. Scared yet? We need to find what makes us unique, but *then* to find out which community will embrace that uniqueness. If you don't, you end up like Homer Simpson, trying to be popular enough to be unique.

I am not condemning all of self-help or psychotherapy. There are strong arguments and testimonials that show it helps the neediest. But a watered-down therapeutic culture that seeks to simply stroke kids and shield them from anything 'too difficult' is doing much more harm than good. It undersells and underestimates our children. Imagine a world that walks behind a baby with a cushion shielding it from the floor as it tries to walk? In the UK today, sixth-formers are being diagnosed with posttraumatic-stress disorder! Some argue this fact points to overwhelming pressures on young people that need to be lifted. I think it points to society's failure to allow these kids to go through stress and realise they are in fact strong enough to live through it. Furedi (2004) deals with this in an excellent book.

Success is often seen as something reserved for a few 'special' people. As Marianne Williamson says in her poem 'Our Deepest Fear' in *A Return to Love* (1996), we often ask, '… who am I to be brilliant, gorgeous, talented or fabulous?' Success is an alien place that is shrouded in a lot of mystery. It doesn't surprise me, then, that most young people associate 'being in the media' with being 'successful'. Where else is success so readily accessible? How is the community valuing success? Are ambition, high achievement (no matter the subject) and forward thinking as important as predicted grades?

Problem 3: Responsibility

I told you I'd get back to this! It's a word that I believed is misused. Responsibility is often used as a synonym for 'blame'. If somebody has been 'irresponsible', the person saying it often means that they feel the 'irresponsible' individual hasn't taken sufficient blame for their actions, or alleviated enough blame from others. Therefore, what they really mean is 'accountability'. Undoubtedly, it is part of responsibility, but it is the aftereffect. Responsibility is exactly what it says on the tin: the 'ability' to choose your 'response'. It is the embodiment of Aristotelian wisdom – the space between stimulus and response.

A girl at a London college summed up the plight for responsibility for me perfectly. 'I'd do better at school,' she insisted 'but all my teachers are crap. And my school is crap. And where I live is crap. And my mum and dad are crap. And I have to go to parties all the time – it's not my fault I'm so popular!' I then asked, who was responsible for the success of her life. She replied more enthusiastically than the first time, 'Me! I am independent.' To which I said, 'No, you aren't. You are telling me that *if* your teachers, school, home and parents all miraculously changed overnight, that then, *and only then*, you would be a smarter worker at school, yes? That means, your life's success is entirely in the hands of others, because you are saying you are powerless to change *them*, but they change *you* on a daily basis.' She frowned.

I then asked her whom she *wanted* to be in control of the success of her life. She said, 'Me. And only me.' To which I replied, 'How can you start doing that?' And suddenly she had all the answers. And they were painful answers. 'I need to put aside time to work. I have to stop blaming everybody. I need to bring my pen to class …' The power of this story is that *she* had the answers, not I, uncomfortable and unpleasant though they were for her to entertain. Teenagers know how to take responsibility. They are often not being challenged enough to do so. They will get it wrong at first, but that's the only chance they have of getting it right in the future.

Intrinsic motivation

All of this would suggest that inherent in responsibility is proactivity. Action. To start. If man's nature is to act, not to be acted upon, then we have a responsibility to our species and our ancestry to be proactive. However, being the semantic little hair splitter that I am, there's a word I prefer to *proactivity*, and that is *creativity*. Creativity has been defined as 'intrinsic motivation' (Abbot and Ryan, 2001). And this is why I end with creativity, because it takes me full circle, back to what I trained to do, and even back to my chat with Bruno. It links all the pieces together. Creativity is 'intrinsically motivating' – the process of creation. Nifty, huh? Back to the whole starting thing.

To act, we must create. To create, we must have vision. To have vision, we need self-understanding, dignity and ambition (let's call that self-esteem or courage, shall we?). Hence, courage is the foundation of any act of creating or starting. Remember the 'Cycle of Change' model from David Keeling's chapter? Lack of courage is the resistance to change, but also the resistance to starting. By starting, you begin the process of destroying the lack of courage in yourself. This skill can be effectively 'taught' only by teachers doing it themselves. Their 'lead' will gain 'followers'. A teacher's methods, mindset and technique will be not only scrutinised, but parodied and lampooned. If your methods, mindset and techniques are not sound, the followers will turn to something more 'real'. But, if you persist successfully, working on yourself and your own process, the followers will become the leaders. This process is known as *modelling*. The great basketball player Dr J said, 'I expect more of myself than everybody else. That way I disappoint nobody.'

The teacher sets the height of the bar for courageous acts. By starting correctly, you build your *own* self-esteem and their self-esteem, and they can begin to manifest their vision. You also start to make mistakes together faster and, by doing so, learn faster. So starting correctly is what makes 'the real world'.

I simply cannot believe that sixth-formers *try* to be, or indeed are, *motivated* to be lazy. Or

stressed. Or bad tempered. They get 'caught up' in a poor vision, fed by the lack of courage. They started badly, and lost the desire to keep going. They often prepare to handle disappointment rather than train their focus to stay on the road they really want to go down.

The solution is not strategies for studying. They come later. The solution is not information saturation. There's already plenty of that. The solution is 'to begin at the beginning' (sorry, Mr Dylan Thomas, sir!) – that is, start by asking, '*Why* should I start?' By starting this way, we demand of ourselves that we act, and so engage immediately with our own ability to take responsibility for that action. We unleash the power in us that is equal to the power needed to move Jonah Lomu 100 metres in 10.7 seconds.

Excuses, excuses

Society maintains no verbal apparatus so extensive or complex as that which excuses the lack of achievement.
– Robert Grudin

The remedy for a lack of responsibility isn't rocket science. It's starting. Do this right now: stand up, balance on your left foot. No, *do it*! I can see you sitting there, so get *up*. Put the book down and put your right hand in the air. Draw the number six with your hand while drawing a figure eight in the air with your right foot. *Go – do it*. Keep trying to get it. Then teach somebody else how to do it before the end of the week. This seemingly silly physical challenge is just about taking responsibility for your own mental state. But, now you are up, what could you do next? Here are a few more things I say to sixth-formers. Try them out.

Every day, turn your mobile phone off, totally off, for three twenty-minute stretches of time. Find the power button (you may not have needed it since you turned it on the first day). And before you say, 'What if it's an emergency?', relax. *They'll* call the police, ambulance or fire service if it's an emergency, not you. Now that your phone is off, what can you do for twenty minutes, knowing you are free to give your undivided attention to something?

Get a stopwatch, a piece of paper and a pen. When you're ready, start the stopwatch and write down five things you can remember about this book so far. What are five reasons you bought it? What are three things you will be able to do in two years that you can't do right now? What is your strongest sense (sight, sound, smell, touch, taste)? If you had £3 million pounds, which charity would you give half of it to? What would you spend the other half on? If you had only five stink bombs left on earth, to whom would you send them and why? You have three minutes.

Decide, today, to make four mistakes tomorrow. You may not know all of them right now. But plan one biggie for sure. And, most importantly, plan how you will handle it. Make it a public mistake. As Billy Connelly told me, 'Do these things, Matt – they improve your life!'

From now until you die, do these three things: if you are hungry, eat; if you are tired, sleep; if you are ill, get better. It was the advice given by a Buddhist master in Ladakh. My father (a life-long card-carrying agnostic) uses the advice every day himself, though he's no Buddhist.

Answer the 14 questions in the 'Vision/motive/mission' section of this chapter again. This time, really go for it, because now you know why it works.

Do not get 'caught up'. The important thing is to ensure that the important thing *always stays* the important thing. That means go back to the beginning and start correctly. It's the advice I gave Bruno. And, in case you were wondering, he went off to New York for a week of interviews and auditions. In two days of activity, he secured

seventeen appointments with New York's elite casting directors and agents. Needless to say, he was overjoyed. And so will you be, if you start. Go on – *now*.

References and bibliography

Abbott, John, and Ryan, Terry (2001), *The Unfinished Revolution* (Bodmin, UK: Network Educational Press).

Clairol Herbal Essences (2004), Online survey of 34,000 teens across the USA from January 2002 to March 2002.

Covey, Stephen (1999), *The 7 Habits of Highly Effective People* (London: Simon & Schuster).

Covey, S., Merill, A.R., and Merill, R.R. (1996), *First Things First: To Live, to Love, to Learn, to Leave a Legacy* (London: Simon & Schuster).

De Bono, Edward (1999), *Six Thinking Hats* (London: Penguin).

Eriksson, Sven-Göran (2002), *On Football* (London: Carlton).

Frankl, Victor E. (1963), *Man's Search for Meaning* (New York, NY: Washington Square Press; Simon & Schuster).

Furedi, Frank (2004), *Therapy Culture* (London: Routledge).

Goleman, Daniel (2002), *Business: The Ultimate Resource* (London: Bloomsbury).

Gorman, Phil (2004), *Motivation and Emotion* (Hove, UK: Routledge).

Graham Scott, Dr Gini (1990), *Resolving Conflict With Others and Within Yourself* (Oakland, CA: New Harbinger Publications).

Greenfield, Susan A. (2000), *The Private Life of the Brain* (London: Allen Lane).

Grudin, Robert (1988), *Time and the Art of Living* (New York, NY: Harper & Row; Ticknor & Fields).

Hanson, Mark Victor, and Robert G. Allen (2002), *The One Minute Millionaire* (London: Random House).

Hart-Davis, Adam (2003), *The World's Stupidest Inventions* (London: Michael O'Mara Books Ltd).

Kelley, Robert E. (1985), *Gold Collar Worker: Harnessing the Brainpower of the New Workforce* (New York, NY: Addison-Wesley Publishing Company Ltd).

McDermott, Steve (2002), *How to Be a Complete and Utter Failure in Life, Work and Everything* (London: Pearson Education).

McKay, Dr Matthew, and Fanning, Patrick (2000) *Self-Esteem* (Oakland, CA: New Harbinger Publications).

Robertson, Ian H. (2000), *Mindsculpture* (New York, NY: Fromm International).

Roskos-Ewoldsen, Beverly (1993), *Imagery, Creativity & Discovery – A Cognitive Perspective*, (Amsterdam: North-Holland, Elsevier Science Publishers).

Russell, Bertrand (1977), *Education and the Social Order* (London: George Allen & Unwin).

Sheldrake, Rupert (2003), *The Sense of Being Stared At and other aspects of the extended mind* (London: Hutchinson).

Williamson, Marianne (1996), *A Return to Love: Reflections on the Principles of a "Course in Miracles"* (New York, NY: HarperCollins).

Introducing Guy Shearer

There's a line I use in the INSET that I deliver about overhead projectors being the 'invention of the devil'. The theory is fine from a technological point of view, but how often have you sat through an INSET day squinting at a skewwhiff slide of a thousand words framed by a brown monochrome haze as the presenter tries unsuccessfully to cover half the text with a sheet of paper while the rest of his presentation blows off the table when the overhead fan kicks in. Used well, it has its place in the classroom, but nine times out of nine and a half it is used appallingly.

And then came PowerPoint or 'overheads on steroids'. Words whiz in from all angles, spin round and melt before your very eyes accompanied by bizarre sound effects and the nadir of off-the-shelf creativity, clip art – the chicken nuggets of the visual arts. But behind all this technological wizardry there's still a complete lack of anything very interesting at all. It's a bit like the Eurovision Song Contest. No matter how much glitz, glamour, starbursts and theatrical trickery you employ, what it boils down to at the end of the day is a moustached Belgian with an accordion.

Guy Shearer, the visionary head of Northampton's hugely innovative Learning Discovery Centre, has a very different idea about the role of technology for learning. For Guy, technology is a tool that liberates teachers and learners to focus on what is really important in the classroom – thinking, learning, creativity, cooperation, getting things wrong and changing the world.

It was 2004, as I was going into a classroom to introduce Philosophy for Children to a group of Year 6 pupils, when I first heard the immortal lines from a primary school teacher: 'OK, children, put your PDAs away and get your chairs in a circle.' It was from that point I knew that, at least for that little corner of Northampton, the future had arrived. And it was thanks to Guy and his team that it had arrived so far ahead of schedule.

A quick look at the Learning Discovery Centre website (www.learningdiscovery.co.uk) reveals the way that the team uses technology not for its own sake but to make learning enjoyable, active, interactive, memorable, inclusive and effective. It also ably demonstrates that there is so much more to IT than computers (IT does not stand for 'It's Typing' no matter what the other teachers tell you.) You can read about the Lego train made of RCX bricks complete with heat-sensitive buffers, digital skim reading, the dark-night photostory, Mars Landing Extreme and a list of the requirements for an 'ICT lite' session at a primary school in Daventry where the project is 'limited' to 'a PDA, an iPod, a 3G camera phone, a portable photo printer, card reader, digital camera and projector'.

The man behind the programmable Lego bricks and the creator of Logo, the first child-friendly computer programming language, is Seymour Papert. He is the Lego Professor of Mathematics and Education at MIT in the States and also the educational consultant behind the $100 windup-laptop programme for children in developing countries. In his seminal book, *Mindstorms – Children, Computers and Powerful Ideas*, he points out, exactly as Guy describes, that IT in the classroom is a wonderful aid for teachers to 'support the development of new ways of thinking and learning', adding that what it can't do is 'produce good learning any more than paint produces art'.

If all you are using technology for in your school is as means of presenting information to children ('e-chalking', as Guy calls it, twenty-first-century chalk and talk, boredom for the new millennium – if more often than not you are using your inter-active 'smartboard' like an ordinary whiteboard then sell it and go back to the whiteboard and save electricity) or as a way of replacing paper and pens that is slightly more motivational for boys (and remember: there is as little evidence that any learning is occurring or brains being actively engaged by children diligently typing into a computer as there is for children writing neatly into books or, heaven forbid, colouring in, even though it looks like a 'lovely quiet class' when the head comes round), then you – and your children – are missing out on one of the most significant breakthroughs in cognitive development for the past thousand years.

What Papert says – and Guy demonstrates – is that technology is a tool to help children think and learn and think about thinking and learning and explore the messy 'let's see what will happen if we do this, oops, that didn't work, let's try it a different way, how have you done it, wouldn't it be better of you did it like that, wow, look at that, I wasn't expecting that, gosh, is that the time ...' approach to cognitive development.

Guy shows that technology is a fantastic tool for active, real-time, whole-class metacognition – help-ing children think about thinking, where scrolling backwards and forwards through their thought processes is as simple as pressing the 'undo/redo' buttons and where different scenarios can be tried out instantly until they find the one that works best. This is the very sort of 'organic' learning that edu-cational innovators such as Maria Montessori and Carl Rogers advocated, giving children tools to help them learn for themselves in a managed and structured way – 'chaordic' even, to refer to an idea in the introduction to Mike Brearley's chap-ter, 'Build the Emotionally Intelligent School'.

What also comes through in this chapter, as it does throughout this book, is that good practice in the classroom may involve challenging the rules or even breaking them as you move from the 'plughole of conformity' to the 'overflow of success', to use Guy's colourful phrases. It involves being daring and having a go and not being afraid to deal with things that don't work out. In fact, modelling to the children the very processes that you are encouraging them to engage in. And because, for many teachers, a fear of letting go and 'losing control' (although in my experience you gain control by giving it away, the same as for respect) is compounded by blind technophobia, Guy also gives a variety of useful hints, tips and software recommendations to help you get started.

And, be reassured, as techie chapters go, this a very untechie techie chapter.

One final question for you: is IT in your school an integrated element of the classroom environment or do you still have the 'IT suite' approach, where all the computers are squirreled away in the computer room to be used for special lessons? As Papert points out, having computers in their own special room with children following a 'routinised curriculum of computer literacy' in this way meant that learning about IT 'often inherited all that was worst in curriculum-driven school practices'.

If this is the case, then it is something that needs to be addressed, tricky though that may be with the security implications that it brings. But once it is achieved then you can really set out to achieve, with Guy's help, what Papert witnessed in his groundbreaking work: 'imaginative pro-gressive teachers who had computers in their classrooms and were prepared to give students time and support to learn often created wonder-fully fertile environments where difficulty was a challenge rather than an obstacle'.

So power up, plug in, hook up, chill out and remember: a machine on which you have to press the START button to stop it can't be too scary.

Chapter 5
Peek! Copy! Do! The Creative Use of IT in the Classroom

Guy Shearer

Introduction

I've always thought that plagiarism gets an awfully bad press in educational circles (although, if you're reading this passage on screen having scanned it into your computer and plan to alter it a little and pass it off as your own, *stop now*!). OK, so there are some bad examples like 'Teflon learning' (search, copy, paste, hand in) and good old-fashioned cheating, but there are times when copying a few ideas here and there is one of the best ways of coming up with something genuinely original of your own.

Truly original, new, non-recycled, non-retreaded ideas are ever so hard to find these days. I go to conferences and events to discuss 'innovative e-learning' and it is rather depressing to see so much orthodoxy and conformity, and I don't pretend not to be part of that.

I have to admit that the thing that really fires me up as a teacher isn't that light-bulb moment, or that sudden-change-of-attitude moment: it's the instant someone says or does something I hadn't expected, hadn't imagined and would never have done myself – a new idea escapes into the universe.

Whether you're hooked on novelty or not, I hope this chapter will be useful, anyway, as independent, free thinking is great when combined with all the power of enlightened approaches to learning (come to think of it, it's pretty good in less enlightened ones too) – and so rarely are creative thought and ICT put together into (or just outside of) the same box. You may not buy into the premise that plagiarism leads to originality, but the ICT ideas may come in handy.

In the next few pages, you'll find a genuinely honest-to-deity original learning model and some ways of linking the use of ICT into that process (and some ways ICT is used to stop it – know thine enemy). I've held back on too many product plugs, but there is a bit at the end pointing you in some good directions.

The peek–copy–do cycle

I have no idea at all where new ideas come from. I'm sure that in the deeper recesses of the brain there are bits that get fired up by all manner of things: talking in good company, an amazing stimulus, a feeling of freedom, an insoluble problem. Many things elsewhere in this book relate to getting into the right state for that to happen; here we're just looking at how to use ICT to throw enough recycled ideas into the air for something else to come out the end. Sometimes these new thoughts get lost because of the way we communicate (chairing a big meeting with a tight agenda and a pile of original thinkers is like herding monkeys) or the way we're encouraged to 'do it right' (or 'do it as I do it'). ICT can help give them an outlet.

For me, the four strongest stimuli for coming up with new ideas rather than simply recycling the old ones in the same way over and over again are:

- having a real need to solve a problem;
- seeing something I quite like that doesn't do what I want;
- seeing something I definitely don't like that tries to do the same thing that I want to do; and
- seeing how someone does something and realising I can apply that to something else.

The process I'd like to describe I call the *peek–copy–do cycle*. It works in a circle, and you can start anywhere on it you like. I see learners working through problems by peeking at ideas and half-ideas from elsewhere (sometimes seeing something you don't like is the best stimulus to help you decide what you do), by mimicking approaches (taking elements without actually duplicating them) and trying those ideas out and testing them.

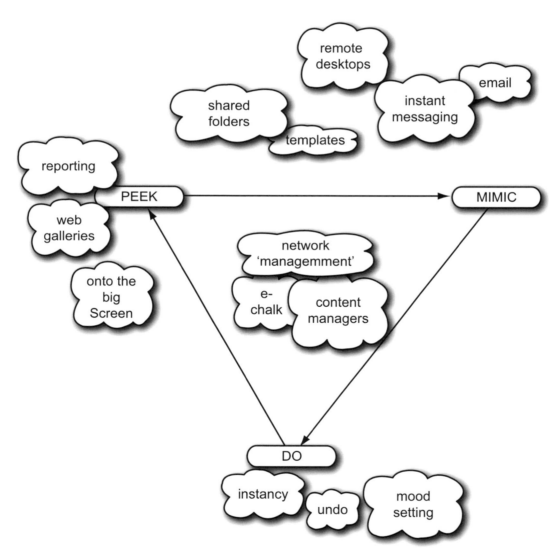

Figure 6.

This process happens all the time although we don't always encourage it – and it happens in different ways in the different stages of our lives. I imagine it like a kind of sink where ideas and people slop around without very much happening. Sometimes we're helped to pick up on the ideas around us, given time to take bits from here and there in true hunter-gatherer fashion and then to try them out to see if they work, and gradually we climb higher to the overflow of success. When a group of learners reach the overflow we get a variety of different solutions to a problem or task that really belong to the people who made them, and often we're surprised by how they did it.

Sometimes we're prevented from pulling ideas in and, given one ('the right one') or none, actively discouraged from using the way the people around us are solving the problems we face (cheat!) and told to stop wasting time and get on with it. This leads to the plughole of conformity – at best our group produce exactly what we wanted, built to the order of our lesson objectives carefully splashed onto the whiteboard, at worst they do bugger all and rebel.

ICT is really good as a tool to support this process because it easily lets us watch many things to see what we do and don't like (we can rewind, transmit, store – for pennies), copy and alter and produce all manner of solutions; but all too often this goes against the grain of what we think is 'fair' and 'right' (hey, let's lighten up a little!).

ICT supporting peeking

Isn't it annoying when you're really into something and someone is looking over your shoulder and maybe asking questions or misunderstanding what you're up to? Good peeking doesn't annoy or restrain the person who is actually doing the doing. Various technologies help us to peek – although maybe we're not using them for that right now (see 'ICT and the war on pedagogy' on page 107).

On to the big screen

Many times I go into a lesson and either the whole class are looking at the big screen or it is being totally ignored (usually it's an interactive whiteboard or projected image, but lower-tech approaches qualify too – they just take longer to draw). In the 'don't peek' classroom, the big screen is used to show what we're supposed to be making, the start and the finish and especially the right answer – which sends an important message:

- My screen is bigger than your screen, therefore …
- I am cleverer than you, which means …
- Do it the way I do it and …
- Don't waste time thinking of your own way (resistance is futile).

By all means use the projector to show learners' stuff, but get them showing stuff there too. Have one group plugged in all through the lesson and encourage everyone to watch what they're doing when they like. Stop the lesson (I want to get off) from time to time and call up different people's screens onto the whiteboard and compare notes; or, even better, don't compare notes but let people decide what to see for themselves from time to time.

Instead of plenaries being about showing the right answer, about showing the answer someone worked really hard to do (ah, bless!), about ticking your learning objectives, highlight some different routes that were taken, because ICT allows you to replay processes really easily.

One good trick for doing this is to save a copy of someone's work, then do lots of undos (hold down the control button and tap Z a whole bunch of times), then use the 'redo' command to replay forwards the whole process that was gone through (practise this with the software you use first – it doesn't work universally!). Another trick that works well is to leave a camcorder pointing at the whiteboard while someone works through a problem, then play the film back to the class at fast-forward speed.

Remote desktops

Most network managers will have a piece of software for what is called *remote desktopping* in their toolbox. Very handy thing for remote-controlling a whole bunch of computers for routine maintenance tasks, sometimes a very useful spying tool for catching *Y* when he should be doing *Z* but he's actually looking at *X*.

All you have on screen is a window with several small pictures of screens on it – click on the screen and you can watch what they see on screen, and can take over their mouse and keyboard if the mood takes you. Your local ICT staff might blanch when you suggest letting children loose with this (and a small element of control probably is desirable, but it is a lot less dangerous than the humble Bunsen burner, and we use them all the time).

In my example above, you probably thought, 'Hang on, how do you pick different people's screens and show them on the whiteboard just like that?' Remote desktopping is how. From the computer plugged into your projector, go through the list picking out machine after machine and either taking over their computer or, even better (and more anarchic), allowing the learner to have their screen splashed large while they can still control it, and without having to stand at the front.

Even scarier, disable the ability to take over someone's computer. Just let any learner see what is happening on any other learner's screen whenever they want – trust me, the feeling of godlike power soon pales, but the ability to watch someone doing something you can't do yourself, without disturbing them or having to ask, is pretty cool. You need to be well in with your ICT staff to do this, and don't expect it to be set up in a few minutes, but if you have a network you really ought to be able to do this – and there are plenty of free or very cheap programs to do it if you haven't got one already. Check out Timbuktu, pcAnywhere, Apple Remote Desktop, RM Tutor, or just Google 'free remote desktop software'.

Web galleries

How many people get to see completed work, good or bad, done in your lessons? How many people learn from the comments you make when you mark the work? Do we get to see only the finished product or can we see the three or four steps we took to get there? A lot of good learning material is lost; the class are generating it constantly.

A really good example of this that I witnessed didn't use much ICT – it was in an art lesson. In it the teacher simply photographs and prints a small copy of everyone's work every lesson and leaves it in a place everyone can access it. It's all there, the work stage by stage (like a flick book), comments, ideas to improve it, the whole thing, and learners were going there during the lesson and browsing – great learner/hunter-gatherer behaviour.

Have a password-protected web page that everyone can upload their work to each session, with a space for you to add comments – and make it as accessible as you feel comfortable with – so while you're spending all night marking when you'd rather be doing something else some of your learners can look through what's there.

Reporting

There is never enough gear for an ICT lesson (probably no longer true everywhere, but it's a comfortable prejudice), so, instead of having quite so many people sharing, let's give them other jobs to do. The above ideas were about not disturbing the doer, but sometimes asking them what/how/why isn't a bad thing. Have a couple of learners wandering around, taking photos, using a PDA or mobile phone as a tape recorder to find out what everyone is up to, their task being simply to tell everyone afterwards the different ways people had worked and why. This has a number of benefits, for instance:

- these people become unofficial 'agents of infection' carrying ideas from place to place; and

- they have the rewarding and useful experience of just thinking about learning for a short time, and a useful learning experience in recording it and synthesising it down.

From my own work, the best example I've seen of this was at the Learning Discovery Centre's Robot Olympic days, featuring fifteen teams of three learners per group plus fifteen more acting as reporters, photographers, scouts and spies for the day. The way that the reporters acted as the eyes and ears of teams, got information about why the designs were going in certain directions that would never make it into a write-up and synthesised the whole thing into their reports was enough to make you think that actually we'd held a reporting day with 45 learners making robots as an extra activity.

ICT supporting do/mimic behaviour

How often have you started a new task by taking 'one you prepared earlier' and adapting it to the new situation (so if you get a Word document letter from me starting 'Dear Mum' you now know why!)? We use writing frames and other similar devices – although often not when using computers (it does make it so easy for them, after all) – but how much further can we take it?

Templates

Remember the time when the joke in the staffroom was that 'IT' stood for 'it's typing'? Well, one of my basic assumptions is that lots of time spent typing is probably a bad thing – when I do it, or anyone else! It does make for a nice quiet lesson, but, really, how much learning is going on? Saving a half-completed file as a template is very useful – everyone can grab a copy and carry on from there – and indeed it can have a pile of sentences/numbers/ideas that the learner can start by thinning out (lots less typing, but, instead, selecting with the mouse and deleting rather than keying it all in). If you always want groups to follow the same pattern (e.g. for a laboratory report, or for a graph) then help them be good bunnies and give them a template.

Are you worried those lazy kids will produce less because you did it for them? Two responses to that. First, use the 'track changes' feature built into most word processors in the last five years so it stands out a mile what they have and haven't done – for you and for them. Second, remember how hard it can be to start on a blank page, and perhaps they'll be encouraged out of sloth by disliking what you've put down enough to write their own. An excellent use of templates I saw in a humanities lesson consisted of a number of quite strongly worded opinions on the page. The group couldn't bear to leave them as they were with their name at the top, and were moved to write their own changes, and then to explain them at length.

Shared folders

Sharing your work on the network is a little like public nudity – disconcerting at first, at times not nice to look at, but once you get used to it quite practical. This is another of those moments when we need to be friendly with those lovely ICT people – we want to be able to share work within our class team and we need them to help us. Traditional school networks allow learners to save work in their own folder and for teachers to publish 'the right stuff' to them.

If you have a folder for your class/subject, get a section freed up so that they can put their work there. In minutes, it will look a mess, but at least it will be full of material. There are a number of advantages to this plan:

- work becomes visible to everyone – another peeking tool;
- progress becomes visible, and you can have a better handle on the 'Sir, I lost my file/password/warthog' moments;
- it avoids the situation, when two people share a computer, of where to keep work: we keep it together; and

- it allows you to put on really quick displays of work.

You will need to insist that learners name their files properly, or somehow structure things – a folder for every project and then some sort of system for naming files where you use your initials at the start or end works for me ('my Egyptian stuff.gs.doc' in the 'Egyptian Work.6G' folder).

ICT purists may be worried by the above, but the way things are going with both Windows Vista and Mac OS Spotlight is for the relation between where a file is kept physically and where you see it when you are working with it disappearing and work being warehoused and accessed by 'smart searching' – so actually young Barry stores his work in 'Sir's Warehouse' but just sees on his desktop a folder that shows all files that belong to him no matter where he left them. So grab the future and share your folders now!

ICT supporting doing stuff

OK, so you can't really peek at anything or mimic it unless someone, somewhere actually did it in the first place, can you? Clearly, ICT helps us 'do stuff' because, as a society, we've spent huge amounts of money on it, to go faster, further and in a wide variety of attractive fonts. What I'd like to talk about is much more how ICT can get us into the mood to do things, and maybe do them in a more creative and original way.

Undo

High challenge, low stress (check out the work on 'flow' of the fabulously named Mihaly Csikszentmihalyi) – if we want to get people to try stuff out we need to make it something they want to do, feel able to do without its being too trivial, and make it so that you can't see the mistakes! The ability to make as many corrections as you like nearly invisibly is awesome – all the daft errors I made writing this are hidden gracefully. The 'undo' key gives us even more power.

Good old control-Z (or the Mac equivalent) sets us free from the 'I wonder if I should try this' problem – and newer software stores a longer and longer trail of undos, allowing all sorts of experimentation. It reminds me of many a weekend spent playing a game on an Amiga (Dungeon Quest or something but, hey, a man's got to have hobbies). If you didn't save the game very often you had to keep repeating the same long chain of movements to get back to where you most recently got digitally splatted – high challenge, but low risk, as we soon learned to hit 'save' before every door and every corner.

There is no real trick to this: when faced with a choice of software make the number of times you can undo one of the criteria; when introducing a task, mention it often (because you can't undo not telling people about 'undo', of course!); and also add a system whereby, whenever a good point has been reached in the evolution of a piece of work, it gets saved with a different name (in our shared folder, of course). If you're paying for your own disk space you might want to delete the rough copies every now and then, but most ICT technicians love installing new hard disks and indeed live for the chance to ask for more money to pay for upgrades, so you're actually doing them a favour by using up all that lovely storage.

Mood setting

Many better words than these have been said about the importance of getting into the right 'state' for learning – whether that's to be positive, cooperative, ready to absorb ideas, whatever. ICT can provide plenty of cues to support doing. And this can be as a general stimulus or a quite specific tool. The advent of the affordable laptop that can actually be carried from place to place without a hernia potentially gives the teacher/facilitator a massive armoury of mood-setting tools that often are forgotten about in the rush to do our admin and check our mail. Try the following:

- Use short film clips and audio files to set the state as a class arrive/settle (or via your web page for them to set their own state when they choose to do so). You can fit so many stimuli on one PC, so there really isn't an excuse. Arm yourself with a long cable with a 3.5mm headphone jack on one end, and whatever on the other end that is needed to plug into the tape machine or speakers wherever you teach. If you've not got a projector but you do have a TV trolley, get a cable to plug your laptop into that.

- Have your lesson objectives on a PowerPoint slideshow for the whole topic or term – so you can go backwards and forwards whenever you want – and, if you have some mind maps to have the big picture, so much the better.

- It doesn't really belong in this section, but PowerPoint isn't just for boring presentations, it makes a great storyboard maker, hyper-book and record of discussion. During a presentation, try clicking on the little tool in the bottom left-hand corner and choosing a pen colour – you can then (or better still they can) scribble notes and ideas to your heart's content and save them for next time.

- Find class background music to match the duration of an activity. Music libraries such as iTunes display song length next to titles, so if you need something exactly 4 minutes 28 seconds long there is no excuse!

Music can be 'borrowed' from your own music collection, of course. As for the material itself, personally, I know that certain types of music probably aren't the best for the classroom because I ought to be using instrumental Baroque pieces, but, heck, I like the Clash! DVDs etc. are always good, too, but your rental agreement with Blockbusters doesn't cover your using a film in school, and if you break the law you're setting a bad example. The same goes for illegal music downloads, so head for Google and search for free music and sound effects and you can get enough stuff to last you for ever without putting anyone out of work or otherwise causing a yin–yang imbalance.

Instancy

How many jobs do we put off because they are just too big or the reward is just too far away? Even worse, before we get to do the cool stuff in a lesson, how often do we have to do the boring stuff first?

- 'OK, everyone, copy the diagram on the board, read Pages 7 and 8, do Questions 11, 13 and 17, memorise the periodic table and then come to the front to collect your sodium. What? Ready already, Jenkins?'

- 'OK, everyone, today we're going to make a movie in which we'll all be killed by aliens, but first we're going to make something really important called a *storyboard* – put that camera down, Jenkins! And that light sabre!'

ICT has taken all kinds of tedium out of my life, but I don't see it doing the same much in lessons. Let's clear out the dullness and get onto the fun bits by:

- using templates relentlessly;

- using digital cameras when a diagram/picture is needed – storyboarding is really fun and easy if you use a digital camera and PowerPoint, and then add your notes under the slide; and

- making it an expectation that we'll use ICT to do the tedious work that doesn't need a teacher away from lessons and do the fun stuff face to face.

The humble projector allows more than peeking and lecturing: it gives a massive hit in terms of rewarding effort. In particular, the digital camera or camera phone can be your very good friend to help keep things moving – let learners photograph things and/or take a voice memo to themselves and move on, and sometimes that might be all the write-up they need.

ICT taking us down the plughole of conformity and failure

I go to events, conferences, working parties and therapy sessions for the whole gamut of what I'd call enlightened approaches to learning, and I also attend similar things for ICT and e-learning, and I don't see a fat lot of crossover going on – worse, more and more, I'm seeing ICT being used to plug holes in poor methodology (I don't call it pedagogy – see below) with bells and whistles rather than empowering people. Much of what appears below makes perfect sense if you are an 'ICT person' – but very little from the point of view of the teacher or learner. The need to have ICT suites that can be managed (and classrooms that can be cleaned) has a lot to answer for in the sense of pushing us into that downward spiral to the plughole of failure.

Managing network management

Managing a network with twenty-odd computers is hard work and not actually that much fun (even for people who wear sandals and anoraks and read computer magazines). You have to do things such as install programs, stop people installing programs, add devices such as printers and stop people installing devices like printers. Hang on, there's a pattern emerging here!

Picture the scene. Barry Jenkins has done his humanities assignment in Flash while on work experience at some web-design company on the eastern side of the motorway and arrives back at school bursting to show it to you – he has it on a USB memory key. Great! We plug it into the computer, and it doesn't work because Barry could be a hacker, and it may contain tools to breach network security, so he isn't allowed to use it. At this point many a teacher will give Barry their password – I don't recommend this – or log in themselves, only to find that they aren't allowed to use the memory key either (in case of course they give their password to a pupil). Assuming

that we haven't got time to burn, we then ask Barry to bring it in tomorrow on CD, which has taken some of the shine off his excitement, but he comes back ready to roll only to find that the school doesn't use the same version of Flash as the PC he uses at home and …

Flippancy aside, the truth is that either the PCs don't work, or they do work by preventing people from doing things. A radical agenda would be to start campaigning for your own network so you can waste hours managing it, too, or to go for a load of computers that aren't on the network (oops, no Google!); but perhaps you're better off working to create a spirit of harmony and support with your ICT gang.

Approaches that work include the following.

- Accepting that there are good reasons for many restrictions but sticking to what you actually want to do and asking how you can work around the restrictions. It may not be possible for the whole class to bring in work on device X, but maybe you could be shown how to do it from one particular computer.

- Remembering that the computers are there to support the learners, not vice versa, so, whenever you hit a wall taking the ICT guy back to first principles, appreciate that you're putting extra work his way, but persuade him that it's worth it.

- Avoiding asking ICT specialists to do any dumb-arse stuff that you could do yourself (finding things on the Web, copying CDs, producing publications) so they can have more time to help you do that learning thing.

Can't get access to ICT when you need it? Don't get mad at the ICT team: get even. Make a note of the time and what you needed, share it with colleagues and get them to do the same; use that to make the kind of ICT you need a priority for your institution.

Managing content management

Not that further down the food chain, we have content management as a problem to contend with. You may want to have a web gallery of work. You might want to make a webpage on a local resource to share in your school. You might just want to publish minutes of meetings. All these situations risk arousing the wrath of the content police – so be prepared.

Is it safe to publish that? You'll sometimes be faced with the objection that, because it is no longer on wood pulp and can now be digitally handled, there is somehow a greater risk. Let's face it: generally we'd be flattered if people wanted to read our stuff! Make sure it is clear who is supposed to see what you want to publish and how you can control that and move on – but don't let that be a reason not to publish at all.

Is it good enough to publish? This one has been going on since before the first printing press. You may be told that somehow what gets published has to pass a test of some kind to make sure it is good enough. I'd suggest you explain the qualifications you have, why as a professional you want to publish it and then see who blinks first.

It needs keywords and categories. Many systems now make you spend longer filling in forms telling you what keywords things relate to, when it should be published (*now*!), how long it should be kept for (*for ever*!), and what subject headings to keep it under than you actually spent making the stuff in the first place. There is a one-word answer to people who insist on this: Google. Computers can index files for you; they have loads of space that's cheap and can find it pretty easily too.

Is it XYZ-compliant? This is the scariest tactic to stop would be teacher-publishers, the idea being that if your stuff isn't packaged in a particular way it is somehow dangerous – the simple response to this is to say yes and, once again, see who blinks first.

ICT and the war on pedagogy

The P-word is thrown around with abandon these days but is it such a good thing? Don't forget that the pedagogy being cited is about the teaching of children – a model of dependence, provider, client, conformity and one-size-fits-all. ICT is a great enabler for pedagogy's big brother, androgogy – the teaching of adult learners – a model of growing independence and peer-to-peer and individual learning. Being charitable. You often have to assume that users of the P-word don't understand what it means, but, with the culture of 'whole-class teaching is good', perhaps not. ICT is time and again being used to support pedagogic models of teaching when that isn't making best use of what technology can do for us.

E-chalkers

I've already hinted quite strongly at a concern that the 'big screen' is becoming the sole preserve of the teacher/expert/gang leader. The sad paradox is that it is often in the schools where the most money has been spent on ICT, where every room has a projector or whiteboard, that you see the worst examples of e-chalking. The e-chalker carries over all the inspirational advantages of the blackboard to the brave new world of the twenty-first century by spending their time either with their back to the class writing on the board, or playing a series of whizzbangpowwow media thingies they downloaded last night (the modern successor to photocopying diagrams on to transparencies or wheeling the video recorder into the room and shushing the naughty boys who talk through it).

Here are some tips for using an interactive whiteboard or projector well.

- Get the learners up there to use it – especially when there isn't a whole-class thing going on. Allow one or two people to work on it rather than a straight PC (very good for kinaesthetic learners).

- Leave it on with people using the computer so at least one example of a work in progress is always on the board. It doesn't matter if they choose to do it wrong or differently – that is a useful teaching point, too.

- Use remote desktop software to make sure that the computer we see there isn't always yours. It is possible to have the system cycle through all the available screens, which is useful and a good way of catching people who like to play games when they should be working.

- Use a tablet PC and wireless link to 'hand the whiteboard' to anyone you like.

- Show the group a short sample of the video or multimedia material available on the big screen and make it available so that they can see the parts they choose as often as they like, in the order they like, when they like (but do have headphones handy).

Avoiding the Google lesson

I've implied great things about Google as a tool to support us – but there is nothing quite so demor-alising as the 'Google lesson' – Teflon learning in its lowest form. People sit at a computer, type in the key words they are told to, copy material or just print it and then do some dispersive activity until the bell goes. It's called Teflon learning because no ideas stick. I saw a much crazier example of this among bilingual Spanish children at a British school in which they downloaded pages of text, ran it through an Internet transla-tor to any language other than English and back again, and then used Word's auto-summarise fea-ture to get to the right length – try it, you cannot tell the piece of text came from the Net even if you have the original and doctored one side by side.

If you make the task one where you're expected to use your brain independently we can avoid this – so, yes, use Google or any other search engine, but then process what you find. So, for example, instead of 'find information about the Battle of Naseby on Google' we have to 'tell the story of the Battle of Naseby from the point of view of a cavalry soldier using Google to find information'.

Voting for good pedagogy with ICT

There are some pedagogic tools that are too good to be condemned. One in particular that is great if used sparingly is the pupil response system ('voting'), in which questions are projected on the board and the group use a remote control to choose their answer. Good for marking free tests, for quick reviews, and above all else for a bit of competitive fun, response systems are an excep-tion that proves the rule, by making an essentially passive 'do this' experience active and individual.

Response systems can do more than just quizzes, though – try a quiz at the start of the lesson with the question, 'Which aspect of our behaviour will we try hardest to improve today from this list?' and let everyone vote and review at the end. The beauty of that kind of process-control use of these systems is that you can make it a secret ballot – nobody can see which one you *picked* so nobody can make anything of it!

More?

Every week we put out articles, resources and examples about the sorts of things you've read about in this chapter on www.learningdiscovery.co.uk – you can also contact us through the site.

Introducing Andrew Curran

Every single aspect of the behaviour of a child in your classroom – from blinking, smiling, laughing or feeling hungry to listening attentively, messing around, nodding off or learning new things and then forgetting them – happens as a result of one thing: electrical and chemical activity in between their ears.

Yet how much about what goes on between these ears do you know about? Amazingly, basic brain function is not a compulsory element of teacher training or professional development and there seems to be no pressure on teachers to know anything about – let alone keep up to date with – the latest insights into brain functioning. Imagine your plumber not knowing about how your boiler works.

Yes, there are teachers who seem to be born knowing the best ways to get more out of young brains, and in many ways the brain research is catching up with good intuitive teaching. But what happens when our best intuitions fail us? Or what has always worked in the past just isn't working now? Or what works with most children just doesn't seem to get through to that one particular child? Or we have no intuition to fall back on? Or Ofsted/government/management/parents are demanding that we work in a way that seems to go against our best instincts but we just don't have the vocabulary to argue our case beyond, 'that just doesn't feel right' or 'I quit!'?

This is where consultant paediatric neurologist and Independent Thinking associate Dr Andrew Curran comes in. But beware: this chapter is not for the faint-hearted. If you're looking for the usual shallow overview of the brain found in most books for teachers (including mine!), then you will be disappointed. For example, within the first few pages you'll find the word *phylogenetically* (I looked it up, and it means 'the sequence of events involved in the evolutionary development of a species or taxonomic group of organisms', so, I'm glad we've cleared that up); and when was the last time you were faced with a sentence that included the unforgettable line, 'cholinergic interneurons that connect with the excitatory efferents from the amygdala to the hippocampus, caudate, substantia nigra, thalamus and frontal cortex'?

But then we are dealing with the most complex organism on the planet and, as someone once said, 'If the brain were simple enough to understand it, we would be too simple to understand it.'

So, in as user-friendly a way as is possible for a man with 'MB, BCh, BaO, MRCPaedsI, MRCPaedsUK, MRCPCH, DipCH, DRCOG' after his name and 'Dr' before it, this chapter will give you the ammunition you need to argue for:

- the vital need for positive emotions in learning;
- the need to reduce – not add to – stress levels to improve memory;
- the need for stimulation – not subjugation – to help learning;
- the need to present information in way that is brain-friendly and not just presenting information;

- the need to move about a bit to improve learning;
- the need to reduce shouting in the classroom;
- the need for an effective process of 'time out' for children who are about to 'lose it';
- the need for an effective process of 'time out' for teachers who are about to 'lose it';
- the need to learn new things in order to accelerate the process of forgetting the old things ('I must not alarm the class hamster unnecessarily' written out a hundred times will not change the behaviour, just reinforce it);
- the need to have self-esteem as an overtly covered part of classroom and whole school practice;
- the need actually to like – nay, love – children in order to teach effectively; and
- the need to think before crossing the road to see an old friend.

In a presentation to a secondary school, Andrew and I were delivering a couple of years ago, a primary headteacher tagged along to acquire, as he put it, the 'vocabulary to argue our case with Ofsted'. (Remember, 'We are not having fun, Mr Inspector: we are simply using positive emotions to obviate negative reptilian brain responses in order to access the limbic system to optimise dopamine release and facilitate autonomic learning.')

This chapter, then, will give you the language, the vocabulary and the support to argue your case for child-centred, enjoyable and engaging lessons with whomsoever it is visiting your classroom telling you that what you are doing is wrong/against school policy/unsatisfactory/not like in the old days.

Apart from backing up your instincts, an understanding of the brain research will also help you get to grips with those children you just don't seem to be able to reach in your classroom. For example, in a 2003 article in *Time* magazine headlined 'Secrets of the Teen Brain', it is clearly apparent that teenagers ... well, they're not people. For example, the bit of our brain that says,

'It's dark – time to go to sleep' is the pineal gland. This is something it achieves by releasing melatonin, which sends chemical messages to the body to start shutting itself down and prepare for sleep. Research has shown that it takes longer for teenagers to reach this critical ready-for-bed level of melatonin, regardless of any external stimulation or exposure to light.

And lecturing young people about the importance of planning ahead and thinking things through may be all well and good, but, hey, talk to the hand 'cos the nucleus acumbens ain't listening. This is the structure in the frontal cortex that 'directs motivation to seek rewards' and is less active in teenagers than in adults. The whole of the prefrontal cortex – the PFC, also known as the 'area of sober second thought' – is the area where our personality resides, where conscious, mature decision-making takes place and where the chemicals originate to calm the amygdala, deep down there in our more primitive brain, which floods with chemicals and is responsible for road rage, David Beckham's sending off against Argentina in the second round of the 1998 World Cup, and Charlotte Church.

What's more, the PFC is one of the last parts of our brain to mature. (The human brain wires itself up in the way that a school hall fills on an INSET day – starts at the back and works through to the front if you're lucky.) Something Andrew doesn't mention in his chapter but I have heard him point out on numerous occasions in his INSET presentations is that it takes 20–30 years for the average human brain to mature. Read that sentence again and think about the pressure we put on children to behave like 'mini-me's'. 'Act your age'; 'You're being childish'; 'Grow up' – how often have you heard yourself say those words. Yet you are talking to a work in progress. They *are* growing up. They just won't have got there by the end of your maths lesson. They are acting their age, just not yours.

In Andrew's unequivocal words: 'You can't be older than your brain.'

On top of that, we know there is a two- to three-year difference in how far along the track of neural maturation children may have reached, even if they share their birthday. Where is it written that every child is ready to sit that SAT on exactly the same day at exactly the same time? It isn't. What's written is that there is a two- to three-year gap and maybe, just maybe, we do so much damage to that child by making her sit that SAT at that time that she doesn't arrive at a state of intellectual maturity intact because we have done so much damage to her self-esteem.

Which brings us to the most important element of what Andrew has to say to us: how *guaranteeing* high self-esteem in children needs to be a fundamental part of every school's development plan. What is coming through among all the long and loud nature-versus-nurture debate is that things that happen to us as children can – and do – produce specific physical effects in the actual architecture of the brain, and, no matter what we are born with (and, as Andrew points out, we aren't born with that much), the effects on our developing, 'plastic' brain caused by the behaviours of adults, especially parents and teachers, will decide how we turn out – for better or for worse.

You, as a teacher, have a huge responsibility in shaping the actual physical structure of the brains of the future of the world. It really is a case of *your* hands in *their* brains. In which case, you really do need to get your head around what Andrew Curran has to say, to help you understand better what you're doing, wouldn't you think? After all – and while we're on the subject of doctors – what's the first rule of the Hippocratic Oath?*

* 'Do no harm.' Interestingly, Google's motto is 'Do no evil'. Either way, make sure you go home with their brains in better shape than when they started the day and with your conscience clear.

Chapter 6
How the 'Brian' Works

Andrew Curran

Introduction

The word in the chapter heading above is not really 'Brian'. 'Brian' was a spelling error that crept into the third draft of a paper that I and a friend, Stephen Gill, were working on to develop a unified theory of brain functioning. Microsoft's spellchecker does not, however, recognise 'Brian' as a misspelling in this context. Obviously, we spotted it before the paper was sent to any of the big journals. Though it did take us three months!

What I want to do in this chapter is to try to give you the lowdown on how basic functions such as memory and the emotional content of thoughts are now believed to work. The aim of all this is to build up a picture of how the brain functions, considering it through its evolution to the present day and explaining how this evolutionary process has allowed humans to develop complex behaviours based on learning. The obvious roll-on from this is how this knowledge can be used to enhance learning in the classroom. I've referenced the whole thing so that you can chase up the literature if you want.

I'm going to divide it up as follows:

Section 1: The evolution of the brain.

Section 2: Normal functioning of the brain in learning and recall with particular reference to the key anatomical structures central to these functions.

Section 3: The hemispheric lateralisation of functionality.

Section 4: Conclusion.

I'll aim to be as gentle with you as I can but I'm also responding to all those teachers I've met who have asked me for the hard science behind all happy-clappy mumbo jumbo so often spouted about the brain.

So, take a deep breath, clear your mind, take your time and engage that brain of yours in learning more about itself than you ever thought possible.

1. The evolution of the brain

About 2.5 billion years ago, when complex living organisms first started to develop, their increasingly sophisticated bodies required a more complex control system than had previously been available. It's hard to get legs to work when all you have is a couple of ganglia and the memory of being a fish. The first step towards this was to evolve a more unified master control system to govern the activities in lesser systems. This structure would eventually develop over millions of years of evolution into the spinal cord, brain stem and corpus striatum (see Figure 7). This is called the reptilian brain and it probably first appeared about 400,000 years ago. This was the first step towards evolving what P. D. MacLean (1990) has called 'the triune brain', the ultimate expression of which is seen in modern man.

Lizard

Compared with the complexity of a modern human brain, the reptilian brain is an unsophisticated and simple structure that is poor at responding to novel situations (MacLean, 1972; 1985). Lizards have only a few behaviours that they do lots of times (I know this bears similarity to many humans, but, believe me, the human brain is actually capable of more!). The corpus striatum (the centre of Figure 7) can store a small number of behavioural responses related to self-preservation and survival of the species, i.e. it is a neural repository for genetically determined forms of behaviour as well as learned behaviours (MacLean, 1972). The actual number of behaviours it can store in lizards is about 27 – not really very many if you think of the number of behaviours we can perform as humans; even words can be seen as a form of behaviour (and there aren't many speaking lizards – outside of politics, that is).

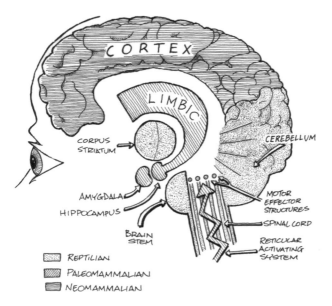

Figure 7.

Interestingly, there are strong parallels to these behaviours in all animals and these behaviours

are also stored in the corpus striatum despite the existence of other phylogenetically younger and more complex higher structures. In humans, it is the reptilian brain that is said to be responsible for 'obsessive compulsive behaviours; personal day-to-day rituals and superstitious acts; slavish conformity to old ways of doing things; ceremonial re-enactments; obeisance to precedent, as in legal and other matters; responding to partial representations, whether alive or inanimate; and all manner of deception' (MacLean, 1970) (as I said, politicians).

The corpus striatum and related structures send their instructions to the body through the brain stem and spinal cord. These two structures act as a signal conduit to and from higher centres in the brain and contain things called *motor effector structures* and the main tracts of the activating systems such as the *reticular activating system* (Garcia-Rill and Skinner, 1987; Reese, Garcia-Rill and Skinner, 1995; Vincent, 2000). These structures do various things. The motor effector nuclei are concerned primarily with giving instructions to the spinal cord so that we can do things such as walking or scratching. The activating systems (of which five have been described) are responsible for the level of arousal of the brain as a whole, i.e. at higher levels of energy, we wake up; at lower levels, we go to sleep. They get their energy from signals that flow into them from the whole body, so both internal and external environments are important. How many times have you felt more awake and aware by standing up and walking around a bit or by doing some 'brain gym'? These activities feed energy directly into the activating systems and from there into the whole brain.

Mammals

The next major step in the development of the brain occurred about 180 million years ago, when the paleomammalian brain started to appear (see Figure 7) (Holden, 1979; MacLean, 1973). This was a huge leap forward in terms of the sophistication of the brain and essentially involved the addition of the main emotional processing structure, the *limbic system*, to the reptilian brain. The limbic system is a common denominator in all mammals and is centrally involved in emotional experience and behaviour allowing feelings to guide self-preservation and survival of the species (MacLean, 1970). For probably the first time in evolution, the arrival of the paleomammalian brain brought with it the desire to care for and nurture the young (MacLean, 1982; 1985) and not eat it.

As the paleomammalian brain developed, it divided into three distinct subdivisions: the two oldest are closely related to the olfactory apparatus and are the *amygdala* (which is concerned with feeding, fighting and self-preservation) and the *septal nuclei* (which are concerned with genital and procreational functions) (Holden, 1979; McLean, 1977). The third subdivision bypasses the olfactory apparatus on its way to link up with what would eventually become the frontal cortex. It becomes progressively larger in higher primates and is concerned with empathy, compassion, and a 'far-seeing concern' for the species (MacLean, 1977). It is felt that this subdivision reflects a change in emphasis from olfactory to visual influences in sociosexual behaviour (ibid.) (which is why we don't wander up to complete strangers and give them a good sniffing – or at least not in an obvious way).

The existing corpus striatum (the centre of Figure 7) became enslaved to the newer limbic and cortical structures and was increasingly used in processing information for behavioural and memory purposes while retaining some of its own independent functionality.

Stone Age

This represents a basic rule of evolution. Later structures do not destroy previous structures, but rather encompass and incorporate their functionality within their own greater abilities (the sum of the parts is greater than the whole). So much of the behaviour you battle with in the classroom is millions of years old – you can take the student out of the Stone Age but you can't take the Stone Age out of the student!

The addition of the paleomammalian brain allowed much more sophisticated behaviours. This increase in sophistication was a direct result of the hugely increased number of neurones that were now available to the animal (a jump from about 15 million to several hundred million).

Humans

Finally, about 3.5 million years ago the first protohumanoids appeared and with them a marked increase in the number of cortical neurones. This was achieved by a massive increase in the amount of cortex. This last part of the triune brain is called the *neomammalian brain* (see Figure 7). It 'provides a vast neural screen for the portrayal of symbolic language' (ibid.). In the human it is represented by the huge bulk of the frontal cortex, the only part of the brain that can look inwards to the inside world (ibid.). This evolutionary development made possible 'the insight required for the foresight to plan for the needs of others as well as the self – to use our knowledge to alleviate suffering everywhere' (MacLean, 1990). It, in its turn, slaved the previous structures to its use and the resulting interrelating system evolved into the human brain as we know it today.

So there you have it – the evolutionary process that ended up with the brain you are using to read this chapter. An intricate, highly complex structure that effortlessly moves between reptilian, paleomammalian and neomammalian functions without your even being aware of what is going on. But how does it all learn? What has evolution devised that enables this mass of cells with the consistency of porridge actually to retain memories? Well that is in the next section.

2. How the brain learns what it does

This seemed to divide easily into two subsections: learning and recall. So, here goes.

A. Learning

As I pointed out in the last section, one of the main differences between the three different parts of the triune brain is the number of neurones that each contains. The reptilian brain has about 15–20 million, the paleomammalian/limbic brain has about 100–200 million, and the neo-mammalian brain has probably 150 billion! Quite an increase in neurones from one step to the next. It is a fact that the more neurones available to a creature, the more sophisticated its behaviour can be.

Why should that be? Well, the reason for this seems to be entirely based on the greater ability to store information that increased neuronal numbers confers. Why does memory equal an increase in sophisticated behaviour? The answer to this is very simple: almost all behaviour seems to be based on the excitation of learned patterns of neuronal firing, i.e. learned templates of neurones are made to fire together and these patterns represent knowledge of whatever sort. And when they fire together, they actually wire together by growing little connections to one another called *dendrites*. These patterns of neurones are called *templates* or *Hebbian assemblies* (Bressler, Coppola and Nakamura, 1993; Damasio, 1990; Kreiter and Singer, 1996; Merzenich and Sameshima, 1993; Rodriguez, et al., 1999; Skrebitsky and Chepkova, 1998; Vaadia, et al., 1995; Varela, 1995).

Disease

Figure 8a represents a group of neurones. (You have to imagine that there are a good 50,000 or so in each diagram. If you can't, I'm not going to draw them for you!). For this example, I have chosen a group of neurones sitting in the basal

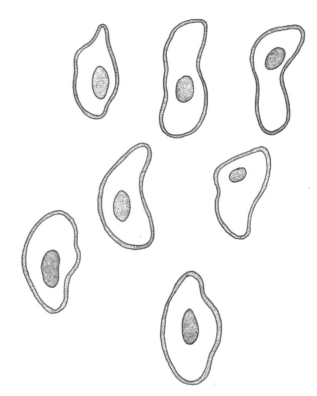

Figure 8a.

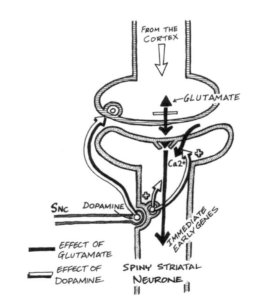

Figure 8b.

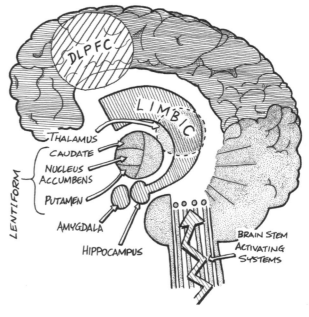

Figure 9.

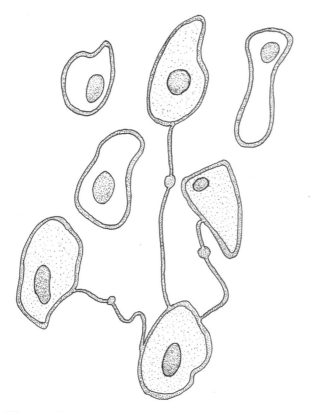

Figure 8c.

ganglia in a nucleus called the *caudate* (the wee circle in Figure 9). The caudate nuclei, the hippocampi and the amygdala are the core structures on which learning depends. They are paired structures, being present in both right and left hemispheres. We know from tragic cases where people have lost these structures through accident or disease that, if they have been damaged or destroyed, that individual will never remember anything again as long as they live – and will be unable to recall anything they learned in the previous 15–20 years.

It has been shown that newborn animals have very little in the way of templates, as their central nervous system has not yet developed to A-level, where higher centres are available for storing new information (Myslivecek, 1997). They can achieve a little bit of crude movement such as the suckling and grasp reflexes, but these

represent brain-stem reflexes and should have disappeared by three to four months of age. The newborn is therefore a *tabula rasa* (which is a very posh way of saying a 'clean slate'). The rest of life is given over to writing on this clean slate all the sophistication of the average human behavioural repertoire.

Think how much of your input as a teacher contributes to the writing on this clean slate, how you are actually moulding the neurological structures of the children you work with almost on a daily basis.

Wiggling

The group of neurones in the caudate (see Figure 8a) therefore exist in the newborn in an unconnected state. They are divided into functional areas (hand, foot, maths, language, love, hate, etc.), and their axons are topographically mapped in a point-to-point way throughout their connection pathways to preserve this functional separateness (Deniau and Chevalier, 1994;

Flaherty and Graybiel, 1991; McGeorge and Faull, 1989; Yeterian and Van Hoesen, 1978). This separateness is functionally very important – it's no good waving your left foot in the air when you are wiggling your little finger. To reiterate that: the reason you don't wave your left foot when you are wiggling your little finger is that the pathways that wiggle your little finger are separate from the pathways that wave your left foot (though waving with the feet is now an unusual thing to do, even where *I* come from). To achieve a long-term memory, these neurones have to form durable, long-lasting connections with one another in a very specific manner. These connections are called *synapses* and they represent the central anatomical fact of memory (Bailey et al., 2000; Kirkwood and Bear, 1994; McClelland et al., 1999; Skrebitsky and Chepkova, 1998).

The caudate nucleus contains relatively few neurones compared with the cortex (probably only a few million as compared with the billions in the cortex). This means that, for all the frontal cortical neurones to connect to the caudate (which they do), each receiving neurone in the caudate (a very specialist neurone called the *spiny striatal neurone*) receives between ten and fifteen thousand connections from the cortical neurones that it is functionally related to (Kawaguchi et al., 1995; Mink, 1996). One could hypothesise that, because of the relative paucity of neurones in the corpus striatum, the caudate and the other components of the lentiform nucleus, the nucleus accumbens and the putamen (Figure 9) store neuronal patterns that represent categories of memories, rather than very specific information (which require significantly higher numbers of patterns to represent all the detail that specificity requires).

Hatchback

In Figure 8a, the caudate spiny striatal neurones are unconnected. So what happened next? I will use the example of a baby starting to form a memory of the appearance of its mother's face (remember, the baby's brain has almost no

formed patterns of neurones – it is that *tabula rasa*). I use this example as it contains the most important ingredient for memory formation in the striatum, the involvement of the limbic system, i.e. the emotions (see below). A single cortical-spiny striatal neurone synapse is demonstrated in Figure 8b (you didn't think you were going to be confronted with neurochemistry, I know, but bear with it: it all comes clear in the end, I hope). It contains two terminal endings. The cortical connection (that's the one at the top of the diagram) utilises *the* major excitatory amino acid in the brain, *glutamate*. As the word *excitatory* suggests, glutamate's only goal in life is to excite everything in front of it as far as it can – a bit like those kids who drive souped-up hatchbacks around your neighbourhood: all petrol and noise and very little brain! This is capable of not only short-term depolarisation of the striatal neurone through its action on fast calcium channels (Murphy and Miller, 1989; Rajadhyaksha et al., 1999), but also, in conjunction with another neurochemical called dopamine, of affecting a set of genes known as *immediate early genes* (IEGs), which can substantially alter receptor and membrane characteristics in the cell (Konradi, Leveque and Hyman, 1996; Lee et al., 2002). However, unopposed glutamate is toxic to the cell and will literally 'excite' the cell to death (Colwell and Levine, 1999), which sounds like fun but I bet you isn't.

Excited

The second terminal coming from the substantia nigra compacta (SNc) releases dopamine (the one coming in from the side in Figure 8b). This seems to be the major 'stabilising' neurochemical in the frontal lobes and basal ganglia (a bit like those Rover-driving, flat-cap-wearing individuals who always drive at exactly three miles an hour under the speed limit). Its release is under the control of the limbic system (Kimura, 1992; Mirenowicz and Schultz, 1994; Schultz and Romo, 1990). It has three major effects. First, it upregulates the glutamate receptor to sustain it at a higher rate of activity (Colwell and Levine,

1995; Surmeier et al., 1995; Snyder, 1998); second, it assists glutamate in its effect on IEGs (Onn, West and Grace, 2000); and, third, it may block further glutamate release through its effect on the presynaptic D2 receptors on the cortical axon (ibid.). This last action prevents glutamate from damaging the striatal neurone. The first two effects are the key elements of two related forms of neuronal activity called *long-term potentiation* (LTP) and *long-term depression* (LTD) (Calabresi, Centonze and Bernardi, 2000). These processes underpin memory in all three structures (striatum, amygdala and hippocampus). As the limbic system to a large extent controls dopamine release, the whole process in the striatum is therefore regulated by the emotional content of any experience (Suri and Schultz, 1999). If LTP and LTD are set up, then the alteration in the gene expression of the striatal neurone will be expressed by the formation of dendrites that sprout from the cell to form connections with similarly excited cells in its neighbourhood (Eichenbaum, 1996; Geinisman, 2000; McEachern and Shaw, 1999).

Let's summarise all that science. Along comes glutamate, which excites the striatal neurone. This is an escalating level of excitation, which, if it isn't stopped, will eventually kill the striatal neurone – not a good outcome. As soon as the glutamate has started to excite the striatal neurone, dopamine is released (a large part of this release is controlled by our emotional systems, underlining the importance of positive emotions in the classroom). This blocks further glutamate release, but works on the striatal neurone to keep its level of excitation high, i.e. glutamate jump starts the system and dopamine keeps it going. Once this increased level of excitation has been set up, then the cell is in a state known as *long-term potentiation* (sometimes this is a decrease in excitation when it is called *long-term depression*). These two processes, LTP and LTD, are the key factors of any learning – if you don't set these going, you can learn nothing. See, you can do neurochemistry. It's like flying – just throw yourself at the ground and miss!

Spiny

A further ability of the limbic system is to stimulate the growth of synaptic connections between a subgroup of caudate interneurones called the *tonically active neurones* (TANs) and the spiny striatal neurones (Aosaki et al., 1994; Flaherty and Graybiel, 1991; Graybiel, 1998; Graybiel et al., 1994; Kimura, 1992; Yeterian and Van Hoesen, 1978). TANs 'tie together' templates of spiny striatal neurones, and when a template has been well learned, surges of dopamine from the SNc are no longer required to perpetuate it as the TANs take over this function (Graybiel, 1995). TANs are directly connected to the limbic system (ibid.; Aosaki, Kimura and Graybiel, 1995), and are another way that the limbic system can exert control over memory. So, once a pattern is formed in the striatum, the limbic system (our emotions) can fire it by activating TANs – dopamine is no longer needed in the same way. How cool is that!

Exposure

So what does all that add up to in the external world of faces and baby goo? Well, the baby is exposed repeatedly to an emotionally important stimulus, the appearance and disappearance of her mother's face. The association of reward or expected reward with the appearance of the mother's face stimulates dopamine release (Mirenowicz and Schultz, 1994; Schultz, 1998; Schultz and Romo, 1990). Over time, this repeated exposure leads to the setting up and perpetuating of LTP and LTD under the control of the limbic system. A pattern of spiny striatal neurones – the Hebbian assembly or template (see the joined neurones in Figure 8c) (Bailey et al., 2000; Hebb, 1968; Merzenich and Sameshima, 1993; Skrebitsky and Chepkova, 1998) – becomes connected together by both direct synapses with one another and through the agency of TANs. This pattern of neurones will now preferentially fire whenever the child sees her mother's face. A final refinement to this summary is to say that the specificity of 'my mother's face' takes many months to develop. Initially, the child will remember 'face', or perhaps just a small subcategory of face such as 'eyes'. The combination of repeated exposure to a specific face with its associated emotional import and the continuing maturation in both the anatomy and biochemistry of the infant's brain will lead this initial generic memory to be gradually refined until the child knows which 'face' is its mother's (Joseph, 1992). The specific details of this face will be stored by patterns in the cortex, the category of 'face' is almost certainly stored in the corpus striatum.

So, let us review all that. A pattern of neurones is established in the corpus striatum by the growth of synapses between spiny striatal neurones and between spiny striatal neurones and TANs. This synaptic growth is controlled by and directed by dopamine released under the influence of the limbic system, i.e. the emotional brain. This pattern means 'face' to the brain when it is fired. Because the striatal neurones are topographically mapped to the cortex, the details of the face can then be stored in the cortex by the neurones that are receiving the LTP and LTD signals from the striatal neurones, also growing synaptic connections with one another. Now, whenever the baby sees her mother's face she has the necessary neuronal patterns to recognise it as 'face' and also as a specific face. And that is basically how all memories work – by the establishment of patterns of neurones facilitated by the emotional brain.

Emotional involvement when learning, therefore, significantly increases the chances of that learning being successful.

In the description above, I have dealt with the corpus striatum, the repository of 'non-declarative' memory, i.e. memory that is not readily accessed by the conscious mind. The other main memory structure is the hippocampus, which deals with 'declarative' memory, i.e. memory that is readily available for conscious recall (Squire and Zola, 1996; Squire, Knowlton and Musen,

1993). This is situated in the medial temporal lobes and is part of the limbic system (Figure 9). The mechanisms of memory formation in the hippocampus also rely on LTP and LTD triggered through the action of glutamate (Malenka, and Nicoll, 1999; Milner, Squire and Kandel, 1998a; Milner, Squire and Kandel, 1998b).

Destroyed

The establishment of LTP and LTD in either striatum or hippocampus is thought to drive cortical neurones to form synaptic connections, i.e. to establish templates representing the memory (McClelland and Goddard, 1996a; McClelland and Goddard, 1996b; Sutherland and McNaughton, 2000). These two structures are the main memory structures our brain has. If they are damaged or destroyed then the individual will never be able to remember anything again as long as they live – and will not be able to recall anything learned in the previous fifteen years. They are therefore highly specialised and it is because of their ability to set up LTP and LTD that they are so central to learning.

To understand memory more fully, two other neurochemicals must be discussed. The first of these is the main inhibitory neurochemical in the brain, *gamma-amino-butyric acid* (GABA). This is also required for the formation of effective synapses (Silkis, 2001). This may exert its effect through the sequence of reciprocal inhibition between striatal neurones that occurs through both $GABA_A$ and $GABA_B$ receptors (Shi and Rayport, 1994; ibid.), and thus the efficacy of inhibitory connections can be modified (Silkis, 1998). Inhibition is extremely important in learning and recall. To learn or recall accurately, the background neuronal 'noise' must be reduced to a minimum. This is achieved through inhibition – you really turn on only the neurones you are going to use in that template. The rest of the neuronal population are kept damped down so they don't interfere.

Lobes

The second neurochemical of importance is *acetylcholine*. This neurochemical is present in large amounts in the brain, especially in the frontal lobes and may have the role of 'synapse control' (Girod, et al., 2000; Girod and Role, 2001; Jo and Role, 2002). Varying the concentration of acetylcholine at a synapse is thought either to increase or to decrease its activity – an essential ability, as recalling previously stored templates is possible only by maximising the number of templates available, while storing a new memory requires previous synaptic connections to be muted so that the same neurone can be used in different templates.

Through this proposed ability, acetylcholine may also be part of the processes of forgetting previously learned data, such as when one changes one's car. By damping down the activity in synapses in the old template, and enhancing the activity in newly formed synapses, the correct 'car' template can be recalled. Over time, the unused synapses will gradually decay. So the more the new behaviour is rehearsed and rewarded in the classroom, the more quickly the old behaviour will disappear.

The final neurochemical involved in the process of learning is *noradrenaline*. Acting through both central brain stem's arousal systems and the amygdala (see below), noradrenaline is responsible for adding 'energy' to memories. Changes in the concentration of noradrenaline, and other neurochemicals such as acetylcholine and serotonin in the brain-stem-activating systems (Figure 9), change our state of arousal and hence wakefulness (Berlucchi, 1997). The reticular activating system feeds up from the locus coeruleus of the spinal cord through the pedunculopontine nucleus (PPN) and into the thalamus and the reticular nucleus of the thalamus (Lee, Rinne and Marsden, 2000; Klemm and Vertes, 1990; Steriade and McCarley, 1990). The more activity there is in this system, the more aroused the brain is. This increased arousal is probably effected by increasing the rate of firing of the so-

called 'matrix' neurones spread throughout the thalamus (Jones, 2002; Jones and Hendry, 1989). This group of thalamic neurones is connected reciprocally to the whole of the cortex via layers I and II (Jones, 2002), and may, in combination with direct connections from brain-stem systems (Berlucchi, 1997), dictate the baseline level of arousal of cortical neurones.

Dream

Put simply, to have an awake, working brain you need to have sufficient levels of activity in the brain stem's reticular activating system. This energy then feeds directly into the main rhythm generator in the brain, the thalamus. This in turn feeds the energy into the rest of the brain, bringing neurones into a state of preparedness. Then, when you want to process templates, everything is ready to go (a state we all dream of creating in the classroom! – see Figure 10).

Learning new templates is of only passing interest if you can't then recall them. The next subsection is looking at some of the science behind recall.

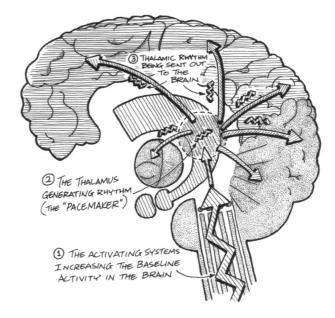

Figure 10.

B. Recall

In the awake, resting state, the frequency of cortical firing is at 10–16Hz (or cycles per second). This seems to represent the 'idling' speed of cortical neurones, and neurones firing asynchronously at this rate do not appear to be performing useful work. This concept of asynchronous firing is of central importance to this section – *so pay attention*!

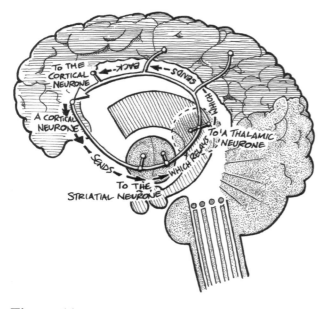

Figure 11.

It is only when groups of cortical neurones are brought synchronously up to higher firing frequencies (the gamma rate – 40–300Hz) that information processing can occur (Bressler, Coppola and Nakamura, 1993; Damasio, 1990; Nini et al., 1995; Rodriguez et al., 1999; Singer, 1993; Singer and Gray, 1995; Varela, 1995). While there is some evidence that cortical networks can achieve these speeds independently, it is likely that, to sustain higher-frequency firing, cortical neurones have to access the subcortical 'processors' represented by the thalamo-cortical and basal ganglia-thalamo-cortical circuits. (This sounds a bit wordy, doesn't it? These loops are the topographically mapped connections I talked

about early on. One passes from the cortex to the basal ganglia to the thalamus and back to the cortex, as shown in Figure 11 and the other is just describing the back-and-forth communication between the cortical neurones and the thalamus, this central brain pacemaker that keeps everything ticking over).

Passage

It can be hypothesised that this passage of templates allows areas of the brain related to the specific area of information being processed to be brought up to gamma frequencies in a 'feed-forward' manner so that they are ready to add to or act on the result of the cortical activity.

How does this transform into a behaviour? The sequence of events occurring in the brain seems to develop as follows. Say an individual perceives an external stimulus, such as a close friend across the street. Visual information travels from the eyes back to the visual cortex in the occipital lobes. Here it will fire neuronal patterns specific to the information arriving at it, and these patterns will be interpreted in the visual association cortex as 'human with specific appearance attributes' (which sounds pretty weird but I think you get what I mean). There will be no emotional context attached to this pattern at this stage because the information has not yet been passed to the limbic system, where such data is stored.

Wee

The information is then passed simultaneously in two different directions: one stream will loop forward to the frontal cortex, and the other will pass via the amygdala into the limbic system. The pattern of neuronal firing that the arriving visual information generates in the limbic system will add emotional weight to it, and this will be fed to the SNc (that wee structure that produces dopamine for most of the brain), which will, in turn, release a dopamine surge in the striatum. This release of dopamine may be one of the core activations that switch our attentional mechanisms from one stimulus to another, as described by Posner and Petersen (1990). Meanwhile, the visual information that has simultaneously been sent to the frontal cortex will generate a pattern of neuronal firing, which will be downloaded into the caudate (part of the corpus striatum – see the illustrations, but especially Figure 9).

It is likely that the following events then occur. The arrival of the cortical download in the caudate at the same time as the limbic-stimulated release of dopamine in the same area of the caudate will rapidly transmit the information back up to cortex via the thalamus and, through a series of neurochemical messages, increase the firing rate of the thalamic neurones specific to the transmitted information to the gamma rate. This will, in turn, sustain the frontal cortical neurones involved in the original download to the higher rate, as well as related neuronal patterns in other areas of the brain. This increased volume of cortical neuronal firing, if it is sufficient, will make one consciously aware that one is looking at a friend across the street, simply because enough neurones are now firing.

Affection

In this example, I am assuming that this particular friend is one that the individual feels affection towards, so sufficient excitation is achieved by the dopamine released by the limbic system in the brain to generate the desire to cross the street to speak with him/her. Even if a stimulus does not enter awareness (i.e. if a sufficient volume of cortical neurones does not come up to gamma frequency), the individual may still be able to formulate a plan of action at a subconscious level.

This planning is known to occur in the dorso-lateral prefrontal cortex (DLPFC) and related structures (Goldman-Rakic, 1996; 1987) (Figure 9). These areas of cortex receive inputs from all of the rest of the cortex and seem to act in a way similar to random-access memory in a computer

in that they can hold information for a period, but once the stimulus is removed the information decays and is no longer available for processing. It is at this stage that the 'feed-forward' effect of basal ganglia–thalamic transmission becomes relevant. Not only will it allow other areas of the cortex and the limbic system that contain relevant information about the friend to come up to gamma frequency and therefore transmit their information to DLPFC, but areas related to possible actions will also have been brought to a state of preparedness. How neat is that?

Next, let's assume that the result of all this cerebral activity is that the individual does wish to cross the street to see the friend. The DLPFC will now send information in a 'chunked' form to cortical areas such as premotor cortex to execute the necessary survival patterns such as looking both ways before crossing the road and the necessary locomotor activity to allow you to walk to the side of the road (Goldman-Rakic, 1995; Petit et al., 1998; Picard and Strick, 2001). 'Chunked' information is like macros in computers. A single instruction to the right part of the brain (say that the instruction is 'walk') will create a flow of templates to the relevant parts of the brain and spinal cord carrying all the details of exactly how those structures should act to walk. They themselves will have their own set of templates covering the details of walking that they deal with. An integrated, seamless, hierarchical communication – how well the brain manages what so many schools fail to achieve!

Very large

Once cortex and limbic system have agreed that it is safe to cross the road, the individual can cross the road and meet with the friend. However, let's assume now that seeing the friend produces a very large and overwhelming desire to cross the street to see them. In this circumstance, instead of arriving at a plan using DLPFC, and reaching the friend in a controlled way, the individual may be overwhelmed by the need to get to their side and impulsively launch themselves into the road without first checking for traffic. This is a very different circumstance. In this situation, the second stream of information from the visual association cortex (i.e. the one travelling to the amygdala) takes precedence.

This brings us onto the amygdala, that little, extremely primitive emotional engine that sits deep in our brains. The amygdala (Figure 9) is a phylogenetically (there's that word again) primitive structure and is thought to be concerned first and foremost with flight-or-fight reactions, though this is probably an oversimplification (LeDoux, 1998; 2000). It has the capability of hijacking the entire behavioural system through its connection with brain-stem-activating systems (Aston-Jones et al., 1996; Gallagher and Holland, 1994) and precipitating impulsive activity over which the individual has little or no conscious control (i.e. if the amygdala is at a high level of activation it will short-circuit out your conscious 'brian' and get you to act in an unconscious way. This is a good survival ability. It is an excellent idea to be running as fast as you can away from a sabre-tooth tiger before you have taken the time to think, 'Oh, look, a sabre-tooth tiger, and it's eying up my right shin' – or, the more likely, 'Oh look – a sab—Aaaaaaaaaaarrrrrggghhh!'). In this sort of circumstance, the amygdala can keep us alive. Unfortunately, because it switches off the conscious brain, any amygdala-driven behaviour is likely to have the same lack of thought. Hence the inability to reason with people lost in the throes of a huge behavioural reaction. So, shouting at the angry child is not going to be a useful strategy. Wait until they have settled down (i.e. their level of amygdala activation has decreased enough for the conscious brain to come back on line), and then try to reason with them.

Explicit

The amygdala can not only get us away from (or into) more trouble than you can shake a stick at, but it is also central to the emotional control of memory. It is part of a system that serves to regulate the strength of memories in relation to their emotional significance (McGaugh, Cahill and Roozendaal, 1996). It is connected to both the hippocampus and the corpus striatum (LeDoux, 1993a; 1993b) (remember that these are the two structures that are essential for the formation and recall of memories). Through these connections and also through direct cortical connections and its connections with brain stem activating systems, the amygdala can modulate the storage of both implicit (unconscious) and explicit (conscious) memories (LeDoux, 2000). The connections to the hippocampus and striatum are glutamatergic (Kita and Kitai, 1990; Krettek and Price, 1977; Pitkanen et al., 2000) (that exciting neurochemical – the hatchback kid of the brain), and their influence on memory is significantly affected by the level of emotional arousal present in the individual (Cahill 2000; Cahill and McGaugh, 1996; McGaugh, Cahill and Roozendaal, 1996). One of the factors that determine this level of arousal is the amount of stress the individual is feeling.

Stress has several effects on the amygdala and hence memory. First, noradrenaline is released directly into the amygdala increasing its activity (Cahill et al., 1994; McGaugh, Cahill and Roozendaal, 1996; Van Stegeren et al., 1998). Second, the systemic release of adrenaline (i.e. into the rest of the body through the blood stream from the adrenal glands, chubby little guys that sit on top of the kidneys) activates nerves going to the amygdala from the vagus nerve (Cahill and McGaugh, 1996; Clark et al., 1999; Packard et al., 1995; Van Stegeren et al., 1998). The vagus nerve is the big nerve that supplies most of our internal organs such as the heart, the lungs and the various bits and pieces of the intestines. This stimulation of the vagus nerve by adrenaline also increases the level of excitation of the amygdala. Third, the release of glucocorticoids from the adrenals also has a direct effect on the amygdala to increase its level of excitation (Quirarte, Roozendaal and McGaugh, 1997; Roozendaal, 2000; Roozendaal et al., 2002; Roozendaal, Quirarte and McGaugh, 2002). Glucocorticoids are also known as steroids and are a central part of the body's reaction to stress.

Enhancement

All these effects have a final common pathway through cholinergic interneurons, which connect with the excitatory efferents from the amygdala to the hippocampus, caudate, substantia nigra, thalamus and frontal cortex (Packard and Cahill, 2001). Stimulation of these nerves enhances memory retention (Kesner and Wilburn, 1974; McGaugh and Gold, 1976). This enhancement can, however become overdriven. In the case of excess stress, the amygdala shifts memory storage from the explicit (or conscious) memory of the hippocampal system to the implicit (or unconscious) memory system of the caudate (Packard and Cahill, 2001). (Just to throw some more words at you, these two systems are also known as *cognitive* in the case of the hippocampal system and *cue-response* in the case of the caudate.)

Finally (I know, you are breathing a huge sigh of relief and wondering if your poor brain will ever absorb all this data!), I will briefly discuss the role of the hippocampus in recall. It has a time-limited role in declarative memory, with memories eventually becoming largely independent of the hippocampus and supported predominantly by the neocortex (Nadel and Bohbot, 2001; Ryan et al., 2001). What this basically means is that templates are laid down in the hippocampi that gradually (through the agencies of LTP and LTD) get transformed into templates in the cortex. Once they are fully established in the cortex, the hippocampus is no longer needed to recall them. It is an essential component of the brain system underlying the conscious recollection of past events (Squire, 1992) and the processing of spatial, configural, contextual and/or relational information (Eichenbaum, 1992; Nadel, 1992; O'Keefe and Nadel, 1978). The particular interest in the hippocampus is that it can encode and store memories that do not have an obvious emotional content, i.e. intellectual facts. It does, however,

receive outputs from the amygdala, so the limbic system can exert some control over it (LeDoux, 2000). It remains true, however, that dopamine under the direction of the limbic system is still required to form the templates that represent long-term learning.

Exogenous amnesiac

The brain also has systems to inhibit memory storage. Gamma-amino-butyric acid (GABA) and endogenous opioids (such as enkephalins and substance P) both inhibit memory storage, as does a huge excess of noradrenaline (Brioni and McGaugh, 1988; Brioni, Nagahara and McGaugh, 1989; Izquierdo et al., 1980a; Izquierdo et al., 1980b; Izquierdo et al., 1984). The benzodiazipine group of drugs, which work on the $GABA_A$ receptor, are an example of an exogenous amnesiac (Izquierdo et al., 1990; Izquierdo et al., 1991; Medina et al., 1992).

Phew! So that just about covers learning and memory and all that stuff. I thought in the last section, I would give you all a quick peak under the stones of lateralisation. After all, why not?

3. The truth about left brain/right brain theory

All really good articles should have a general comments section don't you think, so here's mine.

A. General comments on lateralisation

The hemispheres do contain some functions that are not lateralised, e.g. vision, hearing and the motor and sensory cortices. Each cortex controls these functions for the contralateral side of the body, but these cortical areas do roughly mirror each other, both in structure and function. Superimposed on top of this symmetry, however, are the hemispheric specialisations. The left hemisphere (usually the dominant hemisphere even in left-handed people) deals with linguistic, analytic and sequential processing and the right deals with nonverbal, holistic and parallel processing (Benowitz et al., 1983; Berlucchi, Aglioti and Tassinari, 1997). Why hemispheric specialisation occurred is not known. It can be hypothesised that speed of processing might have dictated a function residing in one hemisphere rather than both – communication between two functionally similar areas of cortex in opposite hemispheres might slow down a behaviour that needs to occur quickly.

Lateralisation, however, should be thought of in terms of complementary hemispheric specialisation (Heilman and Gilmore, 1998): even in visual and auditory cortices, where both hemispheres carry equal functionality, specific items of information are stored preferentially in one side or the other. Information presented to one hemisphere and learned by that hemisphere has been shown not to be available to the other hemisphere when the main connection between the two hemispheres, the corpus callosum, is divided (Corballis, Funnell and Gazzaniga, 2002; Gazzaniga, 1998; Spence et al., 2001).

Posterior

The two hemispheres can, however, process information simultaneously and independently (Zaidel, 2001). Anatomically, the corpus callosum is divided into subdivisions, each of which carries specific information between the two hemispheres. The posterior section carries visual information and, moving anteriorly, auditory and tactile information. The anterior corpus callosum is involved in higher-order transfer of semantic information. For correct interpretation of a stimulus, therefore, by both hemispheres, information transfer must occur both by the posterior corpus callosum, to carry the stimulus itself, and the anterior corpus callosum, to carry semantic information about the stimulus.

The two hemispheres can therefore be thought of as complementary members of the same team

who carry out different functions but sit side by side and communicate with each other all the time via the huge wiring loop of the corpus callosum.

So what do we know about the specialised functions that these two team members get up to? Well, read on and find out!

B. Specialised areas: general findings

Areas that contain a specialist function are inclined to be larger than their corresponding area on the opposite hemisphere and, for the language areas of the left hemisphere involved in phonological decoding and auditory comprehension, this difference is visible shortly after the middle of gestation (Zaidel, 2001). (I've said it before and I'll say it again: How amazing is that?!) It is hypothesised that this asymmetry occurs because of the production of a *small* side rather than the production of a large side (Rosen, 1996). Subcortical areas also tend to be larger on the specialised side, in keeping with their reciprocal connections with cortical neurones (Gazzaniga, Ivry and Mangun, 2002) (i.e. the corpus striatum and the deeper structures of the reptilian brain). Specialised areas also tend to have differences in microanatomical structure such that the specialised area tends to have a greater number of neurones than the corresponding area in the other hemisphere and a more pronounced specialisation in structure (Galaburda et al., 1986; Williams and Rakic, 1988).

Anatomical

It is possible that the microanatomical differences between the right and left hemispheres may be due to quicker early right-hemisphere development but greater left-hemisphere development after the first year of life (Zaidel, 2001). This conclusion is based on the observation that higher-order dendritic branching is greater in the left whereas lower-order dendritic branches were longer on the right, i.e. the left has formed a greater number of connections between neurones while the right has retained a more primitive architecture. It should be remembered, however, that, although anatomical cerebral asymmetry appears in all animals that have been examined, its link with functional lateralisation is not clear (Rosen, 1996).

OK, so enough with the general comments. What does it all mean when you get down to the actual functions that reside in each hemisphere:

C. The left hemisphere

PET

Perhaps one of the most important specialised functions of the left hemisphere is language. This is even true in 50 per cent of left-handed people. For language, the specialised area resides on the superior border of the temporal lobe and includes *Wernicke's area*. The region that has shown to be larger on the left than the right is termed the *planum temporale* and underlies the sylvian fissure near Wernicke's area. This area may be responsible for phonological decoding and auditory comprehension (Zaidel, 2001), according to PET and fMRI studies. (These are two specialist forms of what is called *functional imaging*. This is an extraordinary way of actually watching the brain activity as it performs a task. PET stands for 'positron emission tomography' and fMRI for 'functional magnetic resonance imaging'. Now you wish you hadn't asked, don't you?) The lateral posterior nucleus of the thalamus also tends to be larger on the left (the entire cortex is connected reciprocally to the thalamus, the main generator of frequency in the brain, i.e. the cerebral pacemaker) (Gazzaniga, Ivry and Mangun, 2002). Language can be divided into grammar (the rules of language) and the lexicon (the dictionary). The lexicon is present in both hemispheres, but a larger part seems to reside in the left (Gazzaniga, 1970; Zaidel, 1991). Grammar resides almost entirely in the left, which is also responsible for speech production (Gazzaniga, 2000).

Higher-order cognition and problem solving also reside in the left hemisphere (ibid.; LeDoux et al., 1977), i.e. the left hemisphere is specialised for intelligent behaviour. This is shown in its function in hypothesis formation. While the right hemisphere approaches a task in the simplest possible manner, the left hemisphere tries to make order out of chaos (Gazzaniga, 2000). The left hemisphere is also the interpreter of events, even those generated in the right hemisphere (ibid.). Positive and negative moods generated in the right hemisphere drive the left hemisphere to interpret the present circumstance in a positive or negative way respectively.

Attention is divided between the two hemispheres (Zaidel, 2001). The left hemisphere specialises in spatial compatibility and divided attention tasks and, for motor skills, the left hemisphere is specialised for action.

D. The right hemisphere

The right hemisphere has a better ability to see the whole picture or totality of a problem or stimulus set rather than do a step-by-step analysis (Lamm and Gordon, 1984), i.e. it is where we 'gestalt' situations. Stimuli that preferentially activate the right hemisphere are those that are unfamiliar (Kimura, 1963), spatial (Kimura, 1969), and nonverbal (Milner, 1968).

Smell

As mentioned above, attention is divided between the two hemispheres. The right hemisphere specialises in sustained attention and the orienting of visuospatial attention. The right hemisphere also has a greater specialisation for facial recognition than the left and perception of smell also preferentially activates the right hemisphere.

E. Concluding remarks about lateralisation

Cerebral lateralisation has fascinated neuroscience since the late 1900s and recent work has led to a greater understanding of how it might work. The left hemisphere deals with higher-order functions while the right deals predominantly with emotions, though in many ways it is very 'concrete' in its processes. An example of this is that when a patient with a 'split brain' (i.e. a divided corpus callosum) is asked to decide whether a series of stimuli appeared in a study set or not, the right hemisphere was able to identify correctly items that have been seen previously and to reject new items. The left hemisphere, however, tended falsely to recognise new items when they are similar to previously presented items, presumably because they fit into the schema it has constructed (Metcalfe, Funnell and Gazzaniga, 1995; Phelps and Gazzaniga, 1992). This 'concreteness' is because the right hemisphere does not engage in interpretative processes, maintaining instead an accurate record of events (Gazzaniga, 2000).

Arousing

It is interesting to note that gender differences in lateralisation of emotional memory have recently been demonstrated with females being much more likely to activate the left amygdala after an emotionally arousing memory task, while males activated the right (Cahill et al., 2001). The two hemispheres, therefore, complement each other, allowing elaborative processing to occur without sacrificing veracity (Gazzaniga, 2000).

4. Conclusion

My goodness! There is a lot in all that, isn't there? I have attempted in this chapter to develop the most recent ideas that are present in the literature about how the brain functions, and to apply these to learning and recall.

In a sentence, the literature would seem to suggest that effective learning occurs best in situations of optimal stimulation, where there is sufficient stress to activate learning systems, but not so much that learning is diverted into unconscious tracks and where the student feels an emotional involvement with the material being taught and/or the teacher teaching it.

So, if you think discipline by force, threat and external rewards, teaching to the brain without going through the heart and lifeless chalk-and-talk lessons are the way to teach, think again. After all, you don't teach subjects: you teach children.

And what does all that add up to? Well, the optimal environment for anyone to learn anything in is best summarised by the following algorithm:

- If someone feels **understood** as an individual human being then …
- their **self-esteem** is increased; and if their self-esteem is increased then …
- their **self-confidence** will be good; and if they are in an environment where they feel understood, where their self-esteem is good and where their self-confidence is good then they feel …
- **engaged**; and, if they feel emotionally engaged, then their neurochemistry will be optimised for learning.

And what is this but 'love' in the pure sense of that word?

Everyone you meet is an individual human. The more they feel the four elements above when they are with you, the more they will learn from you. And do you know the best thing about all this? This chapter represents a précis of billions of dollars' worth and many years of research, and what has it told us? Exactly what any village wise woman has been able to tell us for the past ten thousand years.

Neat, huh?

References

Aosaki, T., et al. (1994), 'Responses of tonically active neurons in the primates striatum undergo systematic changes during behavioural sensori-motor conditioning', *The Journal of Neuroscience*, 14(6), pp. 3969–84.

Aosaki, T., Kimura, M., and Graybiel, A. (1995), 'Temporal and spatial characteristics of tonically active neurons of the primates striatum', *Journal of Neurophysiology*, 73(3), pp. 1234–52.

Aston-Jones, G., et al. (1996), 'Role of the locus coeruleus in emotional activation', *Progress in Brain Research*, 107, pp. 379–402.

Bailey C. H., et al. (2000), 'Is heterosynaptic modulation essential for stabilizing Hebbian plasticity and memory?', *Nature Reviews. Neuroscience*, 1, pp. 11–20.

Benowitz, L. I., et al. (1983), 'Hemispheric specialization in nonverbal communication', *Cortex*, 19, pp. 5–11.

Berlucchi, G. (1997), 'One or many arousal systems? Reflections on some of Giuseppe Moruzzi's foresights and insights about the intrinsic regulation of brain activity', *Archives Italiennes de Biologie*, 135, pp. 5–14.

Berlucchi, G., Aglioti, S., and Tassinari, G. (1997), 'Rightward attentional bias and left hemisphere dominance in a cue-target light detection task in a callosotomy patient', *Neuropsychologia*, 35, pp. 941–52.

Bressler, S. L., Coppola, R., and Nakamura, R. (1993), 'Episodic multiregional cortical coherence at multiple frequencies during visual task performance', *Nature*, 366, pp. 153–6.

Brioni, J. D., and McGaugh, J. L. (1988), 'Post-training administration of GABAergic antagonists enhances retention of aversively motivated tasks', *Psychopharmacology (Berl)*, 96, pp. 505–10.

Brioni, J. D., Nagahara, A. H., and McGaugh, J. L. (1989), 'Involvement of the amygdala GABAergic system in the modulation of memory storage', *Brain Research*, 487, pp. 105–12.

Cahill, L. (2000), 'Neurobiological mechanisms of emotionally influenced, long-term memory', *Progress in Brain Research*, 126, pp. 29–37.

Cahill, L., and McGaugh, J. L. (1996), 'The neurobiology of memory for emotional events: adrenergic activation and the amygdala', *Proceedings of the Western Pharmacology Society*, 39, pp. 81–4.

Cahill, L., et al. (1994), 'Beta-adrenergic activation and memory for emotional events', *Nature*, 371, pp. 702–4.

Cahill, L., et al. (2001), 'Sex-related difference in amygdala activity during emotionally influenced memory storage', *Neurobiology of Learning and Memory*, 75, pp. 1–9.

Calabresi, P., Centonze, D., and Bernardi, G. (2000), 'Electrophysiology of dopamine in normal and denervated striatal neurons', *Trends in Neuroscience*, 23(suppl.), S57–S63.

Clark, K. B., et al. (1999), 'Enhanced recognition memory following vagus nerve stimulation in human subjects', *Nature Neuroscience*, 2, pp. 94–8.

Colwell, C. S., and Levine, M. S. (1995), 'Excitatory synaptic transmission in neostriatal neurons: regulation by cyclic AMP-dependent mechanisms', *The Journal of Neuroscience*, 15, pp. 1704–13.

Colwell, C. S., and Levine, M. S. (1999), 'Metabotropic glutamate receptor modulation of excitotoxicity in the neostriatum: role of calcium channels', *Brain Research*, 833, pp. 234–41.

Corballis, P. M., Funnell, M. G. and Gazzaniga, M. S. (2002), 'Hemispheric asymmetries for simple visual judgments in the split brain', *Neuropsychologia*, 40, pp. 401–10.

Damasio, A. R. (1990), 'Synchronous activation in multiple cortical regions: a mechanism for recall', *Neuroscience*, 2, pp. 287–97.

Deniau, J. M., and Chevalier, G. (1994), 'Functional architecture of the rat substantia nigra pars reticulata: evidence for segregated channels', in G Percheron, J S McKenzie and J Feger (eds), *The Basal Ganglia IV*, pp. 63–70 (New York, NY: Plenium Press).

Eichenbaum, H. (1992), 'The hippocampal system and declarative memory in animals', *Journal of Cognitive Neuroscience*, 4, pp. 217–31.

Eichenbaum, H. (1996), 'Learning from LTP: a comment on recent attempts to identify cellular and molecular mechanisms of memory', *Learning & Memory*, 3, pp. 61–73.

Flaherty, A. W., and Graybiel, A. M. (1991), 'Corticostriatal transformations in the primate somatosensory system. Projections from physiologically mapped body part representations', *Journal of Neurophysiology*, 66, pp. 1249–63.

Galaburda, A. M., et al. (1986), 'Histological asymmetry in the primary visual cortex of the rat: implications for mechanisms of cerebral asymmetry', *Cortex*, 22, pp. 151–60.

Gallagher, M., and Holland, P. C. (1994), 'The amygdala complex: multiple roles in associative learning and attention', *Proceedings of the National Academy of Sciences of the United States of America*, 91, pp. 11771–6.

Garcia-Rill, E., and Skinner, R. D. (1987), 'The mesencephalic locomotor region. I. Activation of a medullary projection site', *Brain Research*, 411, pp. 1–12.

Gazzaniga, M. S. (1970), *The Bisected Brain* (New York, NY: Appleton-Century-Crofts).

Gazzaniga, M. S. (1998), 'The split brain revisited', *Scientific American*, 279, pp. 50–5.

Gazzaniga, M. S. (2000), 'Cerebral specialization and interhemispheric communication: does the corpus callosum enable the human condition?', *Brain*, 123 (Pt 7), pp. 1293–326.

Gazzaniga, M. S., Ivry, R. B., and Mangun, G. R. (2002), *Cognitive Neuroscience: The Biology of the Mind* (New York, NY: W W Norton & Co.).

Geinisman, Y. (2000), 'Structural synaptic modifications associated with hippocampal LTP and behavioral learning', *Cerebral Cortex*, 10, pp. 952–62.

Girod, R., and Role, L. W. (2001), 'Long-lasting enhancement of glutamatergic synaptic transmission by acetylcholine contrasts with response adaptation after exposure to low-level nicotine', *The Journal of Neuroscience*, 21, pp. 5182–90.

Girod, R., et al. (2000), 'Facilitation of glutamatergic neurotransmission by presynaptic nicotinic acetylcholine receptors', *Neuropharmacology*, 39, pp. 2715–25.

Goldman-Rakic, P. S. (1987), 'Circuitry of primate prefrontal cortex and regulation of behaviour by representational memory', in V. B. Mountcastle, F. Plum and S. R. Geiger (eds), *Handbook of Physiology*, pp. 373–417 (New York, NY: Oxford University Press).

Goldman-Rakic, P. S. (1995), 'Toward a circuit model of working memory and the guidance of voluntary motor action', in J. C. Houk, J. L. Davis and D. G. Beiser (eds), *Models of Information Processing in the Basal Ganglia*, pp. 131–48 (Cambridge, MA: MIT Press).

Goldman-Rakic, P. S. (1996), 'Regional and cellular fractionation of working memory', *Proceedings of the National Academy of Sciences of the United States of America*, 93, pp. 13473–80.

Graybiel, A. M. (1995), 'Building action repertories: memory and learning functions of the basal ganglia', *Current Opinion in Neurobiology*, 5, pp. 733–41.

Graybiel, A. M. (1998), 'The basal ganglia and chunking of action repertories', *Neurobiology of Learning and Memory*, 70, pp. 119–36.

Graybiel, A. M., et al. (1994), 'The basal ganglia and adaptive motor control', *Science*, 265, pp. 1826–31.

Hebb, D. O. (1968), 'Concerning imagery', *Psychological Review*, 75, pp. 466–77.

Heilman, K. M., and Gilmore, R. L. (1998), 'Cortical influences in emotion', *Journal of Clinical Neurophysiology*, 15, pp. 409–23.

Holden, C. (1979), 'Paul MacLean and the triune brain', *Science*, 204, pp. 1066–8.

Izquierdo, I., et al. (1980a), 'The role of opioid peptides in memory and learning', *Behavioural Brain Research*, 1, pp. 451–68.

Izquierdo, I., et al. (1980b), 'Beta-endorphin causes retrograde amnesia and is released from the rat brain by various forms of training and stimulation', *Psychopharmacology (Berl)*, 70, pp. 173–7.

Izquierdo, I., et al. (1984), 'Effect of various behavioral training and testing procedures on brain beta-endorphin-like immunoreactivity and the possible role of beta-endorphin in behavioral regulation', *Psychoneuroendocrinology*, 9, pp. 381–9.

Izquierdo, I., et al. (1990), 'Post-training down-regulation of memory consolidation by a GABA-A mechanism in the amygdala modulated by endogenous benzodiazepines', *Behavioural and Neural Biology*, 54, pp. 105–9.

Izquierdo, I., et al. (1991), 'Memory modulation by brain benzodiazepines', *Brazilian Journal of Medical and Biological Research*, 24, pp. 865–81.

Jo, Y. H., and Role, L. W. (2002), 'Cholinergic modulation of purinergic and GABAergic co-transmission at in vitro hypothalamic synapses', *Journal of Neurophysiology*, 88, pp. 2501–8.

Jones, E. G. (2002), 'Thalamic organization and function after Cajal', *Progress in Brain Research*, 136, pp. 333–57.

Jones, E. G., and Hendry, S. H. (1989), 'Differential Calcium Binding Protein Immunoreactivity Distinguishes Classes of Relay Neurons in Monkey Thalamic Nuclei', *The European Journal of Neuroscience*, 1, pp. 222–46.

Joseph, R. (1992), 'The limbic system: emotion, laterality, and unconscious mind', *Psychoanalytical Review*, 79, pp. 405–56.

Kawaguchi, Y., et al. (1995), 'Striatal interneurones: chemical, physiological and morphological characterization', *Trends in Neurosciences*, 18, pp. 527–35.

Kesner, R. P., and Wilburn, M. W. (1974), 'A review of electrical stimulation of the brain in context of learning and retention', *Behavioral Biology*, 10, pp. 259–93.

Kimura, D. (1963), 'Right temporal lobe damage: perception of unfamiliar stimuli after damage', *Archives of Neurology*, 8, pp. 264–71.

Kimura, D. (1969), 'Spatial localization in left and right visual fields', *Canadian Journal of Psychology*, 23, pp. 445–58.

Kimura, M. (1992), 'Behavioural modulation of sensory responses of primate putamen neurons', *Brain Research*, 578, pp. 204–14.

Kirkwood, A., and Bear, M. F. (1994), 'Hebbian synapses in visual cortex', *The Journal of Neuroscience*, 14, pp. 1634–45.

Kita, H., and Kitai, S. T. (1990), 'Amygdaloid projections to the frontal cortex and the striatum in the rat', *The Journal of Comparative Neurology*, 298, pp. 40–9.

Klemm, W. R., and Vertes, R. P. (1990), *Brain Stem Mechanisms of Behaviour* (New York, NY: John Wiley & Sons).

Konradi, C., Leveque, J. C. and Hyman, S. E. (1996), 'Amphetamine and dopamine-induced immediate early gene expression in striatal neurons depends on postsynaptic NMDA receptors and calcium', *The Journal of Neuroscience*, 16, pp. 4231–9.

Kreiter, A. K., and Singer, W. (1996), 'Stimulus-dependent synchronisation of neuronal responses in the visual cortex of the awake macaque monkey', *The Journal of Neuroscience*, 16, pp. 2381–96.

Krettek, J. E., and Price, J. L. (1977), 'Projections from the amygdaloid complex to the cerebral cortex and thalamus in the rat and cat', *The Journal of Comparative Neurology*, 172, pp. 687–722.

Lamm, O., and Gordon, H. W. (1984); 'Right hemisphere superiority in processing new symbols for arithmetic operators', *Acta Psychologica*, 57, pp. 29–45.

LeDoux, J. E. (1993a), 'Emotional memory systems in the brain', *Behavioural Brain Research*, 58, pp. 69–79.

LeDoux, J. E. (1993b), 'Emotional memory: in search of systems and synapses', *Annals of the New York Academy of Sciences*, 702, pp. 149–57.

LeDoux, J. (1998), 'Fear and the brain: where have we been, and where are we going?', *Biological Psychiatry*, 44, pp. 1229–38.

LeDoux, J. E. (2000), 'Emotion circuits in the brain', *Annual Review of Neuroscience*, 23, pp. 155–84.

LeDoux, J. E., et al. (1977), 'Cognition and commissurotomy', *Brain*, 100 (Pt 1), pp. 87–104.

Lee, F. J., et al. (2002), 'Dual regulation of NMDA receptor functions by direct protein–protein interactions with the dopamine D1 receptor', *Cell*, 111, pp. 219–30.

Lee, M. S., Rinne, J. O. and Marsden, C. D. (2000), 'The pedunculopontine nucleus: its role in the genesis of movement disorders', *Yonsei Medical Journal*, 41, pp. 167–84.

MacLean, P. D. (1970), 'The Triune brain, emotion and scientific bias', in F. O. Schmitt (ed.), *The Neurosciences. Second Study Program*, pp. 336–49 (New York, NY: Rockefeller University Press).

MacLean, P. D. (1972), 'Cerebral evolution and emotional processes: new findings on the striatal complex', *Annals of the New York Academy of Sciences*, 193, pp. 137–49.

MacLean, P. D. (1973), 'A triune concept of the brain and behaviour', in T. Boag and D. Campbell (eds), *The Hinks Memorial Lectures*, pp. 6–66 (Toronto: University of Toronto Press).

MacLean, P. D. (1977), 'The triune brain in conflict' *Psychotherapy and Psychosomatics*, 28, pp. 207–20.

MacLean, P. D. (1982), 'On the origin and progressive evolution of the triune brain', in E. Armstrong and D. Falk (eds), *Primate Brain Evolution*, pp. 291–316 (New York, NY: Plenum Press).

MacLean, P. D. (1985), 'Brain evolution relating to family, play, and the separation call'. *Archives of General Psychiatry*, 42, pp. 405–17.

MacLean, P. D. (1990), *The Triune Brain in Evolution* (New York, NY: Plenum Press).

Malenka, R. C., and Nicoll, R. A. (1999), 'Long-term potentiation – a decade of progress?', *Science*, 285, pp. 1870–4.

McClelland, J. L., and Goddard, N. H. (1996a), 'Considerations arising from a complementary learning systems perspective on hippocampus and neocortex', *Hippocampus*, 6, pp. 654–65.

McClelland, J. L., and Goddard, N. H. (1996b), 'The involvement of recurrent connections in area CA3 in establishing the properties of place fields: a model', *The Journal of Neuroscience*, 20, pp. 7463–77.

McClelland, J. L., et al. (1999), 'Understanding failures of learning: Hebbian learning, competition for representational space, and some preliminary experimental data', *Progress in Brain Research*, 121, pp. 75–80.

McEachern, J. C., and Shaw, C. A. (1999), 'The plasticity–pathology continuum: defining a role for the LTP phenomenon', *Journal of Neuroscience Research*, 58, pp. 42–61.

McGaugh, J. L., and Gold, P. E. (1976), in M. R. Rosenzweig and E. L. Bennett (eds), *Neural Mechanisms of Learning and Memory*, pp. 549–60 (Cambridge, MA: MIT Press).

McGaugh, J. L., Cahill, L. and Roozendaal, B. (1996), 'Involvement of the amygdala in memory storage: interaction with other brain systems', *Proceedings of the National Academy of Sciences of the United States of America*, 93, pp. 13508–14.

McGeorge, A. J., and Faull, R. (1989), 'The organization of the projection from the cerebral cortex to the striatum in the rat', *Neuroscience*, 29, pp. 503–37.

Medina, J. H., et al. (1992), 'Benzodiazepines in the brain. Their origin and possible biological roles', *Molecular Neurobiology*, 6, pp. 377–86.

Merzenich, M. M., and Sameshima, K. (1993), 'Cortical plasticity and memory', *Current Opinion in Neurobiology*, 3, pp. 187–96.

Metcalfe, J., Funnell, M., and Gazzaniga, M. S. (1995), 'Right-hemisphere memory superiority: studies of a split-brain patient', *Psychological Science*, 6, pp. 157–64.

Milner, B. (1968), 'Visual recognition and recall after right temporal lobe excision in man', *Neuropsychologia*, 6, pp. 191–209.

Milner, B., Squire, L. R., and Kandel, E. R. (1998a), 'Cognitive neuroscience and the study of memory', *Neuron*, 20, pp. 445–68.

Milner, B., Squire, L. R., and Kandel, E. R. (1998b), 'A synaptic model of memory – long-term potentiation in the hippocampus', *Nature*, 361, pp. 31–9.

Mink, J. W. (1996), 'The basal ganglia: focused selection and inhibition of competing motor programs', *Progress in Neurobiology*, pp. 381–425.

Mirenowicz, J., and Schultz, W. (1994), 'Importance of unpredictedness for reward responses in primate dopamine neurons', *Journal of Neurophysiology*, 72, pp. 1024–7.

Murphy, S. N., and Miller, R. J. (1989), 'Regulation of Ca++ influx into striatal neurons by kainic acid', *The Journal of Pharmacology and Experimental Therapeutics*, 249, pp. 184–93.

Myslivecek, J. (1997), 'Inhibitory learning and memory in newborn rats', *Progress in Neurobiology*, 53, pp. 399–430.

Nadel, L. (1992), 'Multiple memory systems: what and why', *Journal of Cognitive Neuroscience*, 4, pp. 179–88.

Nadel, L., and Bohbot, V. (2001), 'Consolidation of memory', *Hippocampus*, 11, pp. 56–60.

Nini, A., et al. (1995), 'Neurons in the globus pallidus do not show correlated activity in the normal monkey, but phase-locked oscillations appear in the MPTP model of parkinsonism', *Journal of Neurophysiology*, 74, pp. 1800–5.

O'Keefe, J., and Nadel, L. (1978), *The Hippocampus as a Cognitive Map* (Oxford: Clarendon Press).

Onn, S. P., West, A. R., and Grace, A. A. (2000), 'Dopamine-mediated regulation of striatal neuronal and network interactions', *Trends in Neurosciences*, 23(suppl.), S48–S56.

Packard, M. G., and Cahill, L. (2001), 'Affective modulation of multiple memory systems', *Current Opinion in Neurobiology*, 11, pp. 752–6.

Packard, M., et al. (1995), 'The anatomy of a memory modulatory system: from periphery to brain', in N. E. Speer, L. P. Speer and M. L. Woodruff (eds), *Neurobehavioural Plasticity: Learning, Development, and Response to Brain Insults* (Hillsdale, NJ: Lawrence Erlbaum Associates).

Petit, L., et al. (1998), 'Sustained activity in the medial wall during working memory delays', *The Journal of Neuroscience*, 18, pp. 9429–37.

Phelps, E. A., and Gazzaniga, M. S. (1992), 'Hemispheric differences in mnemonic processing: the effects of left hemisphere interpretation', *Neuropsychologia*, 30, pp. 293–7.

Picard, N., and Strick, P. L. (2001), 'Imaging the premotor areas', *Current Opinion in Neurobiology*, 11, pp. 663–72.

Pitkanen, A., et al. (2000), 'Reciprocal connections between the amygdala and the hippocampal formation, perirhinal cortex, and postrhinal cortex in rat. A review', *Annals of the New York Academy of Sciences*, 911, pp. 369–91.

Posner, M. I., and Petersen, S. E. (1990) 'The attention system of the human brain', *Annual Review of Neuroscience*, 13, pp. 25–42.

Quirarte, G. L., Roozendaal, B., and McGaugh, J. L. (1997), 'Glucocorticoid enhancement of memory storage involves noradrenergic activation in the basolateral amygdala', *Proceedings of the National Academy of Sciences of the United States of America*, 94, pp. 14048–53.

Rajadhyaksha, A., et al. (1999), 'L-Type Ca(2+) channels are essential for glutamate-mediated CREB phosphorylation and c-fos gene expression in striatal neurons', *The Journal of Neuroscience*, 19, pp. 6348–59.

Reese, N. B., Garcia-Rill, E., and Skinner, R. D. (1995), 'The pedunculopontine nucleus – auditory input, arousal and pathophysiology', *Progress in Neurobiology*, 47, pp. 105–33.

Rodriguez, E., et al. (1999), 'Perceptions shadow: long-distance synchronization of human brain activity', *Nature*, 397, pp. 430–3.

Roozendaal, B. (2000), '1999 Curt P. Richter award. Glucocorticoids and the regulation of memory consolidation', *Psychoneuroendocrinology*, 25, pp. 213–38.

Roozendaal, B., et al. (2002), 'Involvement of stress-released corticotropin-releasing hormone in the basolateral amygdala in regulating memory consolidation', *Proceedings of the National Academy of Sciences of the United States of America*, 99, pp. 13908–13.

Roozendaal, B., Quirarte, G. L., and McGaugh, J. L. (2002), 'Glucocorticoids interact with the basolateral amygdala beta-adrenoceptor – cAMP/cAMP/PKA system in influencing memory consolidation', *The European Journal of Neuroscience*, 15, pp. 553–60.

Rosen, G. D. (1996), 'Cellular, morphometric, ontogenetic and connectional substrates of anatomical asymmetry', *Neuroscience and Biobehavioral Reviews*, 20, pp. 607–15.

Ryan, L., et al. (2001), 'Hippocampal complex and retrieval of recent and very remote autobiographical memories: evidence from functional magnetic resonance imaging in neurologically intact people', *Hippocampus*, 11, pp. 707–14.

Schultz, W. (1998), 'Predictive reward signal of dopamine neurons', *Journal of Neurophysiology*, 80, pp. 1–27.

Schultz, W., and Romo, R. (1990), 'Dopamine neurons of the monkey midbrain: contingencies of responses to stimuli eliciting immediate behavioural reactions', *Journal of Neurophysiology*, 63, pp. 607–24.

Shi, W. X., and Rayport, S. (1994), 'GABA synapses formed in vitro by local axon collaterals of nucleus accumbens neurons', *The Journal of Neuroscience*, 14, pp. 4548–60.

Silkis, I. (2001), 'The cortico-basal ganglia-thalamocortical circuit with synaptic plasticity. II. Mechanism of synergistic modulation of thalamic activity via the direct and indirect pathways through the basal ganglia', *Biosystems*, 59, pp. 7–14.

Silkis, I. G. (1998), 'The unitary modification rules for neural networks with excitatory and inhibitory synaptic plasticity', *Biosystems*, 48, pp. 205–13.

Singer, W. (1993), 'Neuronal representations, assemblies and temporal coherence', *Progress in Brain Research*, 95, pp. 461–74.

Singer, W., and Gray, C. M. (1995), 'Visual feature integration and the temporal correlation hypothesis', *Annual Review of Neuroscience*, 18, pp. 555–86.

Skrebitsky, V. G., and Chepkova, A. N. (1998), 'Hebbian synapses in cortical and hippocampal pathways', *Reviews in the Neurosciences*, 9, pp. 243–64.

Snyder, G. L., et al. (1998), 'A dopamine/D1 receptor/protein kinase A/dopamine-and camp-regulated phosphoprotein (Mr. 32kDA)/protein phosphatase-1 pathway regulates dephosphorylation of the NMDA receptor', *The Journal of Neuroscience*, 18(24), pp. 10297–303.

Spence, C., et al. (2001), 'Representation of visuo-tactile space in the split brain', *Psychological Science*, 12, pp. 90–3.

Squire, L. R. (1992), 'Declarative and nondeclarative memory: multiple brain systems supporting learning and memory', *Journal of Cognitive Neuroscience*, 4, pp. 232–43.

Squire, L. R., Knowlton, B. and Musen, G. (1993), 'The structure and organization of memory', *Annual Review of Psychology*, 44, pp. 453–95.

Squire, L. R., and Zola, S. M. (1996), 'Structure and function of declarative and nondeclarative memory systems', *Proceedings of the National Academy of Sciences of the United States of America*, 93, pp. 13515–22.

Steriade, M., and McCarley, R. (1990), *Brain Stem Control of Wakefulness and Sleep* (New York, NY: Plenum Press).

Suri, R. E., and Schultz, W. (1999), 'A neural network model with dopamine-like reinforcement signal that learns a spatial delayed response task', *Neuroscience*, 91, pp. 871–90.

Surmeier, D. J., et al. (1995), 'Modulation of calcium currents by a D1 dopaminergic protein kinase/phosphatase cascade in rat neostriatal neurons', *Neuron*, 14(2), pp. 385–97.

Sutherland, G. R., and McNaughton, B. (2000), 'Memory trace reactivation in hippocampal and neocortical neuronal ensembles', *Current Opinion in Neurobiology*, 10, pp. 180–6.

Vaadia, E., et al. (1995), 'Dynamics of neuronal interaction in the monkey cortex in relation to behavioural events', *Nature*, 373, pp. 515–8.

Van Stegeren, A. H., et al. (1998), 'Memory for emotional events: differential effects of centrally versus peripherally acting beta-blocking agents', *Psychopharmacology (Berl)*, 138, pp. 305–10.

Varela, F. J. (1995), 'Resonant cell assemblies: a new approach to cognitive function and neuronal synchrony', *Biology Research*, 28, pp. 81–95.

Vincent, S. R. (2000), 'The ascending reticular activating system – from aminergic neurons to nitric oxide', *Journal of Chemical Neuroanatomy*, 18, pp. 23–30.

Williams, R. W., and Rakic, P. (1988), 'Elimination of neurons from the rhesus monkey's lateral geniculate nucleus during development', *The Journal of Comparative Neurology*, 272, pp. 424–36.

Yeterian, E. H., and Van Hoesen, G. W. (1978), 'Cortico-striate projections in the rhesus monkey: the organization of certain cortico-caudate connections', *Brain Research*, 139, pp. 43–63.

Zaidel, E. (1991), 'Language function in the two hemispheres following complete cerebral commissurotomy and hemispherectomy', in F. Boller and J. Grafman (eds), *Handbook of Neuropsychology*, pp 115–50 (Amsterdam: Elsevier, 1991).

Zaidel, E. (2001), 'Brain Asymmetry', in N. J. Smelser and P. B. Baltes (eds), *International Encyclopedia of the Social & Behavioral Sciences* (Amsterdam: Elsevier Science, 2004).

Introducing Roy Leighton

You can't look at a government initiative these days without the word *creativity* staring out at you as you throw the document into the bin. Since the heady days of 'Cool Britannia', when Beatles rip-offs and stuffed sheep were what we were all to aspire to, creativity has been a key element of educational expectation. We even have an Innovation Unit, where we can write to the government and ask for their permission to 'break the rules'. We had the DfES report 'All Our Futures: Creativity, Culture and Education', which was actually suppressed by the government because what the creative experts recommended actually contradicted government policy at the time, so they had to bring out a tweaked version. And, of course, we have 'Creative Partnerships', who can pay for a Zulu dance tribe to come in for the day with the Year 5s.

Yet creativity is far more than suspending the timetable for a few hours or playing music in the background during science. The true nature of creativity is about hearts and souls as well as minds and brains. It is about tapping into what makes us human at a very deep level and drawing on resources we may have never realised – or dared admit – we have.

As a species, we evolve through mutation – 'descent with modification', as it is known. It is the same for our thoughts. If we think what our parents thought then, as a species, we are doomed. It is vital for us to think new thoughts, to evolve by thinking about the challenges before us in new ways.

And this is just as much your responsibility as it is ours. The 'secret of success' for me at school was – and still is, as far as I can see – 'Wait to be told what to do, and do it well. Don't think for yourself, no independent thinking. Just sit there, be a good boy, do what you're told and you'll go far.' And in education you do. But, beyond the world of education, those people sitting around waiting to be told what to do will be left behind, sitting there wondering what's happening and why it's happening to other people. If you're like me, as a qualified teacher you will have done well at school in a system that rewards *not* being innovative and breaking the rules. As the creativity guru Sir Ken Robinson pointed out in an article sponsored by CNN and Shell and featured in *Fortune* magazine, 'Most national systems of education weren't designed to promote creativity: their purpose was conformity. They prioritised the subjects that seemed most relevant to working life: mathematics, languages and science.'

That's the system in which you and I did so well and why breaking the rules and thinking 'mutated' thoughts may be problematic for us. Yet, again as Robinson points out, the need for innovation, flexibility and creativity is greater now than ever: 'Young people leaving school in 2005 may be retiring in 2050. They're likely to change occupations several times. Many will have jobs that haven't been invented yet in businesses we can't imagine.'

There's a logical device called a *syllogism* that I have used in teaching creativity to all sorts of people from tax inspectors to convicted murderers.

If A equals B and B equals C, then A equals C. From a creativity point of view, consider it this way:

> To succeed we need to change.
> To change we need to be creative.
> Therefore, to succeed we need to be creative.

Creativity, then, is a necessary part of all our lives and far too important to be simply a question of sitting back and waiting for the muse to descend. There is a story told in creative circles (that would be a square, then) of an engineering company who felt that the creative types within the organisation were more productive and would contribute the most to the company's success. They brought in a team of psychoanalysts and psychologists to identify the really creative employees in order to help them tap this well of lucrative potential. After months of psychoanalysis and psychometric testing the conclusion drawn up by the team of experts was clear: the people who thought they were creative were creative; the people who thought they weren't, weren't.

That will be £30,000, please.

The more, then, you can think of yourself as a creative person, the more chance you've got to bring out your innate creativity. That said, this will be easier for some of you than others.

In October 2005, the august journal of scientific thought *New Scientist* dedicated a whole issue to creativity. In a lead article entitled 'Looking for inspiration', journalist Helen Phillips points out that creativity has little to do with intelligence: 'Creative people are intelligent, in terms of IQ tests at least, but only averagely or just above … IQ does not help boost creativity; it is necessary but not sufficient to make someone creative'. (Remember (see page 73), the government is trying to send everyone to college as a way to boost productivity!) What is needed, however, is a 'high value' placed on 'aesthetic qualities', 'broad interests, providing lots of resources to draw on and knowledge to recombine into new novel solu-

tions', 'an attraction to complexity' along with 'an ability to handle conflict'. She also points out that, 'Creativity comes to those who wait, but only those prepared to do so in a bit of a fog.'

Another key aspect of the creative temperament is the willingness always to look for more than the first right answer. 'Nothing is more dangerous than an idea when it's the only idea you have,' as someone once said. Yet, the education system often encourages this one-right-answer, convergent, guess-what's-in-the-teacher's-head model. (Have you heard the one about the teacher asking her class about the Vikings? 'What did the Vikings come in, children?' she asked, to which answers such as boats and longships were met with the reply, 'No, no, no! Now come on, children, we've done this – they came in hoards!')

Divergent thinking asks for as many right answers as you can possibly come up with because, maybe, Right Answer Number 10 is a much better – righter – answer than Right Answer Number 1. Try saying to a child, 'Is that your first answer or your best answer?' and see what they say. (Small boys, especially, are past masters at wanting to be 'first' regardless of how 'right' or creative the answer is.)

Creative ideas are like press-ups: the first one is easy but it gets harder the more you do. But, as with press-ups, it is the ones that you really have to struggle to achieve that are the ones that really count. As the article points out, drawing on the work of Guy Claxton and Paul Howard-Jones at Bristol University, '… the more we try and are stretched, the more creative our minds can be'.

And this chapter by Roy Leighton will stretch your creative fibres in a number of ways, reaching parts that success at school probably won't have reached. Any of you reading this who have heard Roy speak know that his was not a story of academic success, growing up, as he did, in the West Midlands in the seventies. School for him was a time lived in the shadow of older brothers who had not done well academically and whose behaviours tainted teacher expectations. ('Oh, you're a Leighton, are you? You're a yob, then, aren't you? You know what that means? It's a backwards boy!' And that was his first day at the secondary school.) For Roy, motivation at school was the motivation to get out of Wolverhampton. Creativity – developed through a career in drama, personal development, training and even television – came despite expectations that a job at the local bicycle works was the most he could aspire to.

Drawing on his own experience and successes, Roy wants to take you on a journey to the source of your own creativity guided by creative greats from Leonardo da Vinci to Mark Twain, Buddha to Goethe. All you'll need is an open mind, the knowledge that you are capable of creative genius, the understanding that our commitment to IQ has led us away from the path of real creativity and innovation, a can of Ronseal and a stout pair of walking boots.

Chapter 7
Living a Creative Life

Roy Leighton

In this chapter, I do not propose to look at creativity from a purely workplace-based point of view. The ideas and exercises included here may have an impact on the creativity and confidence that you bring to your work but I want to focus on the person first and the job second. If we want to live a truly creative life, then the starting point has to be ourselves, and not our work.

A few years ago, my father-in-law died. His name was Brian. He was a carpenter, craftsman and an all-round nice guy. He had a tremendous ability to create something both beautiful and practical from lumps of wood. He had the patience of a saint and would look at problems with both a creative and technical eye. He was, in my opinion, a real genius. I was amazed at his ability and gifts. But it was a talent that he did not regard as anything special. He was of the 'old school' that believed that, because, in a classroom environment, he was not good at maths and was not 'well read' (whatever that means), he was not clever or, to quote one of his former teachers, he 'was not the brightest button in the box'.

There is a contradiction here. The very nature of his work required him to possess a great understanding and application of mathematics (you do not build a cabinet by guesswork). He also used interpersonal, intrapersonal, verbal and linguistic skills to get a job done. This fact did not seem to eradicate his perception that he was a low achiever. His educational experience had done a good job of making sure that he did not 'get above his station'.

At the time of Brian's illness, my life had become 'comfortable'. My work was interesting. I was able to travel and had recently helped to devise and present a six-part series for the BBC (www.bbc.co.uk/health and go to 'Confidence Lab') exploring the psychology of change and confidence. The book that had accompanied the series had hit the top of the Amazon.co.uk bestsellers list. Life was good. Despite, or maybe because of, my success I felt I had slowed down. I was getting complacent and this was not doing my creativity much good at all. Yes, the programmes were successful and people were coming back for more, but I had become lazy, smug and content.

That was until my father-in-law and I were sitting in the garden of his bungalow in Northampton in May 2001 because he wanted to have 'a bit of a chat'.

The previous day had been a good one for Brian. He had been quite active. But today he was tired. He had been diagnosed a few weeks earlier with cancer of the liver and was told to 'put his affairs in order' as the doctors could do nothing for him. The day before our chat he had shown Pat, his wife, where all the things went in the shed. He was meticulously organised in every aspect of his life right down to what size nails went where.

The sun was shining as we sat together at the garden table. I was aware that he was dying and I wanted to spend as much time with this man whom I loved and from whom I had learned so much over the few years that I had known him. He turned to me and asked me if I remembered a trip to Hexham we had made a few years before. I did.

My wife and I had spent our honeymoon in Northumbria. We fell in love with the place and decided to return with Brian and Pat and took them on a walking holiday. He loved walking. He was a very fit man before he contracted cancer and he said that when he retired he was going to walk all the major walkways of the British Isles. A few months prior to our trip he bought a pair of walking boots. A fine, sturdy pair of boots that with regular use and the right care would last a lifetime.

'Do you remember my boots?' he asked. I did.

He pointed to the porch at the side of the bungalow – a neat, well-constructed, wooden-framed structure that he had built himself. 'The boots are in there,' he said. 'And do you know how many times I've used them since I retired?' I knew the answer: none. He had other priorities, things and people that needed him and his talents and the time just went. He would always be there for his family and friends. His own life was not high on his list of important activities. His life was always something that was on the to-do list that never got done. There was always tomorrow for the things that he was going to do for himself, or so he thought. Delaying living our life is something that most of us are prone to do.

He went on, 'I said that I was going to go on all these walks, do all these things, and I know now that I won't. I know you're busy, Roy, but you have a young family and are married to my only daughter.' I tried to make some attempt at humour but I could see where he was going with this. 'Don't waste a day. Don't put off doing things for yourself and your family, because you never get a day back, and one day you'll realise that you, like me, don't have any days left.' He leaned forward and looked at me with frustration, fear, anger and love: 'Wear your boots, Roy. Wear your boots!'

Four days after our conversation he slipped into a coma. Eight days later he was dead. He was 69 years old when he died and had led a life planning for an active retirement that he never got to live. I was left with too big a hole in my life and a determination to do what I needed to do to fulfil my potential and learn from this wonderful man's example.

So, what has this to do with creativity and confidence? Everything.

Over the past four years, I have sought to shift my own priorities to be more balanced and creative. This meant that I needed to take new action daily. There was/is no time to waste. This is it. This very moment. Too many of us are either frozen by our past ('This happened so I can't do that …') or fearful of our future ('But what if …?') that we do nothing until circumstances force us to. Even – or especially – the most active of us need to reflect on what we are doing and focus our activities not just on doing, but on doing the *right thing* and doing it *today*.

Being able to live aware of the possibility of change in each moment is the starting point to living a creative life.

In my twenties, I spent time studying theatre in Japan, where I was introduced to the concept of Honin Myo. This is the idea that the starting point for your life is always 'now'. Whatever our past actions, we can choose whether to reinforce a habit or change it.

How many of us are truly able to realise that our life is here and now, not there and then? Brian's advice forced me to review and restructure where I was and where I was going with my life. This required me daily, and in some cases moment by moment, to apply creativity and confidence to the circumstances in which I found myself. It is my experience that it is the development of these two abilities of creativity and confidence that will enable individuals and organisations to become truly 'independent thinkers'.

The starting point for any development has to be the ability to take action in the present and not to be held back by the experiences of the past or concerns for the future.

I realised through the experience of watching this man die that I had more choice over my life than I realised. I therefore intend, in this chapter, to have a look at what real creative intelligence or genius is, how to develop it for ourselves, why so many people lack the confidence to build their potential and introduce some exercises and activities to help you to slow down, refocus and redirect your creative energies to build confidence and achieve real happiness. In short, to create a personal foundation of creativity that will, as a matter of course, impact all other areas of your life, both personal and professional.

I want to make sure that you get something from this chapter that is going to be more that just an interesting academic exercise. At the same time I do not believe that anyone should launch themselves into activities that may have an impact on their lives without having some sound foundation for engaging in the process. It is a bit of a 'three-steps-to …' kind of thing, but I am a firm believer that synergy takes place best in a structure.

1. *Preparation*: What are the motivating factors for reading this chapter and putting the theory into practice?
2. *Understanding*: What is the theoretical argument and research for the opinions I am presenting and actions I am suggesting?
3. *Action*: A series of structured exercises to put the theory into practice over the coming ten weeks.

Preparation: how is this going to work?

Would you regard yourself as 'bright' or 'dull'? What were the expectations of you from the important people in your life (parents, teachers, partners, siblings etc.)? My father-in-law did not regard himself as 'intelligent'. He was 'good with his hands' but 'not a great book person'. Does this make him any less intelligent than someone who is 'good at words'? Intelligence is the ability, given the circumstances and situations in which you find yourself, to come up with solutions to the challenges facing you. It is all relative. If you need a new sash window frame making and fitting in your house, whom are you going to get round: a professor in Greek or a carpenter? Too many people who are not 'academic' have had a frustrating educational experience because they were forced to learn in a way that did not suit their core intelligence.

Harvard University professor Howard Gardner's theory of multiple intelligences is around thirty years old now, and too many organisations and individuals have benefited from this understanding for its credibility to be in any doubt. It is no longer a question of whether people can think and learn in a multitude of ways, because we know they can. The main point is whether the institutions, or rather the individuals running these institutions, have the ability to change, or are holding onto a belief system that is no longer valid. How many people do you know who are tied to systems and procedures that are ineffective and damaging because they lack the courage to admit there is a gap in their learning and lack the humility to ask for advice or help?

This limited understanding of what intelligence is has been a block to the confidence and creativity of thousands, if not millions, of people since the first IQ tests were devised more than a hundred years ago (1904) by Francis Binet in France. He created exercises to support children in their early years and beyond to learn and enjoy the process of learning. Indeed, this aim is, or should be, the key goal of schools today.

While Binet was sincere in his desire to develop and support children through his work, his ideas were manipulated by others to support ideologies that were more focused on segregation and supremacy than the development of the potential that lies within all of us. Indeed, Binet was furious when people distorted his findings to seek to prove such dubious theories, accusing them of 'brutal pessimism'.

In 1912, the German psychologist William Stern developed a formula to arrive at the now familiar intelligence quotient, or IQ:

$$IQ = \frac{\text{mental age} \times 100}{\text{chronological age}}$$

Thus was born the first modern intelligence test and people loved it. It was picked up and applied by countries that seemed to forget the very restricted context of its use. But then, as now, people like a mode of assessment that is clear, logical and neat. Well, learning and life are anything but. Learning is a messy process. To seek to force an overstructured mechanism on people just because it looks good theoretically is naïve, selfish and downright stupid.

Ken Richardson, in his remarkable book *The Making of Intelligence* (2000), explains that America was very keen on using IQ testing to 'help identify and remove "mental defectives" from the streets, curtail "the production of feeble-mindedness" and eliminate crime, pauperism and industrial inefficiency. By using I.Q. testing, the belief in America was that it would "preserve our state for a class of people worthy to possess it".'

Richardson goes on to talk about one Henry H. Goddard, who was

> concerned about the waves of immigrants then entering the United States, and persuaded the authorities to let him set up a testing station at the main immigration port. He thus managed to ensure that every individual was given the I.Q. test as they landed, using the tests in English through interpreters. In his account of the process, Goddard himself gives an ironic glimpse of the objectivity of the process. 'After a person has had considerable experience in this work,' he said, 'he almost gets a sense of what a feeble-minded person is so that he can tell afar off.' By these means, the country came to be told that 83

per cent of Hungarians, 79 per cent of Italians and 87 per cent of Russians were feebleminded. The amount of feeblemindedness he had exposed soon had psychologists pressing ardently for immigration controls, which eventually became law in 1924 … As many historians of science have pointed out, the subsequent growth of I.Q. was that of a blatantly racist tool. Those who followed Terman and Goddard in the I.Q.-testing movement advocated the sterilization of the feebleminded, a policy which was actually adopted by many states in America, resulting in tens of thousands of surgical operations.

Whom, at the time, did the Americans not want in the country? Well, they were not too keen on communists, those with possible links to the Mafia and the very poor. The tests reinforced the calls to keep these types of people out. Even today, if you wanted to become a citizen of the USA, you would have to take an IQ test.

IQ tests were also used by the American government to discern the level and role a soldier would play during World War One (low IQ = cannon fodder; high IQ = commanding officer and strategist). They thought that this was so successful a process that they created an education system where IQ testing was, and still is, embedded. I find it quite intriguing that the millions of men who died during the war were unable to have any detailed assessment of their IQ and learning skills before or after their military experience, which would give a more accurate picture of their perceived and actual abilities. This was partly because they were, in fact, now dead. Therefore, these tests lacked foundation and sufficient research to be credible. They were quick, though. And you could create easy-to-read 'statistical' data sheets, with columns and headings and everything that would reassure those of a very analytical, mathematical nature.

The fact that this mode of assessment and placement devised by the US military became the model for the US education system and one that the UK would eventually adopt gives serious cause for concern. Not only did we adopt it, but we developed it further, to be even more restrictive and divisive. In the same way the US used IQ test to reinforce racial stereotypes, the UK developed testing to support the class prejudices in our society and schools, and Brian, my father-in-law, was one of the many victims of this inadequate process of assessment and education.

In 1938, the Consultative Commission on Education – The Spens Report – in Britain declared,

> Intellectual development during childhood appears to progress as if it were governed by a single central factor, usually known as 'general intelligence' ... Our psychological witnesses assured us that it can be measured approximately by means of intelligence tests ... it is possible at a very early age to predict with accuracy the ultimate level of a child's intellectual power ... It is accordingly evident that different children ... if justice is to be done to their varying capacities, require types of education varying in certain important respects.

This led to the British Eleven-plus, which, even today (2005), is still used in parts of the UK. This affected, and continues to affect, the lives of many British people. When Brian was a boy, these assumptions made on a deeply flawed test were being used outside Britain – especially Nazi Germany – and affected lives in a more blatantly brutal and irrevocable way.

Some people have bought into the whole limited explanation of a person with IQ being someone who can remember stuff and is good at number-based exercises and solving puzzles. This is a profoundly simplistic approach to the understanding of intelligence.

I recently saw a television programme in which a mother had been 'hot-housing' her son in order to raise his IQ so as to make him into a child protégé. She had been doing it since prebirth. Her life since the conception of her child, by her own testament, had been focused on making him a 'genius'. So she and her husband did everything they could to develop this mini-'genius'. The results were impressive if not a little disturbing.

Unfortunately for all of them, especially for her young son, their definition of 'genius' was based on the lie that the only intelligence that is worthy of the term *genius* is IQ – specifically that aspect of genius that is good at logic and facts.

This child by the age of three could remember masses of information and could give the Latin name for caterpillars; he was a marvel with numbers and a very good chess player. But he was not the best chess player, and this was his problem. He was happy when he was winning. He built his whole self-worth on the belief that he was better than everyone else, and if this proved not to be the case he found it very hard. He could not beat everyone, and this is where the need for emotional, as well as academic, intelligence is vital.

There was a scene in the programme when someone beat him at chess and he could not handle failure and disappointment. He was four at the time. He showed severe signs of stress and anxiety because he had to get it right every time. He was groaning and rocking and, according to his mother, he would also self-harm. He had to win, she said, otherwise he would get distressed. Now call me old fashioned, but to turn a child into a self-destructive mini-computer does not equate to developing a true genius.

IQ testing is flawed, limiting and manipulative. IQ is a vital intelligence for anyone who seeks truly to learn and live effectively in the world. However, it is 'an' intelligence and not 'the' intelligence. While I am a great advocate of the development of intelligence, we have, if we are to become a truly independent thinker, to look beyond this narrow definition of what makes someone 'bright' or 'dull' and start to factor creativity into our understanding of intelligence.

The eminent psychologist Carl Jung (1875–1961) puts forward the argument that there are four core ways of engaging with the world that include, but go beyond, IQ. In brief they are:

- IQ – thought/mind;
- EQ – emotional/creative;

- PQ – physical/practical; and
- SQ – spiritual/intuitive.

Don't confuse spiritual with religious. There are some very spiritual people out there who would not regard themselves as religious, and there are some very 'religious' people out there who do not live their lives in a spiritually enlightened way at all.

Let us look at these four personality types and try to see which one best describes you.

IQ: This describes someone who is predominantly conscious-thought-based and sees the world in a very logical, structured, analytical way. Jason Wright, a friend, colleague and leading psychotherapist, describes this using the famous 'does what it says on the tin' advert as an analogy. If you are predominantly IQ-based, then you approach the world with the attitude that it really does 'do what is says on the tin'. If this is you, then you would probably find yourself attracted to, or using words and phrases, such as:

- reason;
- detailed argument;
- logic;
- how things work;
- justice;
- ethics;
- intellect;
- plan;
- narrative; and
- good sense.

EQ: This describes someone who is led more by emotions and is sensitive to how they feel about things. So, continuing with Jason's tin idea, you lead a life that wants to know how you 'feel about the tin'. Words and phrases that you would use or be drawn to are:

- values;
- relationship;
- empathy;
- consensus;
- morality;

- loyalty;
- responsibility to others;
- perceive others needs
- a feel for others; and
- sense of social obligation.

PQ: This describes someone who is predominantly hands-on or practical. For example, my father-in-law would be influenced by what can be 'done' rather than 'thought' or 'felt'. These people engage in the world at a very 'sensory' or 'sensual' manner and would see the tin as 'matter'. Key words and phrases would be:

- objective facts;
- sense events touch, taste, smell sound, sight;
- observation;
- here and now;
- matter is security;
- practical;
- utility;
- literal;
- use past experience; and
- need for physical evidence.

SQ: This describes someone who has spiritual or intuitive intelligence. If this is you, then you would be interested in the 'arena of the tin' and focus on or be drawn to the following words and phrases:

- the big picture;
- underlying patterns;
- imagination;
- vision;
- wonder;
- inspiration;
- enthusiasm;
- ingenuity;
- beyond senses; and
- interest in the unknown.

I should like to share with you a system and sequence of exercises that seek to develop all four intelligences. It is only when we are able to be open to, and engage with, all aspects of ourselves and the world that we become open to profound and effective creativity and deep and lasting confidence.

Brian was truly creative because he had developed these four intelligences, but, due to the negative effects of a confidence-draining education, he was not aware of his genius. How many people do you know who are doing great things, yet, due to their lack of confidence, are unable to recognise what everyone else sees clearly? Like the classroom teacher daily developing the learning and happiness of the children in their care, who in turn return home unaware of what skills and talents they have drawn on during the day. I am referring here to the teacher more than the children. It is staggeringly common to find people who are doing great work virtually unaware of their talents and abilities. They tend to focus more on what they have not done rather than what they have. This is not only inaccurate but exhausting.

Genius and the evolution of our intelligences is not the limited domain of the chosen few. We all have the capacity, depending on where we are, whom we are with and what we are doing, to experience one or more of these states. However, there is, for most of us, one of those intelligences that we feel most drawn to and one that we would not feel too comfortable with. However, if we are to become truly independent in our thinking and our actions, we have to be open to how other people are developing their own individuality and gifts and allow them to do so. When we block or dismiss the lives of others we are, in a very tangible way, limiting our own potential for real and lasting evolution.

Think about it. You spend a good deal of time dismissing the opinions of someone or the lifestyle of a whole group of people and then something happens that forces you to change your outlook. If you are so embedded in a belief system that makes you feel comfortable, you run the risk of not accepting new ideas and understandings because you do not, or cannot, change. Unfortunately, change is the one key thing you need if you are going to develop.

Why do we so often refuse to recognise that we have not got all the answers and are, and will

only ever be, on a path of evolution? It is often because we do not fully understand the process of change. Unless we are aware of this dynamic cycle we will at best achieve *some* of what we could and, at worst, not even be aware of what we are capable of. How many of us live our lives unaware of the impact we could have on the world? Awakening to this potential requires an understanding and application of the process of change, which is a three-stage process:

1. Opportunity
2. Experience
3. Learning

We have, at every second of our lives, the *opportunity* to make a new choice. Every second is another chance to change our minds and to take a new action that will lead us in a direction and to a goal that we dream of. Every second. That means now, this moment. It is not going to come by again. We need, if we are serious about evolving, to take the moment and move forward.

If we take, or create, an *opportunity*, then this will invariably lead to an *experience* of some kind. For example, if we want to learn to sing, at some moment we are going to have to open our mouth and produce a sound, however ghastly or sublime. Without a commitment to action there is no experience, only the *longing* for the experience.

And, as William Blake so dramatically put it, 'He who desires, but does not act, breeds pestilence.'

The longer we avoid engaging in something, the harder it becomes to start it. This can go on for a long time. Even a lifetime. What, at this time in your life, have you avoided doing? You know the thing that you have wanted to do, dreamed of doing, longed to do but have not quite got around to doing. What dreams have you given up on? We all have something.

A survey was done with old people nearing the twilight of their years. They were asked what, if they could live their lives over again, they would do differently. The common response was that they would take more risks. So, how about it? Are you up for risk or are you putting your effort into staying in the same place instead of moving on?

If you take, or make, the *opportunity* for change you will have a new *experience* of some kind. This experience could be a good, bad or indifferent one, but it is an experience, and experience is power because it leads us to *learning*. When we do, we learn. If we do not do, we imagine. Even if our learning has been a sad or disappointing one, it is still a lesson learned. When we gain some learning, because we had the courage to have the experience, we deepen our confidence, which will make us more open to seek more opportunities, which leads to experiences – and so the cycle of evolution continues.

The block between having an opportunity to do something new, different, exciting or radical is FEAR – 'False Expectations Appearing Real'. *Fear* is just another word for our negative imagination. The thing that we imagine and not what we know. We fear failure, ridicule and embarrassment, so we do not do. Should we be able to conquer our fear, then there would be no block to developing our potential, our achievements or our happiness. As Mark Twain said, 'Confront the thing you fear, and the death of fear is certain.' How right he was!

Fear is more our imagination than fact. Our past experiences will influence our future action and no one is advocating action without being aware of the warning signals. After all, our fear mechanism is the means of protecting our survival as a species. It is the balance between being aware of a state of 'fear' and then choosing the correct action to move forward, using our fear as a lever and not a barrier.

Despite all my father-in-law's gifts he was lacking one key skill for his own fulfilment. This was the ability to look beyond the limitations his educational and social experiences had imposed upon him and the vast majority of his generation. It is never too late to change or learn. If you really believe that 'you cannot teach an old dog new

tricks', then you have been well trained to go only as far as you believe you are capable of and feel you deserve.

When a baby elephant is born into captivity, it spends the first few months of its life with a big chain around its leg and this chain is attached to a wall to prevent it from escaping. At this early stage in its life it cannot break free. After a while it stops trying to move away from where it is. Once this belief system is embedded in the elephant's mind the trainer has only to put a chain around the elephant's foot to stop it moving. The elephant believes itself to be chained to a wall when in fact it could walk away at any moment.

So, what belief systems do you have that are holding you back from advancing?

Understanding: the theoretical bit

In his book *The School of Genius*, the eminent psychiatrist Anthony Storr (1988) says that to develop a creative life there are four stages that need to take place:

- the mental state during which new ideas arise or inspiration occurs;
- forming links between formerly disparate entities;
- continuous personal development because 'no creator is ever satisfied with what he [or indeed she] has done'; and
- the need to create time and space for oneself because 'the creative process and the process of individuation are both phenomena taking place largely in solitude'.

Let's work through these four theoretical stages one by one. So, how do we develop a mental state for creating new ideas and being inspired?

Carl Jung was big advocate of creating openings for independent thinking. In fact, he encouraged his patients to engage in what he called 'active imagination'. We have all had the experience of 'sleeping on' a problem and waking with a new thought or idea to help solve an issue. Jung took this several steps further. He would suggest that the state of reverie, sometimes described as being both asleep and awake, was what was needed to start the whole process of 'active imagination'. When you take time to think about it, it is just common sense. Unless, we create time for new thoughts, we will just continue unquestioningly doing what we have done before, or we just do as we are told, with the varying degrees of angst and frustration that this creates.

This openness to new thoughts is one that most of us avoid because, the older we get, the more 'wired' our attitudes, beliefs and actions become. Unless we can allow ourselves the openness to consider new ideas, new paths and new actions, we will for ever lock ourselves into a life of more of the same. As the old adage states, 'If we always do what we have always done, we will always get what we have always got.'

In the past, states of reverie advocated by Jung have been assumed to be reserved for poets and artists, not for the common person, businessperson, administrative type or carpenter, like the Brians of this world. Yeats and Wordsworth may have given expression to this enlightened state, and, as a starting point for true independence, we need to create it regularly for ourselves.

This state of challenge is vital for anyone serious about developing a life, home or work that is creative and evolving. Where that place is will be different for all of us, but all of us need that place if we are to return to a state where we can assess where we have got to and set our sights for where we need now to go. An aeroplane is continually being blown off its path and gets to its destination only by regular checks and changes. We need to do the same constant seeking and refining to keep our own life on course.

The second stage for achieving a creative life, forming links between formerly disparate entities is one that I find fascinating.

Is it possible that no man or woman is an island? Are there really links and pathways that we cannot see but are followed and create connections? Have you ever had that situation when someone is constantly on your mind and the phone goes and it's them? It is just another form of connectivity that we do not fully understand. It does not make it less real, but it makes our knowledge, at this moment, partial and incomplete.

If we are to deepen our capacity to be really *in* the world, then we need to be open to other points of view. Nothing profound or spiritual about that, it is just a statement of fact. We may not feel comfortable around people who do not see the world in the way that we do. However, we have to seek to understand the position and perspective of others and not just insist that they see the world as we do, since this just creates conflict. So many of us never master the art of 'independent thinking' because we are too worried about how others will think and react. What if we listened more to our intuition or gut and took action based on how we felt and not just on what we thought we 'knew'?

There is a link between hard facts and creativity. Leonardo da Vinci was fascinated by the interconnectedness of things. In one of his many notebooks, da Vinci uses water as an image for interconnectivity and writes, 'Every part is disposed to unite with the whole, that it may thereby escape from its own incompleteness.' That is an image worth reflecting on.

Da Vinci was one of the early advocates of 'whole-brain thinking'. Although he did not have the medical evidence to support his statement, 'Seek the art in science and the science in art', he had an awareness backed up by curiosity and investigation. They are connected. You may not be able to hold and touch these truths, but we are able to engage with them, influence them and be influenced by them. This interaction is happening every second. Just because one may not fully understand something intellectually, it does not make it any less of a truth.

Personally, I have an immense mistrust and dislike of the theory of gravity. I don't fully understand it and I don't like the implications that it is influencing my life. Despite this, I am still affected by it and I am still sitting here writing, and nothing, myself included, is floating about defying gravity, despite my ignorance and dislike of the whole gravity thing.

Many individuals, especially artists, have waxed lyrical about the interconnectedness of themselves and their surroundings. This is all well and good and could reinforce the notion that creativity is some deluded romantic, prancing around the countryside in a Mr Darcy outfit (all loose-fitting shirt and tight-fitting breeches), speaking to the flowers and feeling 'at one' with nature. But this sense of interconnectedness is felt and explained by scientists as well. In *The School of Genius*, Storr makes this point clearly:

> This linking process is obvious in scientific creativity, in which a new hypothesis reconciles or supersedes ideas which were previously thought to be incompatible. Kepler had been able to describe the motions of the planets round the sun; Galileo had described the motions of bodies upon the earth. Until Newton, the sets of laws governing theses two types of motion had been regarded as quite separate. But Newton's idea that gravity could operate at vast distances enabled him to combine the discoveries of Kepler and Galileo in such a way that the motions of bodies in the heavens and bodies upon the earth could be seen to obey the same universal laws.

Isn't this great? Newton was making links and breakthroughs, challenging the beliefs of earlier scientific leaders. We now find that Newton's ideas are being challenged further. (Look at the work of Einstein, Stephen Hawking and Rupert Sheldrake for more on this.) Newton was able to link his knowledge of one thing with another memory and come up with a new theory. This is creativity. This is genius. Unlike the pseudo boy genius referred to earlier who was good at chess but challenged in life.

To be able just to 'regurgitate facts' but unable to form creative links between the information you have and the challenge facing you now is not an indication of genius. It is a good party trick or, at its most acute, a mental or neurological disorder. Yes, a good memory is a skill that can be useful and we all need to develop this skill. But if this is the only skill that we give a value to and the other 'soft' skills such as empathy, creativity and interpersonal and intrapersonal abilities are overlooked, then we miss the point of what being intelligent is. We confine ourselves for ever to be shackled to a dark cave of our own making and delude ourselves that we can see and understand the world when we can see only partial truth and shadows of possibilities. (Read Plato's 'The Cave' in book VII of his *Republic* (Plato, 1968) for more on this.)

It is the connections in the brain that make it function, and it is the interconnectedness between ourselves, others and the environment that make us whole. When we are whole we feel confident and when we are confident we are open to create. Indeed, I would go far as to say that to lead a creative life is to live a life of true humanity. Deny a person an environment to create and you deny them the capacity to be fully alive. This stifling of the ability to think and learn in children can have a lasting impact on their confidence and subsequent happiness for the rest of their lives.

My own home life, although for the most part happy, did not provide the best house for learning and thinking. I was brought up in a not very large three-bedroom council house with six siblings and two parents. Five of these were my brothers and all six of us shared one room crammed with three bunk beds, a fitted wardrobe, an airing cupboard, a chest of drawers and a box for each of our personal effects under the beds. When anyone wanted/needed to study, we had to negotiate space.

The kitchen table was the prime spot and was given over to use in order of age. Robert, my eldest brother, would have first call, and then we would work down (Tony, Rosemary, Martin, Steven, myself and last, and very often least, Colin). If you could not get to the table, you would have the table at the back of the lounge. Try concentrating on your homework when you have a television at the other end of the room and anything up to eight other people engaged in conversations/arguments and obviously having more fun than you. If this proved too much, then you could try to claim a bed to work on, where you would often just fall asleep.

Now I do not relate this experience because I want your sympathy (although at a deeper level I obviously do), but to highlight that where we are and the environment that we are in has a direct impact on how we are feeling and how we succeed in the tasks we are attempting to perform. I am fortunate to have been bombarded with extraordinary opportunities and environments since leaving home that have challenged me and forced me to reflect, relearn and refine my understanding, outlook and abilities. It is this constant challenge to our evolution and never just plateauing out when we achieve an 'easy life' that is the essence of living creatively.

We are now at Stage 3 in Storr's guide for developing a creative life. A creative and confident life is the ability continuously to develop a mind of independent thinking for as long as you live because 'no creator is ever satisfied with what he has done'.

This is not to disregard what you have achieved. It is rather to advance continuously and not to get bogged down with a complacent or critical belief system. Never before has the world needed people who can let go of belief systems that they have outgrown. For this to happen, you need to understand the process of managed, continuous evolution and change.

For all of us, to one degree or another, the process of change can be deeply uncomfortable or an exciting and perfectly natural process. We do not like to fail. Like the 'genius' boy referred to

earlier in this chapter, we tend to react badly to the idea that we have to accept new and challenging ideas if doing so reveals a limitation in our current skills or knowledge. But this, like our boy, can make us feel a bit of a failure. Our fear of failure, ridicule or the reactions of other people will block our pathway to action and evolution.

And finally, Stage 4: 'the creative process and the process of individuation are both phenomena taking place largely in solitude'. How are you at creating time for and with yourself? The exercises that I am going to go through in the next and final section are all linked with this fourth stage: solitude. We need to create space for reflection and to ponder on our own needs, or else we run the risk of burnout and resenting those people and places that are taking up our time. If we cannot create time for ourselves, our time with and for others will be the poorer for this. Charles Handy (1999) calls this need for a balance between personal and social gain 'proper selfishness', where the gain in any activity or undertaking is for all parties, including ourselves.

This is not necessarily material gain – in fact, preferably not just material, but other gains as well: how we feel about ourselves; how to work and live better with other people; how the activity is adding to our lives in some way. Why do we, in different circumstances, seem either to give at the cost of our own happiness or to take to the detriment of other people? We need to develop 'proper selfishness' if we are to get to evolve, despite our feelings of low self-worth or concerns about what others might think or what will happen to our world if we did change.

Educators are particularly prone to giving to others and putting themselves way down the list of priorities. If you fall among that number, then have a rethink. You are your best friend and most valuable commodity. Take some time for a period of creative reflection for yourself and see the benefit to those around you.

Action: wear your boots!

The following are a number of exercises that take you through four stages to help let out of the box your own creative genius. I have sought to make them practical and clear, building on the theories and ideas covered in the previous pages. So, if you're sitting comfortably, let us begin.

1. Creating the mental state for new ideas to arise and inspiration to occur

Engage in daily periods of 'active imagination' in order to review, refocus and renew your direction. The inspiration for this exercise comes from the excellent work of Julia Cameron, in particular her book, *The Artist's Way* (1994).

First, look to Leonardo da Vinci for an example of creative genius and get yourself a plain notebook that you like the look of. Once you have your book use it to jot down thoughts, quotations, comments, observations, doodles, drawings and various ramblings.

I would like to introduce you to a ten-week process to assist you in developing your creativity and confidence. The first exercise is for 21 days, as this is, I believe, the minimum time required to change a thought pattern or belief.

Give yourself 20 minutes a day, at the very start of the day, for 21 days, where you are not disturbed and can create 'the mental state during which new ideas arise or inspiration occurs' I referred to earlier. Allow yourself the luxury of stopping. This may require that you set the alarm 20 minutes earlier than usual. Once you are awake, get up, pick up your book and write.

First, ask yourself the question, 'What is taking up my thoughts and how does this make me feel?' Write the answer.

Ask yourself the next question, 'Intuitively, what should I do?' Having done this, write down one specific action that you are going to take today.

This exercise stimulates all your four core intelligences (IQ, EQ, PQ and SQ referred to earlier).

Once you have done that put the pen on the paper and just write whatever you want for five minutes. It could be creative; it could be your thoughts and concerns. It does not matter what you write, just write something. Even if you write, 'What am I going to write?' again and again, then do so. If this is what it takes to lubricate your thoughts, then do it. Action is the key thing here. Do not wait for the muse to descend, and do not criticise your writing. Worry not about the punctuation, grammar or spilling. Once five minutes have gone by, stop and reread everything that you have written so far.

In the evening, return to the book for a further ten minutes and capture your thoughts. Did you do what you said? How was it? If you did not do what you said you were going to do, what stopped you? Was it yourself, others or your environment? How can you move forward to get over any obstacle?

At the end of the 21 days, sit down and read your daily scribbling from beginning to end. Write one thing that you observed about yourself and one thing that you are now going to do to further your own human evolution. Then get on and do it.

If you miss a day, you should be starting the whole process again. Even if you do twenty days and miss the last! This activity is about consistency of purpose and changing habit. You do not do that in well-intentioned spurts of activity. However much of an effort you might find this to be, it is important to go the whole journey. We change habits with consistent effort and constant yearning. Here is an old Japanese saying about completing a task that you might want to write down and focus on to inspire you to keep going when time, circumstances or laziness get in the way: 'The journey from Kamakura to Kyoto takes twelve days. If you travel for eleven then stop, how will you be able to admire the moon over the capital?' (Kyoto, not Tokyo, was the capital at the time.)

Now, I know that some of you will be thinking, 'Where's the creativity in this?'; 'What about breaking the rules?'; 'Too much structure!'; 'Too many rules!' Do not confuse disorder and ego with creativity. Creativity is not the exclusive domain of those of a theatrical bent. It takes many forms. Sometimes it is spontaneous and explosive and sometimes it is analytical, structured and focused. This exercise is demanding because of its structure, and, if it challenges your preferred learning, working and thinking style, then so much the better. If you did only the exercises that you felt comfortable with or were good at, where would be the learning in that?

A common block to creating the circumstances for our own personal development is that we lack sufficient self-confidence and belief in our own value to invest time and effort to change. So we change nothing, reinforcing a negative self-image, and the longer we leave it the harder it is to change. If your belief system is that you cannot learn, change or be happy, then your brain will agree. Henry Ford said, 'If you think you can, or think you can't, you're right.' So, how open are you to considering that things could be other than they are? How open-minded are you to new ideas, processes or beliefs? This question brings us beautifully to our next stage.

2: Forming links between formerly disparate entities

This is a big one, but I am going to focus on our link with the environment. We influence it and it influences us at many levels and I would like to deepen our understanding of the constant dynamic. There are many ways to raise awareness of our relationship with ourselves and our environment, but I would like to suggest three.

Exercise Number 1 for raising your awareness of your relationship with yourself is split into several stages. Do this during the same period of your early-morning writing.

First, find yourself a quiet spot and take out your journal and a pen. Make sure that you can have an hour without distraction, and do it in the first week (if not the first day) of this ten-week challenge.

Without thinking too much, start asking yourself questions and write these questions down. Do not stop until you have reached one hundred. I know that sounds a lot, but do it, and do not let your mind get in the way. Stay there until you have finished and write fast. Your questions can be personal (Why do I allow people to make me feel bad about my life?), work-related (How can I work less and earn more?), family-focused (How can I improve my relationship with my children/spouse/mother-in-law?) or general (Why is the sky blue?). Keep the questions coming and do not leave too long a pause between writing.

When you have got to one hundred, go back and look for any key themes (time, money, confidence, love, work worries etc.). Highlight the key questions and then go through again and choose the top ten questions.

Write the questions big and bold on ten separate pieces of paper and put the papers in ten envelopes. Seal the envelopes, writing nothing on the outside of the envelopes. You should now have ten questions in ten envelopes and no way of knowing which question is in which envelope. This is where the fun starts and a bit of synchronicity may occur. Leave the envelopes for at least 24 hours but make sure you start reviewing the envelopes within the first week. I want you to focus on one question for each of the ten weeks.

When you do decide to come back to the questions, place the ten envelopes on a table and choose one. Put the other envelopes away and focus on the one envelope you have chosen. Imagine that you have an answer or piece of advice about the question or concern posed in this envelope. I know that you will not know what is in the envelope, but this exercise is about refining your intuition and 'gut' feeling.

Give yourself a few minutes to stop and breathe. When relaxed, pick up your pen and write on the envelope the advice or answer that is floating about in your head. It is not important that you know what is in the envelope – just go with what your intuitive voice is saying.

When you have written your answer, open the envelope and read the question. Does the answer make sense? If it does answer your question, then do what you suggested. Take the action that you have advised yourself to take and make sure you do it, or start it, within 24 hours.

If you do not think what you have written answers the question you had in your envelope, then change the answer or advice so that it fits and then take action. Again, once you have written down your advice to yourself, begin the process within 24 hours.

Spread this exercise over ten weeks. Choose one question/envelope a week, using the same technique of intuition, creative reflection and action.

Now, I admit that the above exercise could sound a little weird but all I am seeking to do is to assist you in developing all of your core human capabilities and not just rely on one. This is why I want you to work from the one that is usually least exercised (intuitive/spiritual) towards the most common (thought/mind). I am not seeking to exclude, merely to refocus.

When I did this exercise I found it both intriguing and helpful. It also brought up some challenging and upsetting things that I had pushed to one side earlier in my life. Be aware of this, but not fearful of it. One thing that you can guarantee when you embark on a creative journey is that at some point you will have to confront some of the things that have blocked you in the past and begin to deal with them.

Over the ten weeks you will not only find answers to your questions and take action. You will, if you commit to the exercise, see that, when you allow your intuition to work, your capacity

for problem solving and trusting your own gut feeling is strengthened. This is a vital skill for 'forming links between formerly disparate entities' – Storr's second stage above. Unless, we can engage with the four core aspects of our selves – mind (IQ), heart (EQ), hands (PQ) and gut (SQ) – how are we going to engage fully and develop these aspects of other people and the world in which we live?

This is a demanding task, especially for people whose lives have an impact on the creativity, confidence and learning of others, such as teachers. Whatever we may have achieved up until now, when we are responsible for the development of others we cannot cease from challenging ourselves and deepening our understanding and, most importantly, our capacity to learn. On to the next exercise.

3: No creator is ever satisfied with what they have done

Find a quiet twenty minutes with someone you trust. Have your journal ready and ask them the following three questions. This is a listening exercise, not a dialogue. Jot down notes of what they have said and do not seek to clarify, justify or intervene. Listen. Really seek to hear with every cell in your body and suspend your desire to comment. If you do want to speak say thank you. You can talk about what they have said but only once you have had time to reflect and to 'sleep' on it (see the earlier reference to Carl Jung for the reasons why).

So, pen at the ready, DO NOT DISTURB sign on the door, comfy chairs and a friend? Let's go.

Question 1: What are my strengths? Let them tell you and jot down their answer. Note your reaction to being paid a compliment. Do you get embarrassed? Are you sitting there thinking that they have got you mixed up with someone more capable or that they are just being nice? Remember; say nothing but thank you. Listen and observe yourself and how you respond to positive feedback.

Question 2: What are my areas for development? This is the politically correct way of saying, how am I screwing up? Use the most appropriate language for the person you are speaking with. Again, write down what they say, since you may forget what they said, especially if you do not like what it is that they are saying.

Question 3: How can I be more sensitive? Again, listen and take note.

I would suggest that you have this conversation with family members, friends and work colleagues. Having done this, you will find that your awareness of how you are impacting people, both positively and negatively, will be highlighted. The challenge then is doing something about it.

This exercise should be done once a week with a different person per week for ten weeks, with you taking time to think about what they have said dispassionately, critically and with an open mind. And so to our last, and vital, condition for developing independent thinking and creativity.

4: The creative process and the process of individuation are both phenomena taking place largely in solitude

The exercises I have suggested have a strong element of time for yourself. You may find it a challenge to give yourself time or imagine that you are being self-centred. However, it is these acts of reflective solitude that will give you the space you need to become more of a 'centered self'. Taking daily action for you, others and the place where you are is not only the path to genius, but it is the action of the truly wise.

If anything that I, or my fellow Independent Thinking associates, have written makes you consider taking some action or making some degree of change in your own life, do not delay. Your potential is vast and if you make changes to develop your own confidence and creativity your example to others will be a signal that they can change as well. Do not let your fear prevent you from taking the next step. Do not allow the desire to know exactly where you are going to end up prevent you from starting, or restarting, your journey.

You will arrive at different places and achieve new results and outcomes as you progress. While it might have been reassuring in the past to believe the lie that everything is predictable, from the fact that the earth is flat or that one kind of person is 'more intelligent' than another, this is no longer the case. Celebrate your moments of 'enlightenment', but do not hold onto them as the 'truth'. They may be a 'truth' but 'all truth' is always going to be out of our reach and it is in our stretching that we grow.

Most of all, *do*.

There is a saying of the Buddha: 'If you know, but do not do, you do not know.' Genius is action combined with knowledge and wisdom. If it is merely known but not acted upon, it is not really understood. The inability to put what you know into action is, as I said earlier, not real knowledge, but storage.

Lines, often attributed to Goethe, sum this call to action succinctly:

> What you can do, or think you can, begin it.
> Boldness has genius, magic and power within it.

When you take action things and people will come to support you in a way you could never dream. But you have to take action.

And you have to take action *today*.

Brian was great at taking action, but believed the lie that there could only be one kind of genius. While he derived great satisfaction from a job well done, he seldom, if ever, publicly celebrated his achievements and abilities. He was painstaking in his preparation and his delivery, and the outcomes were often extraordinary. However, because *he* could do it, it never occurred to him that what he did was anything special. If he did have moments of really recognising his genius, then he did not make a 'song and dance' about it. I never saw him say or do anything that could lead anyone to say he was getting 'too full of himself'. He just got on and did it. He acted daily. That was his real genius. He was, in every sense of the phrase, a man of action.

So, in the words of my much missed, much loved father-in-law, 'Wear your boots!'

References and select bibliography

Cameron, Julia (1994), *The Artist's Way* (London: Souvenir Press Ltd).

Handy, Charles (1999), *The Hungry Spirit* (London: Random House Business).

Hochswender, Woody, Martin, Greg, and Morino, Ted (2001), *The Buddha in your Mirror: Practical Buddhism and the Secret Search for Self* (Santa Monica, CA: Middleway Press).

Jung, Carl (1961), *Memories, Dreams and Reflections* (London: Collins, Fount Paperbacks).

Plato (1968), *The Republic of Plato*, translated with notes and interpretive essay by Allan Bloom (New York: Basic Books Inc.).

Richardson, Ken (2000), *The Making of Intelligence* (New York: Columbia University Press).

Storr, Anthony (1988), *The School of Genius* (London: Andre Deutsch Ltd).

Taylor, Ros, Scott, Sandra, and Leighton, Roy (2001), *Confidence in Just Seven Days* (London: Vermilion).

Introducing Michael Brearley

Next time you charge something to your Visa card, spare a thought for one Dee Hock. He's the man behind the launch of Visa in the 1970s, a company that has been referred to as the 'world's first trillion-dollar company'. Dee Hock was the man charged (excuse the pun) with the job of making sense of what was then the chaotic new world of credit cards produced by individual banks all over the US. His achievement is quite staggering, not because of its size – although a trillion dollars is not to be sniffed at – but because of the fact that I bet that you have never really thought about how Visa works or heard of Dee Hock.

One of Hock's favourite party ticks at conferences to demonstrate this point is to ask people, 'Raise your hands if you recognise this.' And he holds up his own Visa card. Of course every hand goes up. It is one of the most recognisable brands in the world, up there with Coke, McDonald's and Chorley FM. 'Now,' Hock goes on to say, 'how many of you can tell me who owns it, where its headquarters are, how it's governed or where to buy shares?'

It hasn't entered anyone's mind even to consider the questions and, of course, no one knows. Which is exactly the idea. As Hock points out, 'The better an organisation, the less obvious it is.'

I mention Mr Hock and his credit-card company at this point because the secret of Visa's success draws on exactly the same sorts of ideas and innovations as Mike Brearley so ably brings together in this next chapter. What both Mike and Hock advocate is a style of leadership that is nothing to do with confrontation or challenge, with

rallying the troops and leading from the front, over the top and into the breach, dear colleagues, where the leader is at the pointy end of a hierarchical chain of command that stretches from the head's office to the far-off distant reaches of the school (the bits where new carpet invested in for the reception area hasn't quite reached).

In fact, you may be interested to know that such a hierarchical organisational structure is based on the one used by the Prussian army to get messages to the front line, and was hijacked by the newly emerging world of industry in the 1870s, since it was the only large organisation structure around at the time.

With our foothold now well established in the twenty-first century, leadership needs to change quite significantly. Increasingly, it is becoming apparent that the only management expertise that really counts is, first and foremost, the management of one person – yourself. And that management of self means managing, in Hock's words, 'one's own integrity, character, ethics, knowledge, wisdom, temperament, words and acts', adding, 'Without management of self no one is fit for authority no matter how much they acquire, for the more authority they acquire the more dangerous they become.'

Sound like someone you know? I worked in advertising for a while and met people who wouldn't recognise integrity, ethics or temperament if it slapped them in the face with a rolled-up copy of *Campaign* magazine, let alone manage them. I didn't stay long.

In fact, a quick look at Hock's list of management priorities reveals the following: (1) manage yourself; (2) manage those who have authority over you; (3) manage your peers; and (4) no, that's it – management of the people below you in your chain of command is irrelevant if you focus your management skills on the things that really matter.

The school that Mike Brearley describes, the emotionally intelligent school, is one that Dee Hock would be proud of. More than just a system of systems with a pecking order that stretches from the governors to the children, it is a community that learns together and grows together and places as paramount the fact that we are creatures who work best when we are in tune with our own and others' emotional needs.

Mike writes from the point of view of someone who not only has worked in the school system from the inside, reaching the dizzying heights of headship, but is also collaborating very closely with schools around the UK, helping them to take on board these messages and integrate them in a meaningful way into the very fabric of the school community. More than just a one-off INSET hit, he develops a powerful relationship model with schools that not only supports them in their effective development as 'emotionally intelligent' organisations, but also furnishes him with the sorts of insights that make this chapter so relevant, readable and even poignant.

Drawing on educational greats, including Lao Tzu and Carl Rogers (and, if you haven't read Carl Rogers's *Freedom to Learn* and you've got this far in your career, then shame on you!), as well as pointing out what we can learn from Homer Simpson, Harry Potter and a flock of geese, Mike also shares with you a whole series of questions and questionnaires to help you ascertain exactly how far you have come in your school's journey from Industrial Age factory-method learning unit to emotionally mature learning community built on real foundations, consisting of proper management of self, respect for others and positive relationships all round. Easy when you say it quickly!

So, as not to steal Mike's thunder and reveal any more of the essence of his chapter, let me finish by returning to Dee Hock and share with you a few of his thoughts on what he calls 'chaordic leadership'. (A chaord is something you find at the place were chaos and order meet successfully. The Visa corporation has proved itself to be successful in working like this, Independent Thinking strives to work in this way and the Chuckle Brothers have made a living from it.)

Power: True power is never used. If you use power, you never really had it.

Human Relations: First, last and only principle – when dealing with subordinates, repeat silently to yourself, 'You are as great to you as I am to me, therefore we are equal.' When dealing with superiors, repeat silently to yourself, 'I am as great to me as you are you to you, therefore we are equal.'

Ego, Envy, Avarice and Ambition: Four beasts that inevitably devour their keeper. Harbor them at your peril, for although you expect to ride on their back, you will end up in their belly.

Position: Subordinates may owe a measure of obedience by virtue of your position, but they owe no respect save that which you earn by your daily conduct. Without their respect your authority is destructive.

Creativity: The problem is never how to get new, innovative thoughts into your mind but how to get old ones out. Clean out a corner of your mind and creativity will instantly fill it.

Listening: While you can learn much by listening carefully to what people say, a great deal more is revealed by what they do not say. Listen as carefully to silence as to sound.

Leadership: Lead yourself, lead your superiors, lead your peers and free your people to do the same. All else is trivia.

– Dee Hock, 'The Art of Chaordic Leadership', *Leader to Leader*, No. 15 (Winter 2000)

Chapter 8
Build the Emotionally Intelligent School
or The Art of Learned Hope

Michael Brearley

The future is not some place we are going to, but one we are creating. The paths are not to be found, but made, and the activity of making them, changes both the maker and the destination.
– John Schaar, American writer and scholar

This chapter will show:

- why we *must* build emotionally intelligent schools;
- what is an emotionally intelligent school;
- how to understand and use emotional intelligence in leadership;
- leadership in the school;
- leadership in the classroom; AND
- how to build the emotionally intelligent school.

This chapter tells the developing story of the work I have done with a consortium of schools across the North of England who set out to build and sustain emotionally intelligent schools. Their aim: to transform their schools; to create environments where our intrinsic motivation to learn will flourish; where students become self-directed learners; where risk taking, failure, excitement and joy are all part of a daily experience of learning. They set out to teach hope.

This project is now developing into accredited programmes that are described briefly towards the end of the chapter, which are running in Newcastle, Enfield and Surrey. If you want to know more then please contact the Independent Thinking Ltd office (contact details can be found on page xi).

Why we must develop emotionally intelligent schools

Working harder in schools is no longer an option. The work ethic in schools has progressed since the halcyon days in the late 1960s and early 1970s, when table tennis and free expression were king and the individual teacher reigned. It has now run its course; it has gone as far as it can go. Effort alone and a 'try harder' culture now only generate stress, anxiety, a fear of failure and (paradoxically) a fear of success, absenteeism, mediocrity and a blame culture. This doesn't seem to recommend further attention.

Carl Rogers writes of school cultures in *Freedom to Learn* (1969),

> A charade is played out every year, by thousands of teachers of thousands of students. In this so-called educational atmosphere, students become passive apathetic, bored – they become tourists in the classroom. Teachers, trying day after day to prevent their real selves from showing, become case-hardened stereotypes and eventually burn out.

There is a paradox in 'trying harder'. We establish that something hasn't worked, decide what we were doing when it didn't work and then do more of it. It may not be working now, though if I do more of it it's bound to work eventually!

I worked with some sixth-formers in Hertfordshire to help them prepare for their A-level exams. I asked them what they were going to do. They all knew. They all had a way of revising and preparing for the exam.

'How long have you been doing it this way?' I asked.

'Ten years,' they said.

'Is it working?' I asked.

'No,' they said.

'OK – A-levels, kind of important, doors to your life – what are you going to do?' I asked.

'We'll do more of it,' they said. 'We'll try harder.'

'Trying harder' is the uninspired chasing the unattainable and makes habitual the behaviour of mediocrity and failure. Homer Simpson put it succinctly when he said, talking to Bart, 'To try is the first step to failure.' It is also the first step to insanity – to do more of the same thing strangely expecting a different outcome.

Trying harder creates mediocrity. Does your performance equal your potential? Does the performance of the children in your classrooms equal their potential? Tim Gallwey writes in his book *The Inner Game of Tennis* that the thing that prevents our performance equalling our potential is the personal interference that we all create that limits what we achieve. The interference is the emotional baggage we build up from trying and failing.

To move away from the 'try harder' school, school leaders need to become emotionally intelligent; to understand and apply our intrinsic motivation to learn in the classroom and the staffroom; to teach teachers and students to be leaders of learning; to use the power and acumen of their emotions to achieve excellence; to create schools that are truly organisations of learning rather than mere authority; to create the emotionally intelligent school, where people are working together to learn continually about learning.

The emotionally intelligent school doesn't give something that isn't already there: it takes something away and creates a new organisation. It takes away the interference that inhibits our performance, the fear of failure and the fear of success that get in the way of what we can achieve. It allows us to explore and use the potential that we all have within us, though may not be fully using.

Does your school have a low EQ?

Keep the pencil handy and see if you think you are working in an organisation that may have emotional intelligence (EQ) issues that need resolving in order to bring out the best from both teachers and learners. For each of the common organisational EQ problem areas coming up in a moment, give your school a score along the following lines:

1 = Never
2 = Rarely
3 = Often
4 = Always

I am my position

Have you ever come across colleagues who, when asked to look at school improvement, begin every sentence with, 'Well, that's not my problem, I'm a …'?

This is because, when asked to describe what they do, most people describe the tasks they perform. They chunk down their role to their behaviour. They define their territory, defend it, blame others who perform outside of that territory, limit their own expectations to the boundaries they have drawn for themselves and fail to see the real purpose of their role. They see the bits but not the whole picture.

The Johnny Depp character in *Pirates of the Caribbean* said, 'A keel, a hull, a deck, a mast, a sail – this is what a ship has. Freedom – this is what a ship is.' People who see themselves as their position will fail to see the 'freedom', they fail to see the connections they can make with others to create the bigger picture and fail to motivate themselves or engage others.

I have a friend, Paul, who is a manager of a B&Q warehouse. He recently went to see and hear a motivational speaker talk about the potential power of human energy and endeavour. Paul bemoaned the difficulties in getting people in his store to commit their creativity and energy to the cause. Perhaps even Johnny Depp may have difficulties in helping the staff of B&Q to find a greater meaning, though the answer may lie with a quarry worker, breaking stones with meticulous care, focus and determination. Asked what he was doing, he said, 'Building a cathedral.'

What are schools building and what is preventing your colleagues from committing to that greater good and sacrificing their own professional ego on the alter of altruism? It may be that when we apply and develop our own emotional intelligence we start to see that meaning and make the connections that will deliver it.

Do your colleagues see themselves as the bits or the purpose?

If the person with responsibility for the budget spoke at your senior leaders' meeting, would others listen and contribute effectively to the debate?

| 1 | 2 | 3 | 4 |

Do academic and pastoral leaders meet together?

| 1 | 2 | 3 | 4 |

Do staff frequently engage positively with the students in the dining hall at lunchtime?

| 1 | 2 | 3 | 4 |

Is there self-directed sharing of good practice among departments?

| 1 | 2 | 3 | 4 |

Are meetings traditionally adversarial, with people defending their position?

| 1 | 2 | 3 | 4 |

Ready, aim, blame

This is described in the 'not with the kids round here' view of life, where every issue has an external point of reference and blame. Where the enemy is always 'out there' and we don't have to look very hard to find it.

The extent to which people are engaged in 'Ready, Aim, Blame' will determine how open they are to learning, how strongly they take responsibility for their actions and how willing they are to see their own growth as an essential part of the school's success. It will determine how strongly they view their own personal power or feel disempowered, see themselves as the victim and blame others.

If asked to improve results next year, do departments consider what they can do differently rather than seeking extra resources?

1   2   3   4

Are plans within school focused on desired outcomes, creating a future, rather than on mending current problems?

1   2   3   4

Do meetings focus on desired outcomes, creating a future, rather than on problems and their solutions?

1   2   3   4

Is the language of the staffroom one of creative solutions to issues rather than blame?

1   2   3   4

Do people at meetings take a constructive, positive and supportive stance, rather than allowing them to be dominated by the negative?

1   2   3   4

Checking for thongs

A head I have worked with over a number of years has a vision of an empowered staff, with distributed leadership throughout the school. The staff know what he wants – they don't want it. They want him to take charge, they want him to react to events and sort them out, to rescue them. They want him to be there to take the blame when he fails to meet their expectations or to stand still and receive his next assignment should he succeed.

He recently attended a rather agitated staff meeting where a number of colleagues had become rather exercised by the conspicuous wearing of thongs by some sixth-form girls. They wanted him to do something about it – the

greater good was being threatened! The last time we spoke, he was on 'thong patrol' confronting the transgressors. Ho, hum!

Do your colleagues do all they can to resolve problems rather than sending the children to senior staff when there are problems?

1   2   3   4

When senior staff have been asked to intervene, do they spend more time working with the teacher, rather than the child, helping the teacher develop their own competence?

1   2   3   4

Are staff in the classroom waiting for the children after break and lunch?

1   2   3   4

Do meetings have a clear futures perspective where they are building the school rather than reacting to the events of the week?

1   2   3   4

Do staff lead their groups into assembly and make sure they arrive behaving appropriately and on time?

1   2   3   4

'Events, dear boy, events'

We often focus on events and respond to them, though often without really resolving the real cause of the problem. The consequence is that we end up reworking problems as they appear. Is your school development plan focused on the outcomes you want or the resolution of the problems you have? It may be only a matter of time before events overcome us if we do not take time out for the strategic, long-term view. Harold Macmillan, when asked what his biggest problem was, replied, 'Patience! Events, dear boy, events.'

Are the major issues that occupy the leadership's time new ones that show the growth of the school rather than the reworking of old ones?

1   2   3   4

Does you behaviour policy lead to observable improvement in behaviour rather than providing a structure to punish and blame?

1   2   3   4

Are meetings dominated by strategic planning and thought rather than the reaction to events?

1   2   3   4

Is the leadership and management of the school based on real teams, where the outcome is more than the total of the individual parts, rather than groups meeting reluctantly?

1   2   3   4

Is the management and administration of the school smooth, effective and a reflection of total-quality management rather than dealing with regular and predictable stress and difficulty?

1   2   3   4

If it ain't broke, you're not looking hard enough

Charles Handy, an expert in organisational change, tells the story of the frog and boiling water. If you place a frog in a bowl of boiling water, it will immediately try to get out. If you place it in a bowl of cold water and gently heat the water, the frog won't notice the change in temperature until it is boiled. The frog's internal mechanism for spotting environmental change is geared to detect sudden changes, not gradual ones. Are there people in your school happy to carry on doing things as they have always been done, unaware of the arrival of the twenty-first century, unaware of the changing needs of the society that the children leaving school will go into? How many frogs do you have in school?

Do you lead change when things are going well rather than wait for things to go wrong and then change them?

1   2   3   4

Are the staff continually reviewing their own practice even in the light of observable success, rather than being complacent or defending their success and blaming outside influences?

1   2   3   4

How often has your school been able to celebrate real change in the way you do something over the last ten years?

1   2   3   4

Do the staff see change as an exciting opportunity rather than a threat and inconvenience to the current way of doing things?

1   2   3   4

Do the governors work innovatively to create new strategic outcomes rather than reviewing the results of past events?

1   2   3   4

Results

Score 25–50: You have a possibly terminal case of low organisational EQ and should seek help immediately. Call Independent Thinking straightaway!

Score 50–75: Your school has a learning problem but it's not too late – give us a call sooner rather than later!

Score 75–100: Your school is developing brilliantly into an emotionally intelligent organisation – well done! Give us a call anyway and tell us how you did it!

What is an emotionally intelligent school?

A school that is continually expanding its capacity to create its own future. Where survival or the status quo is never enough and whole-school generative learning continues to enhance the school's capacity to grow.
– Peter Senge, *The Fifth Discipline*

The emotionally intelligent school is created by the combined impact of outcome thinking, individual learning and team learning. The relationships that bind both team and individual learning unite the emotionally intelligent school. It is all about relationships with ourselves and with others.

Outcome thinking – a sense of personal mastery: if I believe I can, I will

The ability to lead myself and others.

O'Brian says of staff at Hanovers and perhaps of many other schools, too (Cooper and Sawaf, 1998):

> People enter 'school' as bright, well-educated, high-energy people, full of energy and desire to make a difference. By the time they are 30, a few are on the fast track and the rest put in their time to do what matters to them on the weekend. They lose the commitment, the sense of mission and the excitement with which they started their careers. We get damn little of their energy and almost none of their spirit.

Personal mastery is based on the reciprocal connection between personal learning, leading the learning of others and organisational learning. This happens only when there is a shared vision and common values that align the school as an organisation.

Where there is no vision the people perish.
– Proverbs

Where there is a shared vision, where the school is aligned through shared values, the school creates the opportunity for self-directed learners to flourish in the classroom and in the staffroom.

Mental models, flexible leaders of learning, individual learning

We all have mental models of how the world works, how learning and schools work, mental models about what can be done 'with kids from around here'. If we change our mental models and help others change theirs, perhaps we begin to see possibilities that are there though sometimes remain hidden from view because we are looking in the wrong place.

In a modern version of a Sufi story, a passer-by comes across a drunk on his hands and knees under a street lamp. He offers to help and finds out that the drunk is looking for his house keys. After several fruitless minutes, he asks the drunk where he lost them. The drunk replies that he lost them outside his front door. 'Then why don't you look for them there?' asks the passer-by. 'Because', says the drunk, 'there is no light in my doorway.'

The answer is not always where the light shines brightest. Working harder, doing more, blaming others, leading through authority are all bright-light responses. In the emotionally intelligent school, individuals see possibilities and explore them. Individual learning creates the culture of continual growth.

Blessed are they that aim at nothing for they shall succeed every time. The self-directed learner takes risks in learning, and, if they fail, they have merely successfully found a way that doesn't work! We are all intrinsically motivated learners; we cannot stop ourselves from learning. We are all driven by a desire to understand and gain mastery over our world. We are, unfortunately, also cursed with a brain that is designed for survival rather than excellence. The consequence is that some of our efforts to gain mastery owe more to the Bart Simpson school of excellence than to that of Jedi Masters. We get stuck halfway through our learning. We seek to survive and achieve what we seek, survival. This clearly is some way from the personal excellence we all are capable of. There is an emotional barrier in our learning that often prevents us moving from survival strategies to personal excellence. It is our emotional intelligence that allows us to break through this barrier and complete our learning.

Stage One: I don't know how dumb I am

The learning cycle begins at the point of being 'unconsciously incompetent'. Do you know those people who don't know how bad they are at something? They are unconsciously incompetent. They live in a wonderful delusional world where they believe they are spreading light, largesse, order and happiness and are blissfully unaware of the chaos and mayhem that surrounds them. Should they catch a glimpse of it, they are quicker than a viper's tongue to blame others and tut loudly as they continue their sanctimonious way through life.

Stage Two: I do know how dumb I am

As self-awareness grows, we become more aware of those things we don't do well. We become 'consciously incompetent'. This may not be too bad a place to be – we are surviving. We may not be doing it very well but we have developed coping strategies. They may not work but this is how 'I' do it, so I carry on. These coping strategies help us survive and distract us from excelling. We all

have some element of this in our lives, which is why emotional intelligence is something that applies to all our learning. It is not a pity party for the emotionally fragile but an exercise in personal, team and organisational excellence for everyone.

We all have some of these coping strategies, things that we don't do very well. I may not remember names at parties very well, so what will I do next time I go to a party? I'll try to remember names in exactly the way I did last time. Did it work for me then? No! Will it work for me now? No! And what will I do next time I go to a party? I'll try to remember names in exactly the way that I did last time, but this time I'll try harder! Brilliant, now you have a dumb strategy and anxiety! We survive, we cope, but rarely do we excel.

Stage Three: I'm not dumb, I just have to think about it

It is only when we move from coping to excellence that we begin to build the paths of the self-directed learner, the excellent learner. Here we break through the barrier that separates the 'consciously incompetent' from the 'consciously competent'. We start to learn when we are consciously competent a little like a four-year-old starting to tie their shoelaces. Our learning is mechanistic and responding to conscious prompts, but we are learning.

Stage Four: I can be not dumb without thinking about it

Moving beyond this, we become 'unconsciously competent'. We are generative learners, able to learn about learning, to see failure as feedback and embrace our success. Embracing failure as feedback allows us to grow and move on. We reframe failure, we are able to say, 'Wow, I've successfully found a way that doesn't work.'

This is not always a useful approach for skydivers!

Team learning

How would the classroom be different if the learning were done in real teams, where the individual learned to learn with others, though may still be assessed individually? How might this change both the fear of failure and the fear of success? What might be the outcome of team learning in the classroom and throughout the school?

There are times when good intentions in the classroom and in the staffroom build up barriers in the learning cycle. Teachers implore their students to try harder because they know the value of learning and desperately want their students to achieve. Senior leaders add bigger numbers to targets so that the students, the community, can benefit from the fabulous contribution the school can make. These barriers can be overcome through team learning.

Carl Rogers writes of the classroom,

> Now the question I want to raise is, is this angry dissatisfaction necessary? Can a classroom be a place of exciting, meaningful learning, related to live issues? Can it be a place of mutual learning where you learn from others and they learn from you, where the instructor learns from the class and the class from the instructor?

Where teachers are learners leading learning, there is team learning. A place where the magic of teams pushes everyone to go through the learning barrier and become self-directed learners.

The team culture is crucial because real teams learn better and faster, and go further than individuals. This does not have to conflict with the current national assessment agenda. We learn in teams and are assessed individually. We don't have to look far to find powerful evidence of our willingness to embrace team learning. If your local hostelry advertises a pub quiz, people will pay and invest their own time to go.

'What did you do last night?'

'I went to the pub quiz, to be asked questions I didn't know the answer to with my friends.'

'How did you get on?'

'Had a great time!'

How many would turn up if your local advertised 'Tonight – a pub test'? What's the difference? Questions, answers, success and failure are writ large in both. The difference is that one is done individually and one in teams. We are prepared to learn from failure in teams and embrace success in a way that we find difficult as individuals We challenge convention, take risks, explore more ideas, learn from and contribute to the learning of others. The emotionally intelligent classroom is where the learning is done in teams. It may be assessed individually, though by now each individual has learned more, and learned more about learning, than he or she would have otherwise.

A teacher in a school in Devon said, 'Ah, great idea, but not with the kids round here.' He then told me in detail about the behaviour of the students that meant that team learning would fail. The problem may not be with the students who haven't yet learned how to use teamwork to grow their success. It may be with the staff and schools where there is not enough trust in the capacity of young people to learn and in their desire to do something constructive and positive with that learning. If we don't give trust, we don't get it back.

Schools sometimes take a partial view of learning and end up dragging the cart because they haven't noticed that the wheels have fallen off. If someone is not very good at maths, we give them more maths. If they are not very good at English, we give them more English. If they are not very good at responsibility, we give them less responsibility.

Exercising responsibility in learning, being a leader of my own learning, is more readily accepted in teams than individually. Emotionally intelligent teams take the ego out of learning and the wheels go back on the learning wagon. Taking responsibility for our own learning is crucial if we are to achieve excellence in the classroom. Pupils and students have to be given the opportunity to exercise it. When they are given this opportunity by teachers who are leaders of learning, responsibility becomes a powerful tool in learning rather than a great burden. It becomes and is expressed in its true sense, as response-ability, the ability to respond. Now failure and success are embraced because I have the skills in learning to understand what is working and do more of it, and to understand what is not and change it.

Emotional intelligence in teams, team learning, is not only for the classroom but also for the whole school. Do you have teams in school with an average individual IQ of 120 and a collective one of 43? How might your school be different if these teams achieved more than the sum of the individual parts? How might it be if young people leaving school were able to learn in teams, to create dialogue rather than discussion (which has the same root as concussion), to deal with confrontation without its causing conflict, to think in parallel with others rather than antagonistically, to understand and continually grow the performance of the team?

Five lessons we can learn from geese about working together

1. As each bird flaps its wings, it creates uplift for the bird flying behind. Flying in a 'V' formation adds around 70 per cent greater flying range than if the bird were flying alone.
Lesson: People who have a common direction can get where they are going more quickly and more easily by getting a 'lift' from others in the team.

2. Whenever a goose falls out of formation, it suddenly feels the drag and resistance of trying to fly alone, and quickly gets back into formation to take advantage of the lifting power of the bird in front.
Lesson: It is wiser to stay 'in formation' with those who are headed where we want to go, and be willing to accept their help as well as give ours to others in the team.

3. When the lead goose gets tired, it rotates back into formation and another goose takes the lead.
Lesson: It benefits all in the team to take turns doing the hardest task and sharing the leadership.

4. The geese at the back of the 'V' honk to encourage those up in front to keep up their speed.
Lesson: Give your leader only positive honking – no one likes a backseat driver!

5. If a goose gets shot down or becomes sick, two others drop out of formation and follow it down to help and protect it. They stay with it until it is either able to fly again or dies.
Lesson: We too should stand by each other in the difficult times as well as the prosperous ones.

In the emotionally intelligent team, learning happens in the classroom and throughout the school. Leadership of learning is based on the success of real teams rather than the myth of teamwork, where people become brilliantly skilled at keeping themselves from learning!

If the teams aren't learning, then neither is the school; if the school isn't learning, then the interference is growing.

The thread that binds the school as an organisation, that creates the relationships throughout the school that leads learning, is woven from inter- and intrapersonal intelligence (see Howard Gardner's *Frames of Mind* (1983)). Teachers and students learn to excel in these areas and create the environment where personal, team and organisational learning can flourish. Aspects of inter- and intrapersonal intelligence may be (from the work of Tim Sparrow at the School of Emotional Literacy in Frampton on Severn, Gloucestershire):

Intrapersonal

- mood management;
- self-motivation;
- dealing with setbacks;
- avoiding depression and addictive behaviour;
- using your intuition;
- managing your energy; and
- dealing with stress.

Interpersonal

- relationship management;
- motivating others;
- leading others;
- developing others;
- collaborating with others; and
- confronting others.

If you were to choose one strand from either inter or intra, ask yourself, 'If the teachers or students had even a little bit more of this, then what would be different?' Then, whatever your answer, ask the same question again: 'If the teachers or students had even a little bit more of this, then what would be different?' Then, say a third time.

You may start to see how even a small step can bring large results, both in terms of the outcome and in the way that growth in one area has a direct impact on other areas too. Small steps become the basis of transforming schools.

An emotionally intelligent school is one that learns about learning, where people seek outcomes that they truly want and believe will add value, where collective aspiration is identified and nurtured and where people work together.

If this is what an emotionally intelligent school is, what are the beliefs and values that align the school? These are:

Intelligence is the sum total of the habits of our minds, it can be taught and learned – we can achieve personal excellence when we lose habits that inhibit and develop new ones. The teacher is then a leader who learns about learning. Teachers and support staff are learners who lead learning. And a learner leads their own learning, takes responsibility for the habits they have and the goals they set. So, a learning school learns about learning together through team learning.

The place emotional intelligence has in developing this school is crucial. Conventional wisdom may see emotions as an inhibiter, while emotional wisdom will see them as a strength.

What are behaviours of the emotionally intelligent school?

Conventional wisdom	Emotional wisdom
Emotions:	Emotions:
• are a sign of weakness • have no place in learning • confuse • interfere with good judgement • are a sign of vulnerability • are a barrier to control • complicate planning • undermine authority	• are a sign of strength • trigger learning • clarify understanding and learning • are essential to good judgement • make us real and alive • build trust • spark creativity and innovation • generate influence

Table 3.

Teachers as learners leading learning

The fallible leader

The teacher as a leader of learning will give the students 'the freedom to learn' and allow learning teams to flourish. We all have fabulous teachers whom we remember with great affection, sometimes as our 'best teachers'. There is an issue about those teachers who helped us learn most and sometimes those teachers who just helped us the most. Research by Carl Rogers shows that, while we remember the teacher who helped us the most, we don't always remember what they taught us. Carl Rogers writes of his research,

> I am fascinated by the fact that those students (ones who talk of positive learning experiences) make no particular mention of their teachers but simply of the psychological climate in which they were enveloped. The rewards of an excellent facilitator (leader of learning) are different from the rewards of a brilliant teacher. One study has shown that years later people can vividly remember their brilliant teachers but are quite unable to remember what they learnt in those classes. They can however remember in detail every learning experience they themselves initiated.

I knew a home-economics teacher, Marylyn, who was high on the 'teacher who helped us best' list for many students. She would come into her area and tell the students what they were going to do that lesson. She would then show them how to do it and then the students would begin to model the learning. As they were doing this, Marylyn would go round making a cut here, adding some ingredients there, altering, shaping, remodelling. She just wanted each student to do the very best they could. What the students knew was that they were achieving the very best that Marylyn could make. She left her footprints all over their learning.

She stopped them taking risks in learning, from embracing failure and learning from it, from finding success and celebrating it. She, for the very best of intentions, deprived them of the experience of real learning.

I ran a training programme at Marylyn's school that led to a training programme for the students led by the staff. Towards the end of their workshop, a student from one of the learning teams approached Marylyn and asked permission to do something. The old Marylyn would have either said no or done it for the student. Now Marylyn smiled warmly at the student, gave an open-palmed gesture of permission and said, 'If you want to.' She gave the student the freedom to learn. We remember learning when we believe we started it ourselves, when we are given the freedom and trust to be self-directed learners.

Emotional intelligence isn't something you will do to someone else: it is something you and they do together. The teacher with worksheets for the week tucked reassuringly under their arm, marching away from their fix at the photocopier declaring the students have 'their learning for the week', will have no positive effect. If you look around your photocopier you will find the murdered ideas that were once in the worksheets and have been electronically squeezed out.

Emotional intelligence in leadership is described by Giles Pajou, a writer on leadership, as being 'to create a world to which others choose to belong' (Dilts, 1996). How might learning be different, relationships improve, achievement be raised, the emotional climate of a school be changed if leadership were successful in this way?

The emotionally intelligent leader of learning

Moving from the fallible leader to the emotionally intelligent leader in the classroom and the staffroom can be understood by applying the four pillars of leadership. These are:

- self-awareness;
- leading self;
- other awareness; and
- leading others.

Figure 12 demonstrates how they relate to each other.

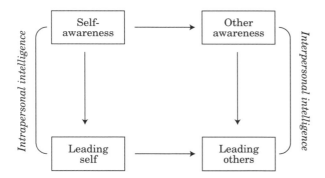

Figure 12.

	U	**I**
I	Public self	Private self
U	Blind spot	Potential

Table 4. Johari's Window

There is a sense that leadership is something we do to someone else. The focus of our leadership is the person or people I will lead. When I can sort out their weaknesses, solve their problems, make them the icons of my world, then, and only then, will real learning take place. Leadership becomes the great myth of altruism, the belief that we do this for others in order to help them make the contribution we know they really can to make. This, of course, is straight from the *Beano* book of leadership and here leadership does nothing but limit performance and massage the egos of the self-obsessed.

Emotionally intelligent leadership is developed through the four pillars.

Pillar 1: Self-awareness

As a leader of learning, I form one pole of a magnet and who I am will determine whether I attract learners or repel them. These learners may be in my classroom, my team or my school. Whether I have followers or misguidedly spend my energy pushing students and staff to where I believe they should go will determine the success I have. What I achieve may be inversely proportional to the extent to which I want to change other people. The paradox of leadership is that we cannot change other people – authority doesn't work. To have influence, we must first give up authority. Johari's Window in Table 4 shows how the emotionally intelligent leader creates both power and influence.

The top left-hand quadrant is the me that we both see and agree on, the *public* me. We may disagree about how often this part of me is on display and for what reasons, though we would agree that it is indeed there.

The *private* me is the part of me that I know and you don't see. The part of me that requires trust for me to reveal – or three glasses of red wine will usually do the trick! I may demonstrate trust by revealing more of my private self. If I show I trust, it may be that I get trust back. If I don't show that I trust I certainly will not get trust back.

The *blind spot* is the part of me that you see though I do not. You might 'know' that I can do something, though because I don't believe it I won't. You can say what you like though, I won't hear it.

The *potential* I have, which by definition currently remains unfulfilled, is the part of me that neither you nor I can see, at the moment – it is achievements on hold.

Pillars 2 and 4: Leading self and leading others

As I grow as an emotionally intelligent leader, I learn to reveal more of my private self; I trust more and get more trust back; I understand others through their eyes and ears; I discover more about myself and others and start to discover the potential that we all have though so rarely use. As I have the courage to reveal myself to others, I give them the courage to do the same. Scary thing to do? Threat and risk here? A change of attitude and expectation needed? Maybe so, though it is only the emotionally courageous leaders who will create the authentic environment for learning.

Public self and performance	Private self
Blind spot	Potential

Table 5. A Leader's profile in Johari's Window

The importance of this profile of Johari's Window in leading others is dramatically told in Cooper and Sawaf's book *Executive EQ*. In the Prologue, Robert Cooper tells of a climbing trip he made to Tibet. When he arrived, his guide took him to the top of a local hill and, looking down, showed Robert the communal grave of his extended family. He explained that in 1959 the Chinese had banned all prayer in the country. One day while walking, the guide had met an old friend and out of instinct had put his hands together and said, *'Tashi deley'*, which means, 'I honour the greatness in you'. A Chinese officer saw the exchange and had the guide arrested for spreading religion. For this crime, the officer felt a suitable punishment would be for him to watch as all of his extended family were killed in a truly horrific way. Full of compassion for the man, Robert Cooper asked his guide why he had told him the story. The guide replied, 'Without knowing this, you do not know me. The deep me, the real me. I could never be a leader to you. And you could not wholeheartedly work beside me or follow me. But now, if you choose to, you can begin to know me, and work with me, and trust me. Now I am real,

I am not just a name. I have a heart and a voice and a life story.'

The story is both moving and the very essence of the relationship between leadership and what you might call 'followership'. There may be boundaries within which you choose to disclose the real you within school, though we can all recall that teacher who hid themselves behind the façade of authority, who did the leader's walk, wore the leader's clothes, had the leader's voice and showed nothing of themselves. They led no one, pushed everyone and changed nothing. Leadership starts with self, and that leadership takes courage.

Johari's Window is the tool that allows us both to know ourselves and to lead others. It is the power that is within us that creates change in others.

The leader of learning in the classroom understands the power and influence they have and uses it to positive effect. This is beautifully described by Ginotti, who says of the teacher,

> I am the decisive element in my classroom. It is my personal approach that creates the climate. It is my daily mood that makes the weather. As a teacher I possess tremendous power to make a child's life miserable or joyous. I can be a tool of torture or an instrument of inspiration. I can humble or humour, hurt or heal. In all situations it is my response that decides whether a crisis will be exacerbated or de-escalated – a child de-humanised or humanised.

> Leadership is the art of allowing others to become who they truly can be.

The German philosopher Martin Heidegger (see Rogers's *Freedom to Learn* (1969)) writes of the teacher as a leader of learning:

> Teaching is even more difficult than learning … and why is teaching more difficult than learning? Not because the teacher must have a larger store of information, and have it always ready. Teaching is more difficult than learning because what teaching calls for is this: to let learn. The

real teacher, in fact, lets nothing else be learned than – learning. His conduct, therefore, often produces the impression that we properly learn nothing from him, if by 'learning' we now suddenly understand merely the procurement of useful information. The teacher is ahead of his students in this alone, that he still has far more to learn than they – he has to learn to let them learn. The teacher must be capable of being more teachable than the apprentices. The teacher is far less assured of his ground than those who learn are of theirs. If the relation between the teacher and the taught is genuine, therefore, there is never a place in it for the authority of the know-it-all or the authoritative sway of the official. It still is an exalted matter, then, to become a teacher – which is something else entirely than becoming a famous professor.

How, though, can we be aware of others, how can we know another person in a way that informs our own leadership?

Pillar 3: Other awareness

We can truly do this only when we see others through their eyes and hear them through their ears and not our own. When we see people through our own eyes, and hear them through our ears, we see and hear a distorted and incomplete picture and then make assumptions about who they are and what they need. Assumptions lead to misunderstandings that lead to frustration and conflict. We fail to see the real potential in others. Charlie Chaplin once entered a Charlie Chaplin lookalike competition and came third! It is only when we see others through their eyes that we can understand their values and beliefs and start to work with them. Now we start to see difficult people as exactly who they really are: people who are different.

Teachers who are learners who lead learning have learned that their leadership will continually develop, that they can always grow as a leader of learning. They have learned that to lead others means that they first have to understand before they can be understood. They have to be able to join the students in their world and lead

them from there. Native Americans have a saying that truly to know others you must walk in their moccasins for many miles. I have a small personal-hygiene problem with this, but I'm working with it. On the brighter side, by the time you have tried this, and stood in their shoes, they are miles away and you've still got the moccasins!

The emotionally intelligent leader of learning is the leader described by Lao Tzu:

> A leader is best when people barely know
>   that he exists,
> Not so good when people obey and proclaim him,
> Worst when they despise him.
> Fail to honour people,
> They fail to honour you.
> But of a good leader who talks little,
> When the work is done, his aim fulfilled,
> They will all say, 'We did this ourselves.'

The powerful and positive impact of emotionally intelligent leadership in the classroom is not a wish but a reality. It is powerful in both positive and negative terms. I had the dubious privilege of working with a pastoral leader who proudly proclaimed a new insight when he announced that we needed more of the 'F factor' in school. We need more 'fear', he explained. If boredom is the curse of the classroom, fear is the death of learning. A school in South Wales proudly advertised for a deputy head some twenty years ago. The successful candidate would understand 'the innate evil in children'. It seems a long time, though the successful candidate might still be out there – teaching your children!

Carl Rogers writes (1969),

> In looking back at my own education, I can see that each school year brought different experiences. Some teachers demanded that I learn, others helped me want to learn; some laughed with me, others laughed at me; some made me want to cry, others made me want to cheer; some gave me hope, others gave me despair; some made me feel stupid, others made me feel smart. In other words, some felt they had to control my learning, while others gave me *the freedom to learn* [my emphasis].

Leadership of learning is not based on the myth of altruism, of what I may do for someone else who otherwise could not do it themselves. It is based on the myth of selfishness. Only when I have the qualities in me that I want others to learn, can I lead them. Only when I have compassion, trust, optimism, self-belief, ambition, self-awareness, awareness of others, flexibility and hope, can I help others discover the same. How might someone's achievement in the classroom grow if they had even a little bit more of these?

How to use your emotions intelligently

The brain is my second favourite organ.

– Woody Allen

Emotional intelligence is leadership. Daniel Goleman describes emotional intelligence as, 'the master aptitude, a capacity that profoundly affects all other abilities, either facilitating them or interfering with them'.

This begins to unpick some myths and misunderstandings about emotions and how they affect both our learning and our lives. There is depth as well as breadth to emotional intelligence. This can be seen in the levels of emotional intelligence. These are:

* emotional responsibility;
* emotional leadership; and
* leading others.

Emotional responsibility

Often we empower people and events with the capacity to create an emotional response in us, which then either helps or hinders our learning.

We are stressed by exams, frightened by the dentist, frustrated by traffic jams, creative in the garden. In attributing these outside influences with the power of creating an emotional response in us, we fail to take emotional responsibility for ourselves and let go the opportunity for choice and emotional leadership.

Do you have a 'bloody person' in your life, someone you go and see, and after you have seen them you have to go and find a really good friend and say with just a slightly clenched fist and gently gritted teeth, 'That bloody man – he always makes me feel like this'? Your feelings, of course have nothing to do with 'that bloody man' (or woman): we are doing it all by ourselves; our emotions are ours and by acknowledging this we can begin to take emotional leadership.

You may want to explore a simple principle. All your emotions are created internally, you do it. If you think you have found something external that you believe is the cause of an emotional response, then look again as the real causes are within you.

I was working with some sixth-formers in Enfield and exploring the principle that all your emotions are created internally. One student suggested this wasn't true and cited grief. The students explored the issue and began to realise that grief is not a response to all death but particularly for those we love. It is the love that is within us that becomes grief when someone dies. Grief, like all other emotions, is created internally. Candice Pert, the neuroscientist, wrote in Molecules of Emotion: 'The notion that others can make us feel good or bad is untrue. Consciously, or more frequently unconsciously, we are choosing how we feel at every single moment'.

If this were true, how might schools be if students learnt that worry was an emotion created by themselves, if staff learnt that stress was something they could learn to live without, if motivation in learning you can access at any time you choose? How might schools be then?

The workshops I deliver in emotional intelligence lead delegates to internalise the principles of emotional responsibility. They accept that emotions are created internally. They then begin to explore emotional leadership. If I am doing all this emotional stuff to myself, what could I do if I chose and how do I do it?

Emotional leadership

Emotional leadership starts with emotional awareness. What are the emotions I am aware of? Are they useful to me at the moment? If not, how do I need to feel? Emotional leadership can be exercised by learning some straightforward skills. Understanding one of these, targeted kinaesthesiology, can be done by trying to find a 'yes' to each of the following statements.

1. I know about brain gym – if not, explore the Internet.

2. I accept that brain gym can have an impact on my emotional state.

3. If a general approach to kinaesthesiology through brain gym works, then a more specific approach might have an impact on specific emotional responses.

4. Targeted kinaesthesiology, sometimes called Emotional Freedom Technique or Energy Intelligence, does just this. It is accessible and easily learnt. Reports from a coaching project I ran in Enfield with Key Stage 4 students using these skills describe 'life changing' experiences for some previously demotivated students.

This of course is only part of the story. To some extent we do catch emotions from other people, which is the start of understanding how to lead others. When we catch emotions from others, it is a choice that serves a need for us at that time. Our limbic system, the emotional centre of the brain, is like an open loop and this enables us to sense emotions in others. This can have a very positive impact on our behaviour and experience, and, similarly, the odd negative one. I went into a tourist shop a few years ago and they were selling fridge magnets. One of them read, 'I don't suffer from stress – I'm a carrier.' Do you know that person? Before you meet them you are feeling perfectly centred and at ease with the world; then, after you've met them, you are just covered in their stress! On the positive side, a study done by Yale School of Management reports that cheerfulness and warmth spread easily, that irritability is difficult to spread and depression hardly at all (LeDoux, 1996).

Leading others

If emotional intelligence in leadership is about resonant leaders – those people who become the magnets in schools, who attract others to their learning – then what are they doing to achieve this?

Once we take responsibility for our emotions we then become empowered to exercise emotional leadership and choice. If I am responsible for my emotions, if they are mine, I can extend this to say that I can therefore lead myself to have the emotional response I choose. Research coming from the FBI suggests we have two choices in life. When we seek the third we just generate stress and anxiety because it doesn't exist. The work they did with hostages demonstrates that the choices are either to change the situation we are in or change our emotional response to it. There is no third way.

When Florence Nightingale was gaining some notoriety for her work, she was asked, 'What makes you do this?' She replied, 'Rage, sheer rage.' History will testify that, rather than jump up and down shouting at the gods, she acknowledged her rage (emotional literacy), realised it was hers and not someone else's (emotional responsibility), and then did something positive with it (emotional leadership). She used her emotions as a motivational tool to change the situation, which then in turn changed her emotional state. In this positive state, with clear value-rich goals, she attracted others to her cause. She created 'followership' in others through her own emotional leadership. Leadership starts with myself and when I am choosing to experience an emotional state that is useful to both myself and to others around me then I will become a resonant leader. It is my emotional state that creates the will in others to follow me.

Emotional intelligence is about exercising and taking responsibility for the choices we make. It is ultimately, as Goleman says, 'common sense'. What it is not is 'common practice'. My children are thirteen, eleven and six years old and so I get taken to the cinema more often than I used to, although I don't always get to see the films I want. I was recently taken to see *Harry Potter and the Chamber of Secrets*. Towards the end of the film, Harry is asking himself why he was put into Gryffindor House (good guys) rather than Slytherin (bad guys). He has found out that he has an association with Slytherin, though was still put into Gryffindor. He asks Dumbledore why this happened. Dumbledore asks Harry what he did when the Sorting Hat was on his head and Harry says that he made a choice: he said he wanted to be in Gryffindor. Dumbledore replies, 'It is not our abilities that make us who we are, Harry, but the choices we make.' Emotional intelligence is an exercise in choice. Choice about how I use the human resources I have, how far I choose to let my performance grow towards my potential or how far I choose to create my own ceilings of achievement.

Suspend disbelief and complete the following exercise:

List five things you want in life:

1.

2.

3.

4.

5.

Now write why you haven't got them.

Nothing that you have just written has any purpose, power or influence other than that you bestow on it. There is no reason why you cannot be working towards and achieving those five things. Marianne Williamson writes in a poem in *A Return to Love*,

We ask ourselves, who am I to be brilliant, gorgeous, talented, fabulous? Actually, who are you *not* to be?

Emotional intelligence allows us to decide whether we want to choose excellence or mediocrity in our learning and in our life. Cooper and Sawaf write in *Executive EQ* about emotional leadership. They define emotional intelligence as 'the ability to sense, understand and effectively apply the power and acumen of emotions as a source of human energy, information and influence'.

Emotional leadership is not about pursuing those pure and noble emotions. We can all identify the emotions we would want to be expressed in school. These become the Persil for the limbic system. Emotional intelligence is about honouring all our emotions and making decisions about our behaviour in respect to those emotions.

The emotionally intelligent teacher and student

How emotionally intelligent are you? Want to find out your EQ score? Read on with a pencil at the ready.

Measuring your emotional intelligence

This has been developed by me, from the work of Professor Malcolm Higgs and Professor Victor Dulewicz, two leading UK-based researchers into emotional intelligence. Read the following statements and decide how consistently you can say they reflect your behaviour on a scale of 1 to 5 with 1 being 'consistently exhibits behaviours described as low-level', 3 being 'exhibits behaviours that consistently lie between high- and low-level or find that they vary between the two' and 5 being 'consistently exhibits the behaviours described as high-level'. When you have decided, fill in the chart below.

	1	2	3	4	5	Total
Self-awareness						
Emotional resilience						
Motivation						
Interpersonal sensitivity						
Influence						
Decisiveness						
Conscientiousness and integrity						

SELF-AWARENESS

High-level

1. Aware of your feelings and emotions in a wide range of situations.
2. If you become aware of feelings or moods that disrupt your performance, you believe it is possible to change.
3. In general, you have an optimistic outlook on life.

Low-level

1. You tend not to spend time reflecting on your feelings and are generally unaware of them in a work context.
2. Overall, you do not believe it is feasible to manage your feelings.
3. In general, you have a pessimistic outlook on life.

EMOTIONAL RESILIENCE

High-level

1. You can adjust to new situations or circumstances and retain a focus on your overall performance.
2. You can balance the need to get a job done with the needs and concerns of those who you have to persuade to help you.
3. In the face of criticism or rejection, you continue to focus on your overall goals and aspirations.

Low-level

1. You find it difficult to deliver consistent performance across a range of situations.
2. When under pressure, you can become irritable or volatile.
3. If you are faced with personal criticism or challenge, you tend to find that your performance suffers.

MOTIVATION

High-level

1. You consistently focus on outcomes and work to overcome problems in ensuring that you attain your goals.
2. You tend to set yourself challenging goals.
3. You encourage others who work with you to set challenging goals.

4. You are able to achieve high levels of performance in a variety of situations.
5. You believe that the potential of individuals far exceeds what is normally expected of them.

Low-level

1. Problems become barriers and distract you from achieving your goals.
2. You dislike committing to goals for yourself.
3. You are unwilling or unable to encourage others to commit to challenging goals.
4. You do not believe that you can achieve truly stretching objectives.
5. You believe that our potential is determined by our working environment, which is controlled by others.

INTERPERSONAL SENSITIVITY

High-level

1. You invest time and effort in discussing issues with others.
2. You are willing to value the views of others or their explanations or interpretations of situations.
3. You are willing to lay aside your own preferred solution when presented with a clearly better one.
4. You actively listen to others and check that you have understood them.
5. You involve those who work for you in setting goals and objectives.

Low-level

1. You impose goals and objectives on others.
2. Even when discussing an issue or topic, you tend to ensure that your view prevails.
3. You stick to your solution come what may.
4. You hear others but stick to your view.
5. You are conscious of your hierarchical relationship with others when setting goals.

INFLUENCE

High-level

1. You can persuade others to accept your viewpoint on problems or issues.
2. In listening to others, you are able to use their needs or concerns as a way of changing their behaviour.
3. You are successful in getting others to change their perception of a problem or situation.
4. You find it relatively easy to develop rapport with others.

Low-level

1. You find it difficult to persuade others to accept and buy in to your ideas.
2. You are rarely able to get others to change their perception of a situation.
3. You find that your perception of a situation and that of others rarely move closer together.
4. You do not find it easy to develop rapport with others.

DECISIVENESS

High-level

1. You are able to make decisions in difficult situations and build support for these decisions.
2. It is more important to make a decision and implement it than to have all possible information available.
3. You use your intuition in decision making.

Low-level

1. You find it hard to make decisions in complex situations.
2. You are uncomfortable in making decisions unless you are certain that you have considered all the angles.
3. You do not trust intuition or those who use theirs.

CONSCIENTIOUSNESS AND INTEGRITY

High-level

1. You demonstrate a high level of commitment to agreed goals and methods of working.
2. What you say and what you do are the same.
3. If things go wrong, you ask what it is that you could have done differently.

Low-level

1. You are willing to compromise on your values to achieve a goal.
2. There are gaps between what you say and what you do.
3. If you underperform, you find reason in circumstances and the behaviour of others.

Conclusion

The emotionally intelligent school is a practical possibility. Intrapersonal intelligence provides teachers as emotionally intelligent leaders of learning and students with a clear sense of personal excellence and the skills to deliver it. The interpersonal excellence creates relationships in the staff room and the classroom where success can flourish. Dorothy Law Nolte writes in her poem 'Children Learn What They Live':

> If a child lives with criticism, he learns to
>   condemn.
> If a child lives with hostility, he learns to fight.
> If a child lives with fear, he learns to be
>   apprehensive.
> …
> If a child lives with encouragement, he learns to
>   be confident.
> If a child lives with tolerance, he learns to be
>   patient.
> If a child lives with praise, he learns to appreciate.
> …
> If you live with serenity, your child will live
>   with peace of mind.
> With what is your child living?

The novelist Frances Hodgson Burnett wrote in *The Secret Garden* (1911):

> At first people refuse to believe that a strange new thing can be done, then they begin to hope it can be done, then they see it can be done and then all the world wonders why it was not done centuries before.

The emotionally intelligent school is both a necessity and achievable. The workshops I have run on emotional intelligence in whole-school leadership and in intrapersonal leadership, and on emotional intelligence in coaching and in building the emotionally intelligent team have all had positive and at times powerful evaluations.

To make the emotionally intelligent school real, it will take courage, self-belief, optimism, emotional resilience and trust. For this to grow in the students, it must first be found in the leaders of the school. For school leaders to find this, they must first overcome the fear that sometimes inhibits us all. As Marianne Williamson wrote in *A Return to Love* (1996):

> Our deepest fear is not that we are inadequate.
> Our deepest fear is that we are powerful
>   beyond measure
> It is our Light, not our Darkness, that most
>   frightens us.

Marianne Williamson then continues with a powerful message to leaders in schools. These may be formal leaders, teachers as leaders of learning or students as leaders of their own learning. She writes:

> As we let our own Light shine, we unconsciously
>   give other people
> Permission to do the same.

As you think about what could be done in your school you may wish to reflect on the emotional resources that you have that can make this happen. Small steps lead to big outcomes.

References and bibliography

Beck, D. E., and Cowan, C. (2005), *Spiral Dynamics: Mastering Values, Leadership and Change* (Oxford: Blackwell Publishing).

Blanchard, K., and Shula, D. (2002), *The Little Book of Coaching: Motivating People to be Winners* (New York: HarperCollins Business).

Bohm, David (1996), *On Dialogue* (Oxford: Routledge).

Burnett, Frances Hodgson (1995) [1911], *The Secret Garden* (London: Penguin Books Ltd).

Chevalier, A. J. (1995), *On the Client's Path: A Manual for the Practice of Solution Focused Therapy* (Oakland, CA: New Harbinger Publications).

Cooper, Robert K., and Sawaf, Ayman (1998), *Executive EQ: Emotional Intelligence in Leadership and Organizations* (New York: Perigee Trade).

Csikszentmihalyi, Mihaly (1990), *Flow: The Psychology of Optimal Experience* (New York: Harper and Row).

Dilts, Robert (1996), *Visionary Leadership Skills: Skills and Tools for Creative Leadership* (Capitola, CA: Meta Publications).

Gardner, Howard (1983), *Frames of Mind* (New York: Basic Books).

Goleman, Daniel (1996), *Emotional Intelligence: Why It Can Matter More Than IQ* (London: Bloomsbury).

Harris, Thomas A. (1976), *I'm OK – You're OK* (New York: Avon).

Jaworski, Joseph (1998), *Synchronicity: The Inner Path of Leadership* (San Francisco, CA: Berrett-Koehler).

Kohn A. (1993), *Punished by Rewards: The Trouble With Gold Stars, Incentive Plans, A's, Praise, and Other Bribes* (Boston, MA: Houghton Mifflin).

LeDoux, Joseph (1996), *The Emotional Brain* (New York: Simon & Schuster Ltd).

Perkins, D. (1998), *Outsmarting IQ* (New York: Riverhead Books).

Pert, Candace B. (1999) *Molecules of Emotion: The Science Behind Mind–Body Medicine* (New York: Scribner).

Quick, Ellen K. (1996), *Doing What Works in Brief Therapy: A Strategic Solution Focused Approach* (London: Academic Press Inc. Ltd).

Rand, Ayn (1961) [1943], *The Fountainhead* (New York: HarperCollins).

Rogers, Carl (1969), *Freedom to Learn* (Columbus, OH: Merrill).

Selegman, Martin E. P. (2006), *Learned Optimism: How to Change Your Mind and Your Life* (New York: Vintage Books USA).

Williamson, Marianne (1996), *A Return to Love: Reflections on the Principles of a "Course in Miracles"* (New York: HarperCollins).